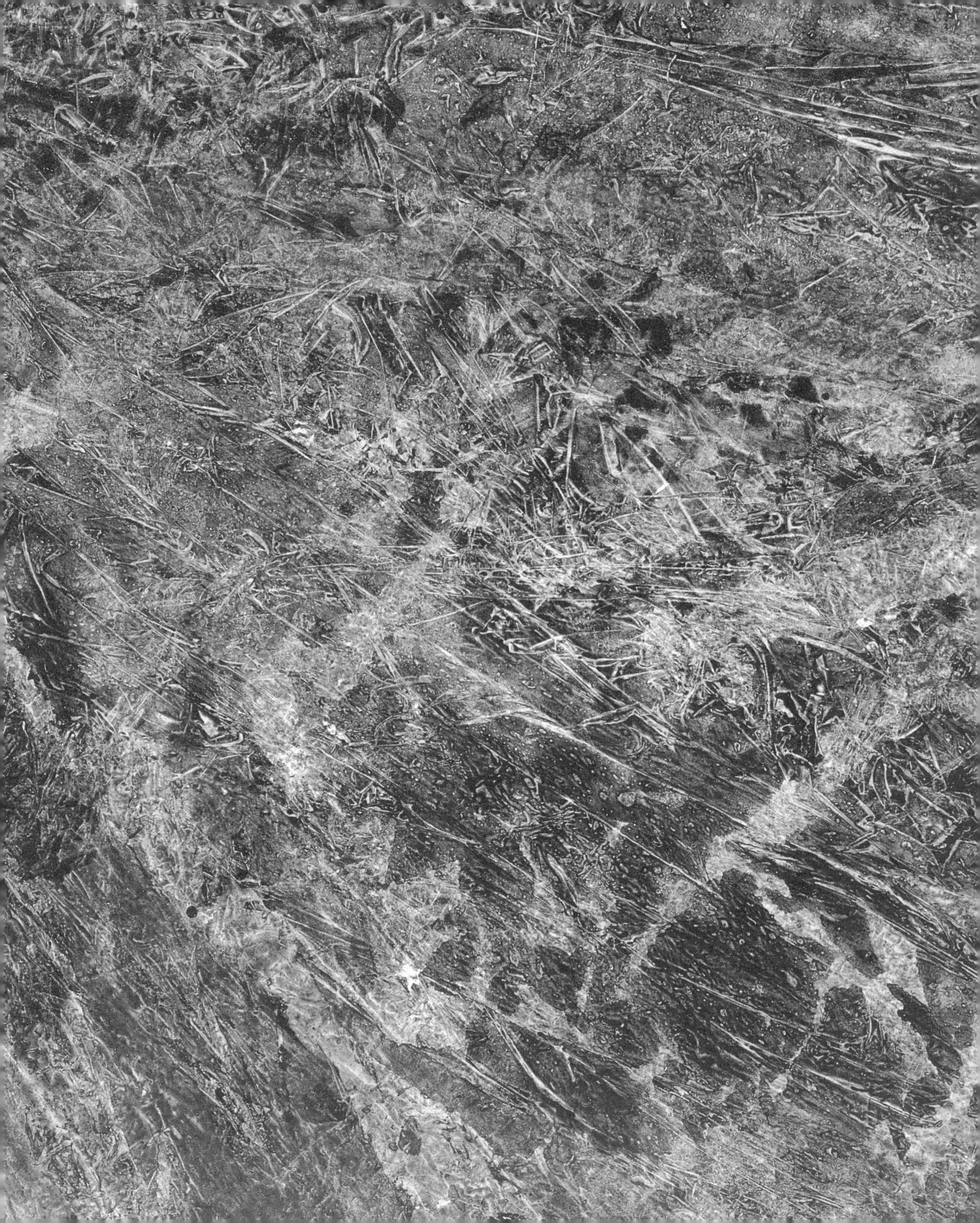

CANADIAN HOUSE & HOME

HOME STYLE

A HANDS-ON GUIDE TO DECORATING

CANADIAN HOUSE & HOME

HOME STYLE

A HANDS-ON GUIDE TO DECORATING

LYNDA COLVILLE-REEVES
WITH DAVID MACFARLANE & JANICE LINDSAY

A LORRAINE GREEY BOOK

RANDOM HOUSE
TORONTO

A Lorraine Greey Book

Canadian Cataloguing in Publication Data

Colville-Reeves, Lynda
Home style: a hands-on guide to decorating

ISBN 0-394-22206-7

1. Interior decoration. I. Macfarlane, David, 1952- . II. Lindsay, Janice. III. Title.

NK2110.C64 1991 747 C90-095453-1

Design and art direction by Andrew Smith
Page composition by Joseph Gisini/Andrew Smith Graphics Inc.
Endpapers by Andrejs Ritins/Ritins Studio
Illustrations by Tina Holdcroft
Section Two chapter openers and jacket styled by Janice Lindsay

Published by Random House of Canada Limited
1265 Aerowood Drive
Mississauga, Ontario
L4W 1B9

Produced for Random House of Canada Limited by
Lorraine Greey Publications Limited
Suite 303, 56 The Esplanade
Toronto, Ontario
M5E 1A7

Printed and bound in Singapore by Palace Press

123456789PP987654321

CONTENTS

SECTION ONE
FAVOURITE STYLES

SECTION TWO

UNDERSTANDING THE ELEMENTS

SECTION THREE

SOURCES AND RESOURCES

ACKNOWLEDGEMENTS

I am most grateful to David Macfarlane for expressing my ideas — in beautifully written prose — and to Janice Lindsay for her tireless work and creative energy throughout this project.

Grateful acknowledgement to all the team at *Canadian House & Home* magazine past and present, for their enormous contribution of talent, energy, and dedication. In particular, grateful acknowledgement to Katharine Vansittart, Cobi Ladner, Carolyn Kennedy, Jane Dupéré, Sandra McKenzie, Vicki Lynn Bardon, Rosemarie Rajca, and Kirsty McFarlane. Special thanks to Robin Roger for her contribution to the title. I am especially grateful to Barbara Dingle and Kate Quetton for long hours of research, editing, and assistance throughout the writing of this book.

I would like to express my appreciation to Lorraine Greey for putting her heart and talent into this project; to our book editor, Shelagh Wallace, for her great assistance; and to Andrew Smith who has delighted us with the inspired design of this book.

Special gratitude to the many designers and home owners across Canada who allowed us into their homes and without whom a book such as this would not be possible.

Lynda Colville-Reeves

FOREWORD

PUBLISHING *CANADIAN HOUSE & HOME* MAGAZINE IS SOMETIMES HARD work, sometimes exhausting, but always, for me, a wonderful adventure. Although I sometimes dream of a world without monthly deadlines, I don't think I'd trade jobs with anyone!

Over the years, the magazine has given me, along with our editors, writers, and photographers, a passport to beautiful houses, apartments, and condominiums from Vancouver to St. John's. We have been welcomed by strangers who quickly became friends. We've walked through their homes and listened to their stories. We have inspected their blueprints, marvelled at their ingenuity, and sat with them in the rooms they love, chatting about their decorating inspirations and their design goals.

In each city, we also have interviewed professional designers, architects, and decorators, whom we have prodded for their secrets and tricks of the trade. We've visited shops and showrooms and tracked down the most talented craftspeople. And, always, we are astonished by the dazzling array of talent, materials, and imagination that we encounter in our journeys.

Our travels have also taught us what decorative styles best suit Canadian homes and lifestyles. This book is our chance to share what we've learned. We hope that by showing you these popular and best-loved styles we'll inspire your creativity. We want to encourage you to tackle the projects you've been dreaming about. We want to give you the practical information you'll need to create successful interiors. Helpful hints, useful guidelines, do's and don'ts — they're all here. Our resource file of products and services (pages 219-225) will be an invaluable tool whether you're renovating or decorating.

This book is a celebration not only of design and decoration but of the impulse to create rooms that delight the eye, satisfy the imagination, and make homes work — for the people who live in them. At *Canadian House & Home*, we have been privileged to witness this creativity flourishing from coast to coast. Now we want to pass that excitement along to you.

Lynda Colville-Reeves

ENGLISH COUNTRY STYLE

"It was an aesthetic experience to live within those walls."

EVELYN WAUGH, NOVELIST,
BRIDESHEAD REVISITED

MOST OF US HAVE NEVER SET FOOT IN THE SITTING ROOM OF A COUNTRY HOUSE IN England, and yet one of the reasons for its enormous appeal is its cosy familiarity. Movies, plays, and books have made it a grand and irresistibly romantic image of home. Designed for warmth, comfort, and serendipitous elegance, compounded over the generations with furnishings, collections, and curios, it is a room with only one absolute purpose: to accommodate the idiosyncrasies, tastes, habits, and pleasures of the families that inhabit it.

In many ways, the sitting room represents the epitome of English Country style. Its comfortable splendour and gracefully accumulated whimsy will exceed even that of the rest of the house. In a home filled with collections and curios — a hallmark of English Country style — it is probably the sitting room that will feature the collector's prizes. In a house where the deep duveted beds look too comfortable ever to get out of, and where the bathtubs seem to encourage extravagantly long baths, it is the sitting room that is especially

luxurious — layered in carpets, enclosed with drapes, and warmed by the glow of a fireplace. Or, in a house where every bedside table is stacked with three or four beautiful books, it will be the walls of the sitting room that are lined with bookshelves. In a style renowned for its individualism, the sitting room is the most individual of rooms.

Still, a room's function is the most straightforward clue to its appearance, and the question remains: What exactly does one do in the sitting room of a country house in England? For most of us — unfamiliar with the ways of horses and hounds, an ocean away from the nearest village green — the answer is largely outside our experience. We know, of course, that one sits in an English Country sitting room. But beyond that we can only imagine how it must feel to sink, with our skin still tingling from an afternoon tramp across wind-blown fields, into the faded silk pillows and the abundant chintz slipcover of a vast sofa. It is cold and damp outside, but we warm ourselves in front of the fire and let our gaze wander over the mahogany tables and walnut cabinets, the pale walls and the cream-white plasterwork, the urns filled with casually arranged bouquets, the cotton spreads, the woollen throws, and the rich deep patterns of Persian carpets. Perhaps we curl up with a book from one of the room's ceiling-high bookcases, or pour a cup of tea from an ironstone pot. Or perhaps we stand at the large bay window, between swags of full-length

PRECEDING PAGE: A formal sitting room in the English Country style by designers Nancy Raeburn-Paul and David Rollins. Rich jewel tones are a dramatic backdrop for fine porcelain. LEFT: This typically English-style sitting room, by designers David Rollins and Nancy Raeburn-Paul, is anchored by a needlepoint rug of floral motifs within a grid pattern.

ABOVE: Blue and white is the theme for a collection of English china and Chinese porcelains. OPPOSITE, LEFT: Elaborately gathered tie-backs above a small chest embellish this feature window. OPPOSITE, RIGHT: A close-up of trimmed and tasselled drapes that puddle generously on the floor.

chintz curtains, and watch a chill mist drift across the rambling beds of delphiniums and foxglove and roses.

We're new to the game, after all. But the English have been perfecting country life for centuries. The fortresses of feudal lords were the first centres of English rural communities. Cold, smoky, and damp, these vast stone halls bore little resemblance to our notion of country homes today. However, they did establish the definitively English connection between a house and its surrounding countryside. Peasants owed their allegiance and their tithes to their lords who, in turn, oversaw not only their own house but the environs and the surrounding rural community as well. A view of the land has always been an integral part of the country house in England.

Passed from generation to generation, the ancestral homes of English nobility represent the remarkable continuity of English history. For almost one thousand years — and almost without interruption — the monarchy has ruled England, and the institution of aristocracy has remained remarkably intact. According to the laws of primogeniture, which passed titles and estates intact from father to eldest son, the great houses came down through the centuries as the most cherished symbol of a family's birthright and tradition. William Shakespeare could describe the entire political, military, and economic domain of the powerful dukes of his plays with the simple, all-encompassing "House of Lancaster" or "House of York." And this reverence for tradition and for the architectural symbols of a noble family's history became not only a way of life for the ruling class, but also a model for the wealthy but untitled landowners of grand homes and country estates.

"Oh God, leave us our luxuries even if we must do without our necessities.... Let house parties burgeon once more in the stately homes of England!"

CHARLES RITCHIE,
DIPLOMAT/DIARIST,
THE SIREN YEARS

LEFT: The greenery through this Palladian window harmonizes with the soft green palette of this formal dining room by designer Robert Dirstein.

By the Elizabethan age, the country home began to resemble the image we have of it today, although it still bore its unequivocal relationship to the countryside. The Elizabethan fascination with glass opened the house's vistas to hedged gardens and distant commons. But comfort became increasingly important. The monarch was a frequent visitor to the grand estates of her most eminent subjects, and houses vied for the favours that followed a particularly pleasant and comfortable royal stay. Architects were as involved in furnishing a house and commissioning its ornamentation as in designing its structure. Rush floor-matting and canvas screens cut the chill of draughts.

CHINTZ

Nancy Lancaster, the celebrated American decorator, seems to have best understood the appeal of chintz.

The glazed, printed cotton fabric — intricately patterned with colourful floral designs — was imported from India in the seventeenth century and enjoyed immense popularity in England. But when it was mass-produced in English textile factories in the nineteenth century, its quality declined so much the very word "chintz" became the source of "chintzy," meaning cheap. It was rediscovered in the late nineteenth century by William Morris, the artist, writer, and designer who celebrated traditional English art and craftsmanship. Restored to its former glory, chintz was eventually championed by the British textile house Liberty & Co., by the influential English decorating firm Colefax and Fowler, and by Nancy Lancaster.

Lancaster recognized that chintz aged beautifully; its colours softened with passing generations, its backgrounds became richer. She knew that it was this — the subtle and elegant patina of time and use — that evoked the charm, the traditions, and the effortless comfort of country life in England. Our palette, especially in North America, tends to be more vibrant. But, as a clue to the sensibility that we now call English Country style, it's worth remembering Nancy Lancaster; when she used chintz, she often insisted that it be left out in the rain before being made into slipcovers, or washed in tea before being hung as drapes.

LEFT: Loose slipcovers on dining chairs can change with the seasons. They bring a lighthearted, fresh appeal to traditional English Country decorating.

CHIPPENDALE

Thomas Chippendale, one of the greatest English cabinet makers and furniture designers, was born in 1718. Two years later, as if preparing the way for the young Chippendale, the British government repealed the heavy import duty on woods imported from the Americas. Chief among these was the mahogany of Central and South America. Beautiful, strong, and ideally suited to the needs of a master carver, mahogany was featured constantly in Chippendale's settees, armchairs, breakfronts, highboys, tables, and bookcases.

The influence of Thomas Chippendale on English furniture was so profound his name is synonymous with elegantly carved, majestically finished pieces. The famous claw and ball feet of a console table, the pediment of a secretary bookcase, and the ornately carved ribboned back of a side chair are recognizable as the marks of Thomas Chippendale. Interestingly though, there is really no such thing as a single "Chippendale style."

Chippendale was an extremely successful businessman and a shrewd arbiter of taste — the Ralph Lauren of eighteenth-century cabinet making. His book of furniture designs, *The Gentleman and Cabinet-Maker's Director*, was an enormous success. But although he influenced popular styles, he wasn't interested in setting them. During his lifetime, he responded to five different shifts in fashion: from the early Georgian style to the straightforward architectural elegance of the classic style. In fact, so diverse were the styles of Thomas Chippendale that a roomful of his work could look as if it had been accumulated by half a dozen different collectors. The unsurpassed excellence of his carving and the rich perfection of his finishes would be the only give-aways.

Tapestries were not only treasured works of art, they were also convenient insulation. Fireplaces became the focus of rooms, drawing the furnishings away from the cold stone walls and deep-set windows. Doors were heavy and magnificent because heavy, magnificent doors kept the cold on one side and the warmth on the other. Bedchambers were hung with drapery and sumptuous bed-curtains because such adornments were luxurious — but also because, when a bitter wind was howling off the heath, they kept guests warm enough to sleep. Comfort and classicism, proportion and order prevailed. Under the influence of designers such as Inigo Jones, Christopher Wren, and Thomas Chippendale, the seventeenth and eighteenth centuries were the golden years of the English Country home.

Our notion of the English Country home is one of artful, pleasant clutter: bookshelves are crammed with books; sofas bulge with oriental pillows; flat-weave kilim rugs are set against thicker, hand-knotted Persian carpets. In part, this is due to the natural accumulation of many generations; an English Country house, it has often been said, is a never-finished process. But

Collecting and displaying memorabilia is a typically English detail.

Designers Cally Bowen and Suzanne Davison let the vibrant colours of a floral chintz by Cowtan & Tout inspire this dramatic sitting room, with its strong pink sponged walls.

RIGHT: Designer Henry Liska mixed marble, fine wood detailing, nineteenth-century engraving, and Art Deco accessories in this very sophisticated bath. BELOW: An antique dressing table and accessories add elegance and character to an English Country bathroom. OPPOSITE: White lace is the theme for this bedroom by designer Murray Oliver. The room is dominated by an elaborate carved four-poster bed.

ORIENTAL RUGS

The caravans of the silk route first brought oriental carpets to Europe. For seven hundred years, the rich colours and exotic patterns of Persian, Turkish, Afghani, Pakistani, Chinese, and Indian rugs have remained staples of Western interiors.

Western craftsmen have never successfully copied the art of their production. As they were for the Victorians and Edwardians, the carpets therefore remain souvenirs of the East. The less bulky and usually geometrically patterned kilims, made in Turkey and Afghanistan, are woven on looms, but the thicker, more sumptuously dyed and intricately patterned rugs that have always been so popular in English homes are finished by hand-knotting. The ancient technique is painstaking. A fine Persian or Turkish rug can have eight hundred knots to a square inch and can take a skilled craftsman years to produce.

There are as many geometric, floral, and animal patterns, and as many colour combinations of rugs as there are tribes and villages in the Near, Middle, and Far East. Many of the tribes were nomadic, and so patterns, colour combinations, and dying techniques have spread from region to region. The ability to say where, exactly, a rug comes from is usually the result of years of study, travel, and careful observation.

To discern whether a rug is an Ouchak or a Lilihan or a Belutsch or a Hamadan, a rug expert will immediately look at the knotting on the back. The barely visible differences in knotting techniques are the only reliable way to know where a rug has been made.

it is also due to the English fascination with collections, curios, and souvenirs. In the nineteenth century in particular, with the Empire at its height, the keepsakes of travelling Englishmen — worldly civil servants, far-flung diplomats, businessmen, journalists, and soldiers — gave their country homes a uniquely exotic and eclectic flavour.

"It was an aesthetic experience," said Charles Ryder, the narrator of Evelyn Waugh's *Brideshead Revisited*, "to live within those walls, to wander from room to room." Brideshead was, of course, a country house — perhaps, in North American imaginations, the quintessential English Country house. We think of it as the real thing — a refined and ancient retreat from the rigours of city life.

The opulent, brilliantly coloured fantasies of the modern North American proponents of English Country style seem overdone in comparison. The decorator largely responsible for the urban popularity of chintz and drapery and throws and comfy sofas is Mario Buatta. Thanks to him, it is now possible to find English Country sitting rooms in high-rise Manhattan apartments and suburban homes. And although purists, with their insistence on the English penchant for understatement, have criticized Buatta's exuberant exaggeration and vibrant colours, it's worth remembering that fantasy has always been an essential ingredient of English Country style. "I piled it on rather," Evelyn Waugh once said about writing *Brideshead Revisited*. And, so perhaps should we.

RIGHT, TOP: The country kitchen of designers Frank Codd and Will Ryan centres on an island counter of reclaimed architectural elements. RIGHT, BOTTOM: A single floral chintz pattern dominates this light-filled sitting room.

"I've always liked Mario Buatta's answer to how to achieve the perfect English Country look. He said that first you have to have the perfect chintzes, and the perfect antiques, then you lock two poodles in the house for the weekend!"

RICHARD SALTER,
RICHARD SALTER INTERIORS

FRENCH COUNTRY STYLE

"He who takes leave of Avignon takes leave of his senses."
PROVENÇAL PROVERB

AS MUCH AS ANYTHING, FRENCH COUNTRY IS A PLACE THAT EXISTS IN OUR IMAGINATION. PART dream, part memory, it is the romance we conjure when we breathe the scent of fresh rosemary. It is the land we visit when we glimpse a splash of sunshine on an old stone wall. It is the destination we invent when we crave simple elegance, spirited generosity, and sheer exuberance.

For some, the epitome of French Country style may be a souvenir of a visit to France — a remembrance of a perfect *auberge* in Avignon, a cottage glimpsed through the cedars near Arles, or the memory of the crisp taste of cider in a golden orchard in Normandy. For others, it may be pure fancy — and this is what makes it such a delight. French Country can be studied on walking tours of Provence or on bicycle trips through the Auvergne, but you don't have to be an avid traveller to love it. Some people simply have French Country — abundant bouquets, rooms full of comfort and romance, sunlight and colour — in their hearts.

Which is not to say that French Country can be anything anyone wants it to be; its

CHURCHES OF CANADA

characteristics are distinct and unmistakable. They grow out of a deeply felt love affair between the people of the French countryside and their surroundings, and they draw on an ancient tradition. French Country colours are as old as the landscape itself: the deep hues of well-worked soil, the bright blue of the summer sky, the soft purple of lavender, the quiet green of olive groves, the brilliant yellow of van Gogh's sunflowers. The pretty, delicately patterned fabrics, dishes, wallpapers, and accessories that are typical of French Country were inspired by the abundance of French villages and farms. Animal motifs, fruit motifs, and — in a land that is never far from the sea — shell motifs are everywhere.

Amid this profusion of colour and texture, the furniture maintains an unadorned, rural simplicity. The hand-carved armoires, the woven rush seats, and the vast fruitwood tables possess a beauty that is almost sculptural. They can become as central to a room as a much-loved work of art. Yet they also seem content simply to perform the tasks for which they were made: they hold clothes, they seat friends, they support hearty, lively meals. They have a decidedly human charm.

In our homes today, much of French Country's appeal is based on its generosity of spirit. There is nothing restrained or exclusive about it. It sweeps together historical periods and geographic distinctions in a pot-pourri of style and design. During the 1980s, when French Country established itself as one of the

PRECEDING PAGE: French Country prints and simple carved seating add whimsy to this soaring foyer by designer Harold Babcock. LEFT: This sitting area is part of a French Country kitchen. The effect of *faux* stone walls is achieved using wallpaper with a stone block design.

THE ARMOIRE

Sometimes over three metres (ten feet) tall and ornately carved, sometimes the size of a refrigerator and perfectly simple, the armoire is an essential element of French Country style. No household in rural Provence or Brittany was complete without one. In fact, so valued were these beautiful pieces that not only were they often used to store a young girl's treasure of laces, linens, and silks, but frequently the armoire itself was a cherished part of her trousseau.

Today, the French armoire is at home in almost any room. In an age obsessed with utilizing space, it can be appreciated not only as a thing of beauty, but also as a wonderful problem-solver. Tall, gracefully carved, and elegantly panelled, a formal armoire is a romantic and stately addition to a bedroom. It also happens to be a perfect place to hang clothes and store linens. Its more modest cousin, the simple, unadorned kitchen armoire — painted in soft washes of blue, green, and grey, and unembarrassed by its age — acts as a friendly and informal cupboard in a modern kitchen. But it can also be used in the living room for stylishly storing the stereo, the television, or even the bar.

most popular interior design trends in North America, shops in Manhattan, Toronto, and Vancouver overflowed with faience pottery, Souleiado and Les Olivades prints, *cotton indiennes*, and oak buffets. These stores saw nothing wrong with putting a nineteenth-century wash basin from Normandy on an eighteenth-century *buffet Provençal*. And the joy — indeed, the point — of French Country is that different styles can be pulled together. The style has always relied on an accumulation of influences, periods, and locales. It has no rigid laws. As much as anything, it depends on our trust in our own sense of beauty.

Throughout French history, fashion always emanated outwards from Paris. Trends in clothing, music, furniture — whatever the latest pursuits of nobles and Parisian sophisticates — eventually found their way to the provinces. Once there, these fashions were copied and adapted by local craftsmen and artists.

Unlike Paris, these regions did not abandon the styles and adaptations with every shift in the winds of fashion. In the countryside, people tended to be frugal. They built things to last. And last they did. Thus, a solid armoire built in the seventeenth century, and bearing a carved allusion to the elaborate tortoiseshell-and-ebony decorations popular in the court of the day, was passed down from one generation to the next until it found itself in a room of rounded, graceful tables and chairs that were a hundred years younger. No one imagined that anything was wrong with this. In fact, the casual collection of inherited styles had a

RIGHT: A French Country dining room in the Toronto townhouse of designer Harold Babcock. Flowers nestled in the chandelier are a romantic gesture.

SOULEIADO AND LES OLIVADES

If there is a single element that says French Country, it is the bright, intricately patterned fabric of its drapes, pillows, curtains, and bedspreads. Originally inspired by the colourful, hand-printed calicoes and chintzes imported to France from India in the seventeenth century, these cotton prints are a wonderful combination of naïvety and sophistication. The strong colours of their flowers and fruits, geometrics and paisleys, are an important part of the French Country palette.

In Canada, French Country prints are available under the brand names of Souleiado and Les Olivades. The name Souleiado — which means "sun breaking through the clouds after a rain storm" — was coined in 1938, when Charles Demery took over an old family textile business in Tarascon, just north of Arles, and began production. Les Olivades continues the tradition of the *Société Avignonnaise d'Impression sur Tissus*, founded by Pierre Boudin in 1948. But both companies have based their production on the long-established tradition of local craftsmen who hand-painted carefully selected cotton with blocks carved from fruitwood. Today the patterns and colours of the best French Country prints are based on the original fruitwood blocks.

certain charm. It was relaxed, straightforward, and as generation added to generation, abundant. It bespoke tradition and craftsmanship and cherished heirlooms. It had a charm that today we call French Country.

"Fantasy and earthiness are very difficult to marry," says Arouna Lipschitz, the manager of Toronto's Pierre Deux store, "but French Country does it." And, in large part, it is this combination of elements that explains French Country's undiminished popularity. As early as the 1960s, adventurous travellers and discerning buyers were drawn to the authenticity of rural French furniture and design. The grand, antique styles of Versailles and the provincial affectations of the affluent bourgeoisie seemed out of step with a more casual, less élitist age. In North America, the quest for real — real food, real furnishings, real lifestyles — was on. It continues still, and French Country suits the mood perfectly. Kitchens aren't hidden from dinner guests; on the contrary, French Country kitchens welcome visitors with their gleaming copper pots, their bowls of fruit and vegetables, their well-scarred cutting boards and massive fruitwood sideboards. Living rooms do not dictate with rigid precision the number of guests they will accommodate; the generous and apparently casual appointments of a French Country living room — with its cascade of colourful drapery and throw of pillows, its banquettes and armchairs — are cosy enough for a romantic evening *à deux*, and yet expansive, elegant, and comfortable should the numbers

RIGHT: Furniture in the typically French bedroom is kept to a minimum. Dried herbs are hung on the wall above the bed, which is dressed in the freshness of pale linens.

*"So I lived, and drank deep draughts of the balmy air of Nice.
Life and happiness came flooding back to me,
music sought me out, the future beckoned."*

**HECTOR BERLIOZ,
COMPOSER,
FROM HIS LETTERS**

ABOVE: This dining room by designer Gary Zanner combines French Country antiques with *faux* animal fabric for a dash of wit. RIGHT: Toile de Jouy and a black-and-white palette were the inspiration for this eclectic bedroom by John Manuel.

FAIENCE

A pine harvest table from as un-Mediterranean a place as rural Ontario can be magically transformed to French Country style by the addition of a single accessory: a beautiful faience vase overflowing with a sumptuous bouquet. The bouquet can be purchased at your local florist, but the faience comes from farther afield. This hand-thrown or hand-moulded pottery is made from the red clay of the mountains of northern Provence and was originally produced by local craftsmen for day-to-day use in country homes. Created in the seventeenth century in Moustiers, the distinctive bowls, place settings, and ornamental vases were mostly blue and white. Then, in the eighteenth century, polychrome techniques were developed, and today its opaque glazes include mustard yellow, emerald green, and white. Decorated with multi-coloured motifs of flowers, fruits, or pastoral scenes, faience has a charm and friendly elegance all its own. It is the perfect French accent.

grow. An art historian might have to be consulted to decide exactly what sort of silver tureen to put on the brecciated marble top of a Louis-Quatorze commode; but within the context of French Country, if a Japanese stereo system finds a home inside an eighteenth-century armoire from Provence, no one — probably not even the ghost of the original cabinet maker — would think the decision anything other than perfectly elegant, practical, and right.

Lovers of French Country style are passionate

RIGHT: A breakfast table set with faience and Souleiado linens. FAR RIGHT: A more sophisticated version of French Country style in a porcelain palette. Modern in its spareness, antique in its detail.

about its colours, its textures, and its flair. They cherish its hearty, unfussy friendliness and straightforward grace. And yet its appeal is something that even those who surround themselves with its bright, lively warmth find difficult to describe. On a grey, cold day in downtown Toronto, the owner of a shop that specializes in the rich fabrics, sumptuous laces, solid furnishings, and pretty china of rural France was asked to explain why she loves French Country as much as she does. She looked around at the full drawers and piled counters and open, full armoires of her store. Then she considered the chill, wet sidewalk beyond her window.

"Sunshine," she said. And that seemed to say it all.

BELOW: A French day bed upholstered in a mellow gold velvet displays a sumptuous collection of antique pillows. OPPOSITE: Two versions of the French Country approach to kitchen design: one light, one dark, both using natural materials and the honest beauty of kitchen wares.

"Il fait beau aujourd'hui.... I've just been for a walk on my small boulevard and looking down below at the houses all bright in the sun and housewives washing their linen in great tubs of glittering water and flinging it over the orange trees to dry. Perhaps all human activity is beautiful in the sunshine."

KATHERINE MANSFIELD,
SHORT STORY WRITER,
FROM HER LETTERS

Grand Marnier

SOUTHWEST STYLE

"O for a beaker full of the warm South."

JOHN KEATS, POET,
ODE TO A NIGHTINGALE

CANADIANS, ESPECIALLY IN THE WINTERTIME, ARE DRAWN TO THE SOUTH. WHEN THE MERCURY drops and the winds howl, we head for Mexico, the southern United States, the Greek Islands, or the Caribbean. Hot sunshine, cool shadows, warm expanses of sand, and cloudless blue skies are irresistible beacons to snow-weary northerners. And when Canadians dream of how they want their homes to look and feel, their imagination often takes the same direction. Call it fantasy, call it wishful thinking, or call it the celebration of qualities we cherish because in our climate we possess them so fleetingly — for whatever reasons, the warm simplicity of the South has entered into our interiors.

The sun-drenched, white-washed walls and the happy-go-lucky accent colours of hot, southward-looking styles have found their way into North American palettes. These styles are the products of climates where the strongest visual elements are the pure hot light of the sun and the dark, sculptural contrasts of its shadows. Usually, southern styles are furnished simply because the transition from indoors to outdoors — from the stone floor of

a dining room to the stone floor of a veranda — is intentionally unclear.

Southern styles such as Greek and Caribbean have popularized plain, rustic wooden ceilings and white beds enshrouded in fantasies of mosquito netting. But in recent years, the distinctive design traditions of Santa Fe, New Mexico, have become the most popular destination of our southern decorating journey. It's now possible to eat *frijoles* in Montreal, to buy Navajo rugs in Toronto, and to discuss the installation of a ceiling constructed of the heavy, horizontal timbers called *vigas* with interior decorators in Vancouver. There's even a store in Manhattan that specializes in bones.

Part of this new trend is the revival of interest in artists such as Georgia O'Keeffe and Ansel Adams. In addition, Ralph Lauren's ongoing celebration of classic Americana, the resurgence of naïve art and native crafts, and even the popularity of the open grills and tangy cuisine of the southern United States contribute to our new Southwest orientation. Homes that were once dark and sombre now have solariums and skylights and are filled with shafts of sunshine, views of blue sky, and the lush year-round green of tropical plants.

Southwest style seems suddenly everywhere. But its thick, sun-bleached walls, sparse furniture, bursts of colour, and its distinctive use of the stones, plants, and dried bones of the desert are really nothing new. This style has been around since 1821, when the Santa Fe trail was opened and travellers and settlers from the

PRECEDING PAGE: The classic beehive fireplace is a staple of Southwest style. LEFT: A canvas-and-wood market umbrella, used indoors, is a dramatic addition to this solarium room.

NAVAJO BLANKETS

The Navajo blankets that are hung on the walls of stylish, modern living rooms are the products of a thousand-year-old tradition. The Navajos — or, as the Spanish called them, the Pueblos — cherished the art of weaving. It was taught to their ancestors, they believed, by the mythical Spider Woman, and its traditions were passed from mother to daughter. Made from the wool of the sheep they raised, and coloured with simple vegetable dyes, the blankets were used primarily as clothing — as shoulder blankets, as serapes, and as ponchos. The intricate geometric designs were always created spontaneously on the rough looms.

The introduction of the oily, synthetically produced aniline dyes late in the nineteenth century brought a bright new palette to the Navajos: the startling reds, vibrant yellows, and dark blue-blacks. But their sense of design and function remained unchanged. The blankets were made to follow the soft contours of shoulders and arms, or, possibly, to be used as a temporary seat on the cold ground. But now that their use tends to be more decorative — providing splashes of eye-dazzling colour amidst the sun-washed Southwest palette — the blankets' gentle past shouldn't be forgotten. Hang your blankets with care. Nails, staples, or carpet tacks will damage the weave and upset the Spider Woman.

eastern United States met the Spanish and Indian influences of the Southwest. Nor is it really a very recent discovery for most of us. The desert colours and the weathered textures of mission walls, the colourful blankets, the turquoise jewels, the brightly painted window frames, the solid Spanish furniture, and the broad stone floors of haciendas have been with us ever since we watched our first western movie.

And yet much of the appeal of Southwest style is the strong, confident, and undeniably contemporary statement that it makes. A cow's skull on a white stucco wall, a curve of brick steps and a series of deep-arched doorways, a solitary wicker basket, a Navajo rug, and a

RIGHT: Bleached bones have long been a part of Southwest style. They are a reminder of the dry, barren beauty of the desert and should not be confused with "trophies of the hunt," which are so objectionable to many.

"I brought home the bleached bones as my symbols of the desert. To me they are as beautiful as anything I know."

GEORGIA O'KEEFFE,
ARTIST,
1939 EXHIBITION CATALOGUE

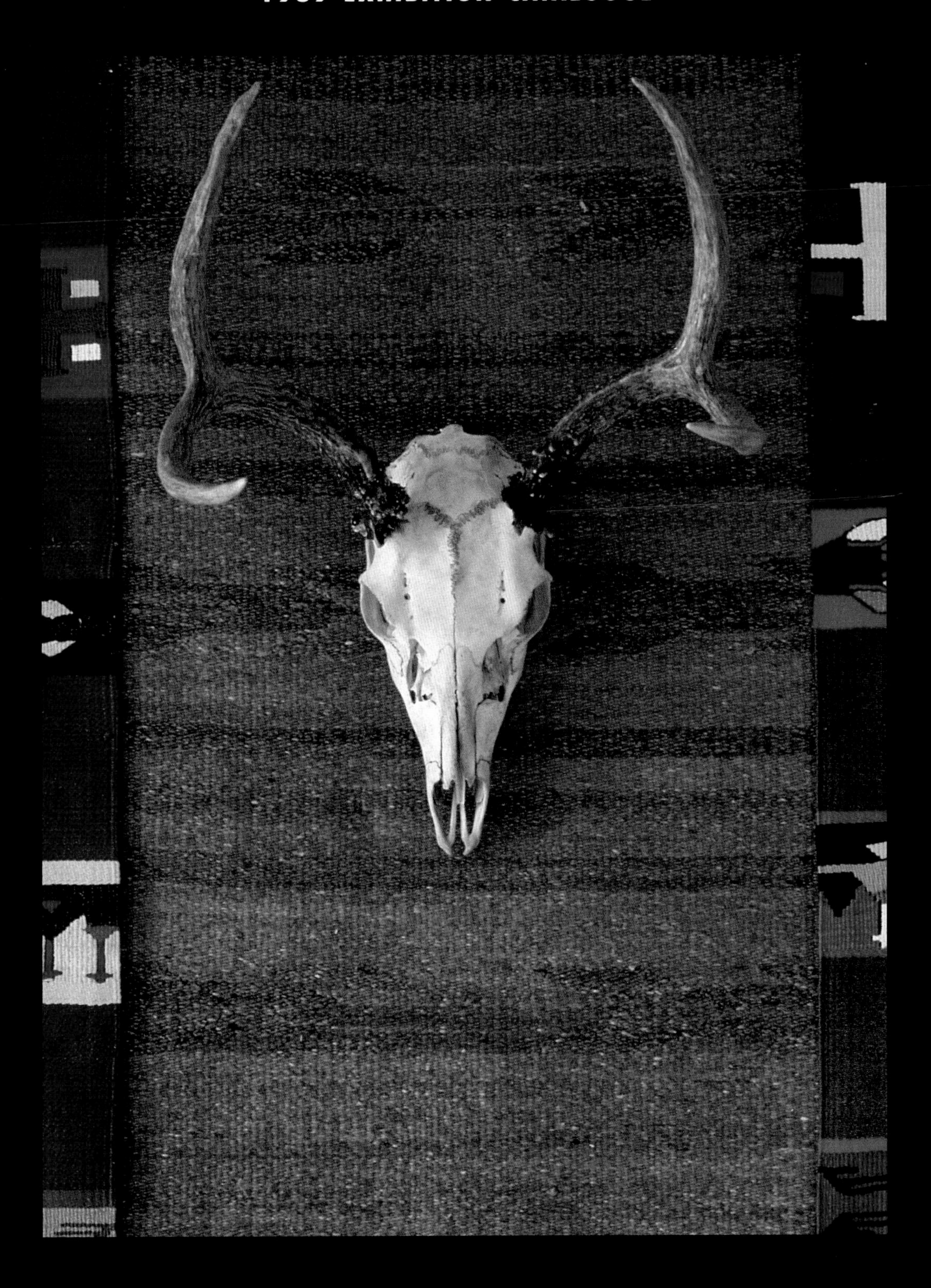

simple unvarnished wooden trunk are not the components of a timid or half-hearted look. They feel as new as the most fashionable downtown restaurant and as bold as the latest New York fashions. Despite its rural origins, Southwest has a snappy, urban appeal and, despite its strong historic roots, it seems to be anything but antique. Someday, historians will look back upon the end of the twentieth century and ponder the intriguing fact that some of the most modern dwellings in the most sophisticated urban centres were decorated with relics from an ancient desert.

Southwest's popularity has as much to do with modern culture as with the natural splendour of its own traditions. It certainly wasn't invented for homes with furnaces, double-paned glass, and baseboard heaters, and it hasn't changed to accommodate us; in the mysterious evolution of trends and styles and lifestyles, we've come around to it. We are, in general, more casual and less stuffy in our approach to our homes and our social lives than we were a generation ago, and Southwest's great appeal is that there is nothing formal or pretentious about it. It's comfortable and relaxed but also curiously modern. In our age of simplicity and sleek lines, its uncluttered spaciousness has the same disciplined quality as minimalism. "I like empty spaces," Georgia O'Keeffe once said of New Mexico, her adopted home.

Yet, in an age that is also drawn to the natural, the unpolished, and the real, Southwest style adds the warm tones of soft, earthy colour

This west-coast home designed by Grace Gordon-Collins gets a Southwest feeling from wicker furniture, Indian blankets, and cotton fabrics in geometric designs. Canadian Indian and Inuit art works well with Southwest elements.

OPPOSITE: "Southwest with a California feeling" is the message in this grouping of rattan and strong vertical cotton prints. LEFT: Although the architecture of this master bedroom suite is Contemporary, the sand-and-cream colour scheme, leather furniture, and Pueblo inspired pottery give this space a Southwest feeling. BELOW: This combination dining-sitting room sports French Country dishes, Contemporary furniture, and eclectic accessories. The Southwest style comes from serape chairs, cactus, Pueblo pottery, Mexican terracotta tiles, and a desert colour scheme.

RIGHT: Hand-painted Mexican reproduction furniture, from Joan Eiley & Associates, is primitive yet sophisticated.
BELOW: Designer Stephen Bailey creates a Western feeling in this guest room of a vacation home. Strong blue walls harmonize with the Roots bed cover. Mexican leather-and-cedar furniture adds a Southwest feeling.

and the friendliness of well-worn textures to minimalism's cool emptiness. It manages to be spartan without being austere, restrained without being inhuman. It manages, in fact, to bridge the gap between two very attractive but seemingly contradictory qualities. It's as new as it is old-fashioned, as surprising as it is familiar.

Southwest is immediately identifiable, and its distinctiveness is one of the reasons a marketer as shrewd and discerning as Ralph Lauren recognized it as a classic. As soon as we see it — whether on a trip to the American Southwest, at a Calgary restaurant where the chicken is grilled on beds of mesquite and the tequila is spiced with chili peppers, during a stroll through Toronto's Designer's Walk, or while watching a re-run of "Bonanza" — we know precisely what it is. The sand-coloured walls and terracotta urns, the tile floors and heavy wooden beams, the rounded, sculptural fireplaces, and the solid, ancient-looking

TERRACOTTA

As old as ancient Greece, as new as the tiled floor of the flashiest downtown restaurant, terracotta has always been in style. This natural ceramic — in the form of vases, jugs, cooking pots, planters, tableware, statues, and friezes — is made from grey clay that turns a distinctive warm reddish-brown when fired.

Many of the vases and bowls that we enjoy today as decoration had purely utilitarian origins. Terracotta, too, has a strong practical side. Because it retains heat and keeps things cool, the Pueblo Indians used it both for cooking and storing water. These properties also make it a wonderful material for tiles. It is dramatic and durable, and on a hot day, nothing feels nicer than cool terracotta tiles underfoot.

Terracotta's simple elegance — whether left in its raw state, glazed, stained, or painted — makes it an extraordinarily adaptable accessory. Terracotta vases and planters are at home on patios, in garden rooms, and on the steps of verandas. But terracotta has a grandeur that also makes it a pleasing addition to a much more formal environment. In a gleaming Contemporary living room or on the landing of a sweeping staircase, it fits right in.

POTTERY

One of the oldest ongoing traditions in Santa Fe is the Indian marketplace outside the Palace of the Governor. There, beneath clear blue New Mexican skies, visitors have been buying the jewellery, blankets, and pottery of the Pueblo Indians ever since trains first brought tourists to the Southwest a hundred years ago.

Today, the popularity of the Southwest look has made the reddish-brown earthenware water jars, figurines, canteens, and bowls available far beyond the New Mexican state line. But even if you are shopping beneath the chillier skies of Vancouver or Halifax, a few tips from the habitués of the Santa Fe market are worth bearing in mind.

There is no such thing as a Pueblo glaze. A vase, a jug, a jar, or a bowl will have either an even matt surface or the smooth sheen caused by polishing the clay with cloth or leather. Sometimes decorated with painted geometric designs, Indian pottery can be easily checked for authenticity. If a moistened finger smears a jar's painting, the painting was done after the firing, which is an undesirable modern short cut. Also, traditional Pueblo pottery is not thrown on a potter's wheel and as a result, its most popular shapes — so integral to the Southwest style — are uncomplicated and usually asymmetrical. The pieces should be well-balanced and solid, but their walls should be thin. And the true test of Indian pottery is the simplest one. A slight tap will make a well-fired, finely crafted vase ring like a bell.

armoires have an integrity that no designer could invent. It is a style born of history and landscape. The colours are those of sand and stone and sky. The accents are the brilliance of Navajo rugs and Indian jewellery. The shapes are the bald, rounded contours of the New Mexican hills. The influences are Spanish and Native American, but Southwest is, above all, a celebration of a vast and spectacular outdoors, and this — to a generation of hikers, health enthusiasts, and spa-goers — is its greatest appeal.

"New Mexico," wrote Roxana Robinson in her biography of Georgia O'Keeffe, "was a sensual feast of heat, color, and air." These characteristics are the essence of Southwest style, and exactly the same qualities lie at the heart of other popular southern styles. They are all styles that are open to the warmth of sunshine, to soft, dry breezes, and to the expansive views beyond their deep-silled, unadorned windows. Their walls are thick in order to keep rooms cool, their floors are stone because the stones will stay warm long after the sun has set. And although no one has ever described a Canadian landscape in February as a sensual feast, there is probably no place on earth where heat, colour, and clear, gentle air are longed for so passionately. Whether in our travels or in the creation of our interiors, it is the promise of something we love that draws us to the Southwest.

RIGHT, TOP: Designer David Thomas combined terracotta walls, cool, creamy white fabrics, antiques, and an eighteenth-century Mexican cowhide trunk in this personal retreat. RIGHT, BOTTOM: A highly functional Contemporary kitchen gets rich textural overtones from a Mexican terracotta floor, primitive pottery, Canadiana accessories, and bamboo stools.

"Oh! That the desert were my dwelling place."

LORD BYRON,
POET,
CHILDE HAROLD'S PILGRIMAGE

FOLK STYLE

"Folk art is what makes people smile."

JIM SHOCKEY,
FOLK ART INTERIORS LTD.

A LUNENBURG COUNTY SEWING BOX, A SHAKER ROCKING CHAIR, A HAND-CARVED DECOY FROM Quebec, a painted wooden salmon from Vancouver — the items seem too unrelated to belong on a single list, and yet all share a common origin. They are all examples of folk art. Each says something about a particular place, culture, or community. Each comes wrapped in history. Once they were functional parts of everyday life. Only later were they labelled primitive or naïve. Now, thanks to a world-wide revival in folk arts, they are as integral to sophisticated and stylish interiors as a Bergère chair, an Italian halogen light, or a Chippendale sideboard.

Canadian, Scandinavian, New England, and Central and South American folk do not belong exclusively in museum exhibitions. They are found in glossy magazine spreads and some of the trendiest stores. The bright colours, simple shapes, and cheerful lack of pretension of folk art have struck a chord with our modern world. Folk art did more than just appear in collections; it began to influence interiors in a more general way. People who

loved folk art found themselves drawn to a look we think of now as Folk style.

Folk style's popularity arises from our curiosity about the past, from our longing to link our lives to the lives of previous generations, and from our own remembrances of childhood. Folk connects us to a real and identifiable past that was created not as high art or ostentatious display, but simply for the use and pleasure of the people who made it.

Time is the commodity we value so much in folk art. Somehow, in an age of such time-saving devices as computers, automatic banking machines, and cellular phones, we seem to be in more of a hurry than ever. Time is what we recognize, almost without thinking about it, when we admire a hand-painted blanket box, a traditional hooked rug, a cane armchair, or an array of patchwork throw cushions — the things made by "unhurried hands."

As well as time, folk art also evokes place. It has a strong regional identity. On old Canadian pieces, from blanket boxes to bread boxes, decorative thistles or shamrocks tell whether the maker was originally from Scotland or Ireland. One Nova Scotian community might have used a different group of decorative motifs than its neighbour. In our modern age, when every shopping mall looks the same, this kind of connection has enormous appeal.

Folk objects made today do not grow out of a real need for a toy or a weather vane as they

PRECEDING PAGE: This is the foyer of an Ontario farmhouse. The church-style window in heritage blue and the Canadian antiques combine to create a dramatic second-floor landing. LEFT: This eat-in kitchen shows how French Country prints on curtains and table-top can contribute to Canadiana Folk style. Often the elements of different country styles complement one another.

SHAKER

Simplicity was the key to the Shaker movement, just as it was the key to the extraordinary furniture it produced. Established in America in the late eighteenth century, the Shaker faith spread from the northeast as far west as Kentucky and Ohio. An astonishingly successful communal Utopian experiment, it had at its height almost six thousand members in twenty communities.

The United Society of Believers — or Shakers, as they came to be called as a result of the joyous dancing they performed as part of their worship — disavowed vanity and the pleasure of possessions. They were a frugal, practical, hard-working people. "Set not your hearts on worldly objects," read one of the tenets of their faith, "but let this be your labour, to keep a spiritual sense."

Ironically, the simple, functional objects they produced for their own use have come to be highly valued possessions today. And it's easy to see why. Shaker furniture has a purity of design that seems almost modern in its economy. The spiritual sense that the Shakers tried so hard to find in every aspect of their lives shines through in the care they took with the things they made. All their pieces were made with painstaking craftsmanship. Pine cupboards and maple cases of drawers, simple boxes painted olive green, birch work stands, and cane-seated chairs — all are the products of unhurried, careful craftsmen who saw no purpose in making something unless it was as perfect as it could be.

once did. Today's folk objects are art forms and the products of cottage industries. However, they retain the friendly personal charm of older pieces and provide an antidote to the monotony of modern life. Folk art represents qualities and standards that seem superior to those of the present. Every time you reach for a big, home-style chocolate chip cookie instead of one from a mass-produced package, every time you choose an "old-fashioned" potato chip over the greasy standard, you're making the kind of choice that draws us to Folk style.

One of the great charms of Folk style is its adaptability. Its origins are informal, practical, and unpretentious. It was never intended to be part of a particular look or fashion, and it can still fit in almost anywhere. It can be as sparse and uncluttered as a Shaker home — a set of plain, splint-seated chairs around a cherry, drop-leaf table in a room in which a shaft of sunlight from the window seems to be the only accessory. It can be a happy jumble of fabrics, textures, and objects — a sofa piled with patchwork pillows, a

RIGHT: The spartan beauty of early Canadiana is heightened by oxblood painted chairs against soft grey-washed walls. OPPOSITE, TOP: Kristin Basso designed a "harvest home" live-in kitchen. An antique armoire filled with preserves is a reminder of the harvest and its fruits. OPPOSITE, BOTTOM: Open shelving turns upper kitchen cabinets into display cases for hand-painted pottery in this very personal country kitchen.

"Anything may be called perfect that perfectly answers the purpose for which it was designed."

SHAKER SAYING

twig side table holding painted dolls and a crockery-based lamp, a blanket-box coffee table next to a window sill filled with oil lamps.

Folk style is also wonderfully accessible. It draws its inspiration from, and is built around, the objects of folk art. In Canada, we have a wealth of folk traditions at our fingertips. You can find wonderful examples of folk art in local flea markets, specialty boutiques, antique stores, and auctions. You can still find pieces piled in barns or gathering dust in attics. Prices have soared for the best pieces in recent years, but there are still plenty of affordable options — from homemade board games to your grandmother's baking tins. And Folk style, like the objects it celebrates, is often more easily achieved and affordable than other more rarefied, less home-grown styles.

The pieces of folk art that are so important a part of Folk style are by definition simple; their design is straightforward. Objects are made to

OPPOSITE: "Folk" collector Joanne Thring created a sun-filled breakfast room in her Toronto home. This was a *Canadian House & Home* cover and the appeal was as instant and broad as Folk style. BELOW: A hallway is often the prime spot for a rogue's gallery of family photos.

ABOVE: This rooster lamp from Cullen Country Barns is a reproduction copied from an original in the collection of the Museum of American Folk Art. RIGHT: This guest bedroom in an Ontario farmhouse designed by Elaine Slater shows the owner's appreciation for the natural beauty of the structure. Furniture is simple and minimal and the sheep are good company.

PATCHWORK QUILTS

There is a shop in Mahone Bay, Nova Scotia, called Suttles and Seawinds which sells some of the country's most beautiful quilts.

Suttles refers to the scraps of material that were traditionally sewn together to create patchwork quilts. It's possible to make an appliqué quilt by sewing pieces of material over a single complete layer of fabric. But traditionally, in pioneer days, a quilt was more likely to be scraps of fabric pieced together. Pioneers were, by necessity, frugal people. Rather than throw out leftover pieces of material or salvageable bits from old clothes, the women would save their scraps until they had enough for a quilt.

These quilts provided warmth and colour, and were also a way that pioneer women could express themselves creatively. Over time, extraordinary patterns were developed — some quite intricate and complex, and some with wonderful names. Kites and Spiderwebs, Log Cabins, Drunkard's Trail, Trip around the World, and Fanny's Fan are a few of the popular ones. Somewhere in their intricate patterns, quilters would make a deliberate "mistake"; one corner triangle might be a different colour than the other three because "only God is perfect."

Designing a quilt, choosing a colour scheme, cutting, and sewing are time-consuming, labour-intensive jobs. That's why we so treasure patchwork quilts. A big quilt can be completed in two weeks of solid work. More likely — because few people have the time to sit down and work solidly on a quilt for two weeks — it will be an entire winter's project.

MILK PAINTS

There was a time, not many years ago, when any wooden antique or antique reproduction had to be stripped. In the 1960s, painting wood — which is, of course, exactly what our ancestors did — was considered a desecration. Robert Danielis, one of the founding partners of Homestead House Paint Company, remembers only too well the comments he received when he sold antiques at Toronto's Harbourfront not many years ago. He loved the look of old painted furniture, and his desire to recapture the distinctive colours took him back to the original pioneer recipes for milk paint. Mixing lime, clay, casein (the bonding agent found in milk), and natural dyes, the celebrated craftsman and folk artist would spend hours looking for the right shade of Mennonite Red for a harvest table or Loyalist Green for a kitchen cupboard, only to have people say, "That's nice. Can you get the paint off?"

But times have changed. Painting wood is popular again, and many of the old heritage colours are available in stores across the country. The milk paints produced by such companies as Homestead House Paint have names such as Barn Red, Texas Rose, Waterloo Green, Acadia Pear, Prince Edward Grey, Mount Royal Blue, and Mustard. Based on the paint that pioneers and farmers made themselves, their soft, peaceful colours recall the days when dyes were made from berries, grasses, iron oxide, animal blood, and coal. The colours have a soft, authentically old-time look, and they're perfect for wooden furniture, kitchen cabinets (covered with a flat lacquer), floors (covered with urethane), and even walls.

Since the paint is mixed at home, both a light wash and a more colour-saturated intensity are possible. A little sandpaper or steel wool can distress the surface to create an antique look.

last. And it is this same unfussy practicality that makes Folk style so appealing. Just as a patchwork quilt seems to suit almost any room, Folk style has an easy-going ability to adjust to almost any scale of decoration or renovation. A modern apartment, an executive boardroom, a suburban basement can be transformed with a few carefully chosen pieces, a little paint, and some imagination.

Like folk art, Folk style is about family life. It's a style for doers, makers, and crafts-lovers, as well as buyers. Its sturdy practicality, plain finishes, gentle friendliness, and simple charm have withstood generations of children, pets, traffic, and activity. It's the perfect style for a busy house.

Our videos, stereos, home computers, and exercise machines have given birth to the term "cocooning." We play at home, exercise at home, entertain at home, amuse ourselves at home, and even work at home. But cocooning isn't an entirely modern phenomenon. In many ways, it's a return to the household that produced the style we think of now as Folk. When the snow was blowing outside, families sat near the fireplace and played a homemade board game. They wrapped in quilts and curled up with books. They busied themselves hooking rugs or carving wooden toys. Much like the most modern family, they enjoyed their own home entertainment, and their interiors reflected this contentment. Perhaps it is for that reason that what they left behind — and the style inspired by this inheritance — so suits our lives today.

RIGHT AND FAR RIGHT: Canadian folk art and simple furnishings provide an honest charm at Manitowaning Lodge. Designer Leo LaFerme chose local artist Angus Trudeau's popular folk art.

"When times are uncertain, people seem drawn to the past. In particular, they seem drawn to things that are made of wood – furniture, gamesboards, decoys, and bowls. There's a warmth and a simplicity to wood, and, in folk art, there's often a sense of humour people find attractive."

DIAN SMITH,
PORT DALHOUSIE TRADING COMPANY

TRUE NORTH STYLE

"You have not seen Canada until you have seen the North."
PIERRE TRUDEAU TO QUEEN ELIZABETH II

MARGARET ATWOOD ONCE REMARKED THAT WHETHER OR NOT WE CANADIANS EVER ACTUALLY leave our cities to head north, the place that the North holds in our imaginations is what makes us Canadian. These days in particular, with the state of our environment so much on our minds, the Canadian North — though by no means immune to the ravages of pollution — remains a symbol of what people everywhere are trying to protect. The tranquil blue of a lake, the magnificent green of the forest, the clear, cool air, the solitude, and the quiet: these are the elements that make the North so appealing. Whether it sits in our memory of childhood summers or in our vacation plans for the week after next, it is often the place we think of when we're riding a crowded subway, working beneath the fluorescent lights of an office, or frantically juggling the demands of busy lives.

The style that has grown out of our northern experience established itself naturally long before anyone thought to call it a style. It's simply a part of the Canadian psyche, and the words we associate with it — "Mounties," "trappers," "furs," "canoes," "Rockies,"

"snowshoes," "trading posts" — conjure the style's images: smoke curling from the chimney of a log cabin, bacon frying in a cast-iron pan, a fishing rod propped against the wooden rails of a veranda.

Today we see it as a particular look. Clothes, architecture, and interior design have been touched recently by northern influences. Having long been told that we had no national style, Canadians are happily acknowledging the one we've had under our noses all along. The miner's cabin, the trapper's lodge, the interiors festooned (long before the days of environmentalism) with animal heads, skins, horns, and antlers — these historical images have inspired a distinctly modern trend. It's now possible, in most major Canadian cities, to buy a beautiful rugged sweater at a Roots store, twig furniture at a fashionable boutique, and sourdough bread, maple syrup, and peameal bacon at a gourmet grocery. You'd have to wrap yourself in a Hudson's Bay blanket to be more Canadian.

The popularity of Roots and of Ralph Lauren's rustic look has brought the northern style to our attention. But originally it wasn't an expression of taste, fashion, or national aesthetics. It was simply the product of necessity and the available materials. People wore woollen sweaters because fleece was obtainable and winters were cold. They ate bread and bacon because there was flour in the barrel and a few pigs out back. They made chairs from twigs because twigs were there. And they built their houses out of logs and stone

PRECEDING PAGE: In Ontario's cottage country, designer Stephen Bailey mixed the rugged elements of stone and wood with weavings and Indian art. LEFT: The charm of a miner's cabin is captured in simple cotton bedding and the beauty of rustic bare walls.

LOG CABINS

Log houses were built in North America long before the coming of white settlers. West Coast Indians constructed log-frame dwelling places, and in the eastern woodlands, log houses often marked the permanent sites of seasonal campgrounds. But it was with the Europeans that the structures we think of as traditional log cabins arrived. In these buildings, short, roughly squared logs were horizontally laid and fitted into slotted corners. This basic construction is still what most people envision today as the traditional rustic woodland retreat.

As picturesque as the traditional log cabin is, it has its drawbacks. Its lines do not allow for the large windows that most modern home-owners enjoy; if you add too many large windows, the structure stops looking like a log cabin. And although pioneers were happy with the insulating qualities of carefully chinked log walls, they compare poorly with the standards of modern construction.

A happy compromise seems to be the prefabricated wooden house constructions that are being made today by companies that use a traditional method of meticulously notching and fitting timbers to form a highly adaptable skeleton. Thus, a house that has the vaulted ceilings, large windows, and insulation standards of a modern home can also have the kind of rustic quality, natural finishes, and exposed timbers that draw people to the romance of log cabins — it's the best of both worlds.

because these were the materials that were available, and because shelter, warmth, and comfort were necessities in the northern climate.

This straightforward approach to building had an obvious secondary effect; houses not only suited their environment, they actually looked like their surroundings. So, by the time log cabins ceased to be the crude shelters of pioneers and started to become the comfortable summer retreats of city dwellers, their appeal was obvious. They echoed — in their colours, textures, and scale — the very qualities that drew people to the North. Their logs were from the surrounding woods; their stone was taken from the land nearby. Their furniture had a

BELOW: A log house can accommodate the comfort of contemporary seating. RIGHT: This country house is a 175-year-old barn that was built in Caledon East, Ontario, and reconstructed in Vancouver. Architect Leith Anderson revived the structure, and the owners – avid collectors of interesting old furniture and relics – designed the warm, whimsical interiors. The furnishings are largely Ontario and Quebec pine antiques. The rough cedar walls were sprayed with a fireproof paint that gives the effect of whitewash.

"In summer it was green, raw greens all in a tangle; in autumn it flamed with red and gold; in winter it was wrapped in a blanket of dazzling snow; and in the springtime it roared with running waters and surged with new life."

A. Y. JACKSON,
ARTIST

rough, unfussy texture. But it was simplicity that was their greatest attraction.

The promise of simplicity has always been what has lured people away from the pressures and complications of city life. A walk in the woods, an afternoon of cross-country skiing, a hearty dinner in front of a crackling fire, a peaceful sleep — these are the pleasures that are celebrated by True North style.

True North has about it the same informal, uncluttered approach as the celebrated styles of the American Southwest. Its colours are darker than the colours of Southwest, its forms and weights are heavier and more solid. But it celebrates Native colours, textures, and crafts in the same way. Brightly coloured Indian blankets provide splashes of colour and warmth. Quill boxes and beadwork are the perfect contrasts to the soft, shadowy browns of wood and logs. And True North enjoys the same easy-going informality and the same openness of design as

LEFT: Logs, lace, and the drama of a spiral staircase are part of the eclectic mix in this rustic retreat by architect Brian Williams.

TWIG FURNITURE

Willow, hickory, or cedar. Painted, stained, or *au naturel.* With or without bark. A twig chair is not as simple a thing as you might think. It can come from Georgian Bay, the St. John River Valley, or the Adirondacks. It can be made by Ojibway Indians, entrepreneurial hippies, or well-financed artisans in Wisconsin. It can cost two hundred dollars or a thousand dollars.

In fact, twig or stick furniture is so diverse and so popular, it's almost impossible to classify. Like wicker furniture, it utilizes a wide variety of styles, materials, and finishes. It has also developed well beyond the traditional bounds of the garden table and matching chairs. Today there's more in twig than a place to sit and a spot to put your gin and tonic; today there are twig beds, twig sideboards, twig armoires, and twig chests of drawers.

Twig furniture's origins were humble and purely utilitarian. It was made by Canadian and American native peoples and by pioneers simply because saplings were readily available. Later, in the late nineteenth and early twentieth centuries, it became fashionable on the patios, along the verandas, and in front of the stone fireplaces of the grand cottages and lodges of the day. Today, twig furniture is everywhere.

Bent by hand, green branches of cedar, willow, or hickory are nailed together and allowed to dry out naturally or in a kiln. There are no particular regional styles for twig furniture; it's an individual craft. Choosing twig furniture depends on what appeals to your eye — as well as to another part of your anatomy. "There's some twig furniture," said one dealer, "that you wouldn't want to sit in for more than five minutes. There are other pieces in which you can happily sit and read all evening."

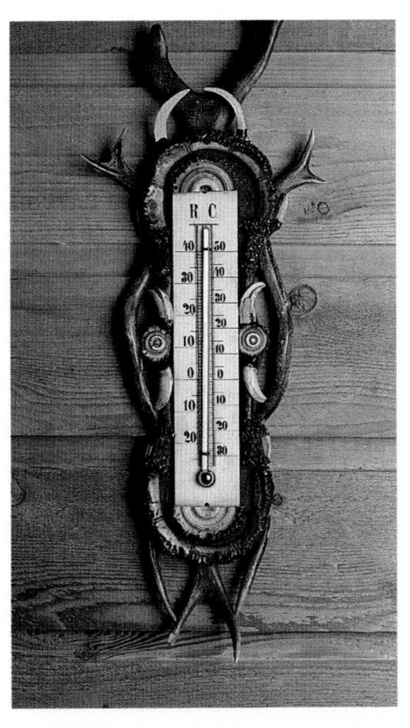

FAR LEFT: Architect William Bennett designed this contemporary retreat with its soaring sense of scale, its abundant sunlight and rustic comfort. LEFT: Accessories can echo the natural beauty of animal horns and the textures of nature. BELOW: Krystyne Griffin created a mix of rich colour and memorable texture in this highly personal family retreat.

QUILLWORK

Indian quillwork is a distinctively North American craft. Used as embroidery on pouches, bags, quivers, head-dresses, moccasins, belts, and jackets, dyed porcupine quills have been a part of Native tradition for centuries. So important were the decorative patterns to ceremonial costumes, the art of dyeing quills was said to have been given to Indian tribes by the great Thunder spirit. The art of quillwork was thought to be sacred and was passed on from mother to daughter.

Porcupine quills are naturally white-ish with black tips. Women cut them into even lengths and coloured them with dyes made from lichen, berries, and grasses. Since the quills did not readily absorb the dyes, the colour was often pressed into the surface by wrapping the quills with the dye in a cloth, and then flattening the bundle for several days beneath the weight of several blankets.

Quillwork — especially the small leather pouches and bags that were covered with bright, intricate patterns — are valuable collectors' items today for two reasons: first, their inherent beauty and craftsmanship, and second, their scarcity. Examples of fine, early quillwork are extremely rare. In the 1880s, beads brought by North American settlers almost completely replaced the quill as a decoration on leather. Quillwork, until a relatively recent revival, was almost a lost art.

the desert and Pacific styles. Because the wood of walls, ceiling, and floor, and the structure of a cabin, chalet, or cottage make so complete a statement, only the furnishings you need and the accessories you love are required to complete the look.

True North differs from Southwest largely because it developed in response to the Canadian winter. Even though today cottages and country retreats might be used more in the summer months, originally log houses were built with long, cold winters in mind. And True North style therefore emphasizes the warmth and cosiness that come from blankets and rugs, throws and eiderdown quilts, Franklin stoves and roaring fires, and homemade patchworks and abundant pillows.

True North can reflect regional differences as well. If the Klondike and the gold rush are the inspiration, then saddle-bags, cowboy boots, ropes, and prospecting gear create the mood. A more eastern look can be developed by echoing the simple interiors of homesteading pioneers — the old irons, the butter churns, the farm tools — or, with its big stone fireplaces and high wooden rafters, it can conjure the grand old resorts of Muskoka or the Maritimes, or Montebello in Quebec.

But, whether ranch, chalet, cabin, or lodge, True North is about taking it easy. It's about fresh air and peace and quiet. And it's about simple, timeless pleasures.

RIGHT, TOP: The spirited ease of the rugged Northwest is captured in furnishings, fabrics, and accessories by Ralph Lauren. Try mixing cotton, denim, lace, and leather on beds and soft seating. RIGHT, BOTTOM: Again from the Ralph Lauren Home Collection, a hand-tooled leather armchair with blanket-stitched trim and cowboy fringe sits dramatically on a Navajo woven rug.

"To be a stylist is to be yourself, but on purpose."

PETER C. NEWMAN,
WRITER

CONTEMPORARY STYLE

"Form ever follows function."

LOUIS HENRI SULLIVAN,
ARCHITECT

THE INFLUENCE OF THE VICTORIAN AGE IS SO STRONG IN CANADA THAT WE STILL THINK OF THE styles that reacted against it as "modern," even though some of them — Art Deco, for instance — are three-quarters of a century old. "Old-fashioned," for most of us, is still the gloomy, cluttered, knick-knacked look our grandparents favoured. And "new-fashioned" can be anything from the clean, geometric shapes of a Bauhaus chair designed in 1924 to the sleek lines of the 1985 Post-Modern icon, the stainless steel "Singing Kettle." Both are "modern" statements, both have their place in our century of dizzying styles and trends. Art Deco, Bauhaus, Modernism, Fifties Free Flow, Post-Modernism, Memphis, and High Tech are some of the century's main design currents. An understanding of these styles allows us to use them as a source of inspiration for our own Contemporary design.

PRECEDING PAGE: The architectural design of this soaring space by architect John Mason provides the aesthetic statement. The emphasis on space, light, and form is the essence of the Contemporary message. LEFT: This vignette is a wonderful example of the dramatic simplicity and rich materials that typify Art Deco design. RIGHT: This converted warehouse space combines Bauhaus seating with Post-Modern and Italian furniture and accessories. Functional steel construction is celebrated and made part of the design statement.

ART DECO

Art Deco became fashionable in France during the Roaring Twenties. Its influences included cubism, the bright colours of the Fauve painters, and the designs for Diaghilev's Ballet Russe production of *Scheherazade*. The razzmatazz of the Jazz Age and the discovery of Tutankhamen's tomb are reflected in Art Deco's vibrant shapes and colours and its love of African images and Egyptian motifs.

Art Deco celebrated the new machine-made materials — bakelite, celluloid, Formica, tubular steel, plate glass, tinted mirror — and combined them with rare and exotic materials such as ebony and amboina woods, snake, zebra, leopard skins, and even "shagreen," which is treated fish scales! Art Deco designers combined technology with quality craftsmanship to produce luxury one-of-a-kinds. Traditional forms were rejected in favour of the new streamlined surfaces, geometric forms, and the zig-zags of Egyptian and Mayan pyramids. When ornamentation was applied — whether graceful female figures, animals, or floral motifs — it, too, was streamlined, flattened, and geometric.

Art Deco embraced the concept of "total design." It was meant to be applied to everything from a clock or a keyhole to an entire building, as it was, for example, at Radio City Music Hall or the Empire State Building. Erte, the most celebrated Art Deco designer and artist, designed everything from rooms and their furnishings to towels and teacups.

As the Depression took hold, Art Deco began to seem too frivolous and too expensive a style. The glamorous Cocktail Age gave way to the more austere Modernist Movement.

BAUHAUS OR MODERNISM

Bauhaus was the style of the Thirties. It began as a school in 1919 in Weimar, Germany, led by designer and architect Walter Gropius. The goal of Bauhaus was to combine quality design with machine technology to create a style that could be mass-produced. According to Gropius and his followers, form would follow function, and function would not be hidden by antiquated

THE WHITE ROOM

Almost every decade of the twentieth century has brought a shift in tastes and styles. In fact, we frequently use the decades as convenient categories for describing styles. One of the century's most celebrated interiors, the rooms of white walls, cream rugs, and mirrors created by Syrie Maugham, the wife of the famous writer Somerset Maugham, is pure "Thirties." This look had its Hollywood parallel in the white satin bias-cut gowns and platinum hair of Jean Harlow.

Syrie Maugham's simple white-on-white interiors with their absence of antiques and sumptuous draperies teach an important lesson even today. Anyone decorating a home or an apartment in Contemporary style need not spend a fortune on costly furnishings and *objets d'art*. Thanks in large part to Syrie Maugham, we accept as perfectly natural the notion that a room should reflect imagination and creativity, not just the size of the owner's bank account.

Syrie Maugham created her white-on-white, *crème-on-crème* look in the years immediately following the crash of 1929. Money was scarce. Servants were too expensive to maintain. Luxurious, hand-crafted furnishings were too costly to purchase. In fact, in many ways the age was similar to our own. And it was Syrie Maugham who, with her white look, created an interior that did not depend on lavish, sumptuous decor, or on faithful reproduction of a period, or on the inherent value of objects for its deluxe appeal. It was glamorous and exciting simply because it had flair. No one had ever thought of a white room before, which is what made it so wonderful. And ever since, we have felt free to follow our own creative instincts. The white rooms became a rage, but the most valuable thing in them was Syrie Maugham's imagination.

decoration. The Bauhaus movement rejected the warmth and luxury of handmade furniture and crafted ornamentation. It celebrated the functionalism of straight lines, geometric forms, hard glossy surfaces, bent plywood, and tubular metals. Its machine-like appearance perfectly suited the school's underlying philosophy of economy of design. One of its most celebrated practitioners, the architect, designer, and artist Le Corbusier, once remarked that a house should be "a machine for living." Everything from a teapot to a living room was stripped to essentials. The words "modular" and "standardization" crept into the design vocabulary.

In the absence of decoration, an object's beauty came from its proportions, from its linear abstraction, and from colour, which was used sparingly but effectively. The Bauhaus palette was revolutionary; it eschewed lively decorative colours in favour of neutrals. The natural colours of materials — wood, metal, unbleached fibres — were an important part of this palette. Burnt orange, maroon, and deep greens added more vivid accents.

The Nazis disapproved of the social and political theories put forward by this "rationalist" design style and closed the Bauhaus in 1933. The school's leaders — Mies van der Rohe, Gropius, Marcel Breuer, and Moholy-Nagy — fled Germany for other European countries and America. At this point, Bauhaus became known as Modernism, and its influence spread world-wide.

FIFTIES FREE FLOW

What we think of today as 1950s style actually began in the 1940s, at the end of the Second World War. The war had created an explosion of technology and mass production. To keep the

ABOVE: Architect Kenney Nickerson designed this renovation of a typical bungalow. Fifties' furniture was reclaimed, and throughout the house period pieces are mixed with new, fifties-inspired, and Italian-designed furniture and accessories. LEFT: "Clean and spare" is the message in this simple grouping of Contemporary elements. Architectural prints and black-and-white line drawings are favourite complements to the monotone scheme of this style.

massive wheels of the economy rolling in peacetime, wartime frugality had to give way to planned obsolescence.

Reacting to the drab and sterile qualities of Bauhaus or Modernism, designers embraced the new materials the war had created: fibreglass and other moulded plastics, wire mesh, and stronger, lighter metal alloys. They took full advantage of new manufacturing techniques to produce the bulging, flowing forms that were so characteristic of the period. Charles Eames, for example, designed chairs with moulded plywood seats on splayed chrome legs. A later chair — asymmetrical with a hole in the plywood — resembled the sculpture of Jean Arp and Henry Moore. Isamu Noguchi's rice-paper lampshade, Harry Bertoia's black wire mesh chair, and Marcel Breuer's tubular steel and cane side chairs remain Fifties' classics. With its curving lines and light weight, Scandinavian furniture was also immensely popular. It could be easily moved — an appealing quality in a mobile world — and its functionalism was balanced with the warmth of natural materials and hand finishing.

The smooth and curving lines of Fifties' furniture were reflected in the period's revolutionary approach to house design. Space opened up dramatically. The kitchen "flowed" into the dining room, which "overlapped" into the living room, which "blended" with the hall.

POST-MODERNISM

The term Post-Modernism was coined in the 1970s, but came into its own as the new wave of the 1980s. Its bursts of colour and quirky, playful ornamentation were largely a reaction against the austerity of Modernism. The turquoise Chippendale crowns and the pastel columns seen in fashionable restaurants, the explosion of primary colours and the crazy angles of bookcases or teapots designed by the Milan-based Memphis Group, the return to mouldings and *faux* treatments and decorative columns were, in part, the wonderful creations of our own age. But they were also attempts by designers and architects to free themselves from the shadow cast by Modernism.

Post-Modernism's aim was anti-design. Past forms and norms were understood but used irreverently: huge columns might hold up tiny

LEFT: A Post-Modern fireplace sports a Tezio lamp, one of the classics of Contemporary lighting design. Items such as this are so distinctive they can come to represent an era of design. RIGHT, TOP: This artful mix of dark and light uses Italian-designed Contemporary furniture, natural materials, and subtle mood lighting. RIGHT, BOTTOM: A dramatic statement in utter simplicity. Plank flooring and finely crafted cabinetry bring warmth to an otherwise stark space.

pediments, and all might be perched precariously on a set of spheres. Colour became playful: walls could be pink and window frames turquoise with a window sill of black-and-white check. Post-Modernists believed that the products of machines didn't have to look like machines: a steam iron could be pink with a yellow curve for a handle and a baby-blue dial.

Patterns, which Modernism had rejected, became vital elements of Post-Modernism. Surfaces were covered with little squiggles, computer-like graphics, timeless stripes and checks, or geometrics that gave a three-dimensional look.

MEMPHIS

Memphis is a Post-Modern style first seen in 1981 at a now-famous Milanese furniture show. Ettore Sottsass, with his group of irreverent, irrepressible young Italian designers, rocked the design world with outrageous, radical, often whimsical furniture. The name Memphis was chosen for its reference to the Tennessee home of Elvis Presley, the ancient Egyptian city, and the lyrics of a famous Bob Dylan song ("...stuck inside of a Mobile with the Memphis blues again...") — a cultural hodgepodge that typified the Memphis Group's rule-breaking "hot" style. In Memphis style, the Op-Art love of black and white was mixed with the bright colours of licorice all-sorts. Shapes were drawn from the 1950s' atomic style, from pure neo-classicism, and from so wide and playful a variety of stylistic and architectural sources that it shook the serious world of modern design to the core,

This Contemporary living room by architects Thomas Payne and Bruce Kuwabara combines glass block, exposed ducting, and Post-Modern detailing.

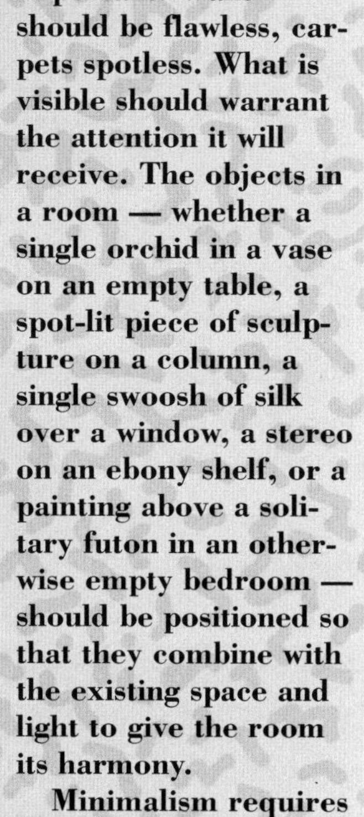

MINIMALISM

Minimalism is a design approach that strictly edits out all the superfluous clutter of everyday life. It is a style that reduces the objects in a room to the bare, beautiful minimum. It combines the Modernist concern with line, proportion, and balance with the Japanese appreciation of empty space and the contemplative serenity of simplicity.

The essentials of life — food, clothes, books, etc. — must be stored inconspicuously. Everything must have its place. Cleanliness as well as tidiness are important. Walls should be flawless, carpets spotless. What is visible should warrant the attention it will receive. The objects in a room — whether a single orchid in a vase on an empty table, a spot-lit piece of sculpture on a column, a single swoosh of silk over a window, a stereo on an ebony shelf, or a painting above a solitary futon in an otherwise empty bedroom — should be positioned so that they combine with the existing space and light to give the room its harmony.

Minimalism requires discipline; this is the most demanding of styles because simplicity is never easy to achieve and once achieved is difficult to sustain. But simplicity has its own extraordinary elegance, and Minimalism is simplicity taken to a dramatic and beautiful extreme.

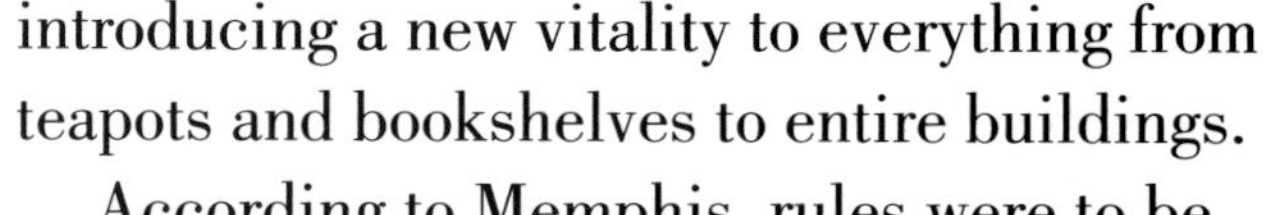

introducing a new vitality to everything from teapots and bookshelves to entire buildings.

According to Memphis, rules were to be broken. The laws of good taste were bent by the new and largely humorous popularity of kitsch. *Faux* finishes were celebrated for their tongue-in-cheek attitude to things grand, lofty, and pretentious. Furniture became almost sculpture, and its beauty came from the witty way it balanced apparent imbalance and found its own sense of harmony in confusion.

HIGH TECH

High Tech, or the use of industrial products in non-industrial situations, was considered revolutionary in the 1970s. Now we take for granted factory lights hung over dining room tables, hospital faucets in the bathroom, and restaurant appliances in the kitchen.

The quality and durability of things made to meet the demands of industrial or commercial use are valued in an age when objects designed for household use look nice but don't last. In a world that embraces jeans, work boots, jeeps and vans, warehouse lofts and offices, High Tech's appeal is its honesty and aesthetic unpretentiousness. The Georges Pompidou Centre in Paris, for instance, looks more like an oil refinery than an art gallery. It flaunts its heating pipes and air ducts. As a building, it is what it is and this straightforward approach establishes its own kind of beauty.

An understanding of different twentieth-century styles is not meant to pin us down to one particular approach. A purist might prefer to

The spa-like purity of this Contemporary bath is achieved with functional design and materials. Note the two banks of lockers framing the stainless steel counter.

ABOVE: A grouping of "classic contemporaries" – the Pratfall tub chair by Philippe Starck, the Driade and Golden chair by Magistretti, the Orio table by Pierluigi Cerri, the Bibip lamp by Achille Castiglioni, and the Aforismi storage unit by Antonia Astori. OPPOSITE: A state-of-the-art Contemporary kitchen by designer Stephen Bailey. The checked iron chair with its animal motif adds humour and whimsy to an otherwise serious interior.

keep each style distinct. A serious collector of Art Deco — someone in love with pale walls and highly polished open floors, low divans and Egyptian vases, exotic rugs and abundant lacquer — would never dream of mixing a bent-plywood Eames chair, designed in the 1950s, or an Italian halogen desk lamp from the 1980s, with a 1925 Macassar ebony, ivory-inlaid dressing table. Most of us, however, are a little less exclusive in our tastes. In furnishing our homes, we tend to blur the boundaries between styles.

One of the reasons we shift so freely from one Contemporary look to another is that there is a strong visual connection between the various "modern" styles. They all celebrate the beauty of strong clean lines and balanced proportions. A thing is not attractive because of the decorations and frills that are added, but because of its shape, its mass — the way it fills space.

The startling, clean lines of a Memphis Group gravy boat, designed in 1982 — and considered quite revolutionary at the time — would have scarcely raised an eyebrow had it been placed on a gleaming Art Deco table in a Paris dining room in 1925. The smooth curves of a 1931 German tubular steel chair would look perfectly at home in a showroom of the latest Italian furnishings. Walter Gropius, had a sparsely furnished office in Weimar, Germany, in the 1920s; its rectangular chairs and desk, vast windows, steam radiator, and bare, wooden floor could be a corner of an extremely chic New York loft today.

Contemporary rooms are not boxes to be filled with attractive "clutter." They are spaces with their own impact and beauty. What is left out can be as important as what is added.

POET,
ADAGIA

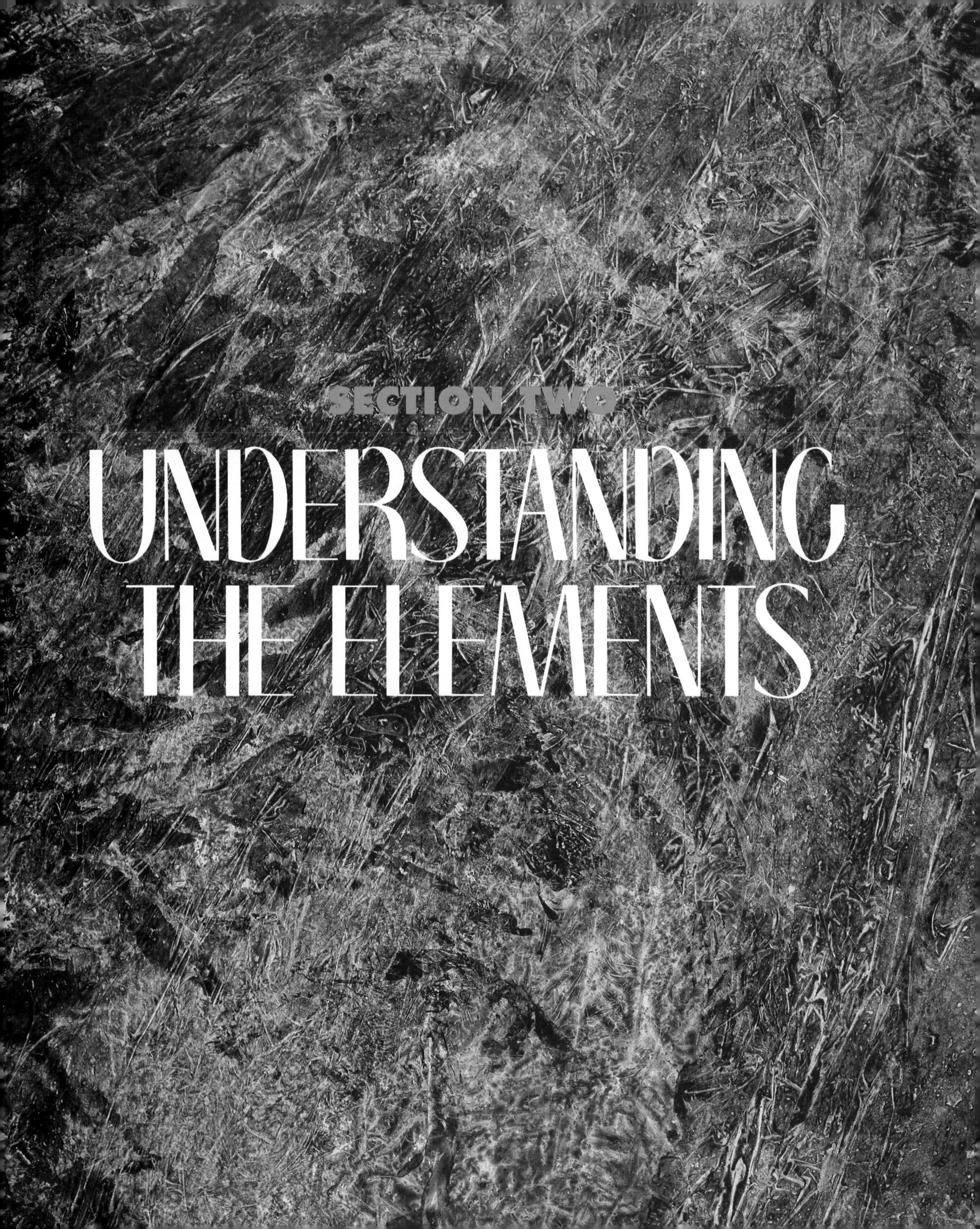

SECTION TWO

UNDERSTANDING THE ELEMENTS

SCENTED ROOM
GARDENING
NOTEBOOK
BARBARA MILO OHRBACH

GETTING STARTED

Approaching Your Rooms with Confidence

YOUR ROOMS ARE REFLECTIONS OF WHO YOU ARE. Over the years, they've accumulated your belongings, adjusted to your needs, and accommodated your lifestyle. Now that you've decided to renovate, redecorate, or establish yourself in a new home, don't be daunted by what might seem an intimidating task. Think of the project ahead as an opportunity to evaluate your lifestyle and express your evolving tastes.

If you take the time to think your project through, organize yourself effectively, and master a few basic rules of design, the results you achieve will reflect the excitement and fun you can have in creating them.

For most people, the mere thought of decorating is frightening and overwhelming. Choices seem too numerous, mistakes too costly, and information too hard to come by. Many people imagine that only professionals are privy to the "tricks of the trade." But even though professional decorators and designers can create extraordinary rooms — and even though there are times when the assistance of a professional is an absolute necessity — many of the loveliest rooms in the country have been created by non-professionals. With a few basics, you'll be well on your way.

Finding Your Style

EVEN IF YOU THINK YOU have no particular decorating preferences, chances are that you do and that, if you look around, plenty of clues are available. A glance at your wardrobe, for instance, might reveal something about the colours you favour. Decorators often use this device to establish clients' true colour preferences over their professed ones. The person who wears only neutrals may not be comfortable waking up to strong pastels. Similarly, clues may come from the style of your wardrobe. If you favour casual chic, you will probably feel most at home in rooms that are decorated with the same approach.

Few people start from scratch when redecorating or renovating a home. The furniture you already possess — and the cherished pieces you intend to make focal points of your rooms — will be excellent jumping-off points in choosing a direction for your design scheme. A Victorian sideboard inherited from your grandmother or two beautiful Art Deco side chairs are strong enough elements in themselves to establish a context for your style.

Of course, furniture is not the only indicator. If you're an avid reader with a huge collection of antiquarian books, you may find yourself leaning naturally towards English Country style. If you're an enthusiastic cook and have a kitchen full of pots, pans, utensils, and herbs, French Country might be the obvious choice for you.

You may simply decide to have fun with objects, collections, or pieces of furniture that you possess. Framed family photographs might become the focus of a wall or table-top display. A collection of Victorian hats or teapots, arranged in an artful and dramatic fashion, might establish the mood of a room. Furniture as ordinary and nondescript as six unremarkable dining room chairs might become an astonishing focal point if painted a lively colour.

The basic organization of your home or workplace will probably say something about whether you prefer cluttered cosiness or open space. These simple likes and dislikes will help point you towards an appropriate style.

Think of your own lifestyle. Do you have small children? Do you entertain a lot? Do you love to cook and want a large, live-in country kitchen? These are the kinds of questions you should be asking yourself as you approach your choices.

Study the basic architecture of your home. Every room conveys a personality of its own — even when it's empty — and lends itself more to one style of decorating than another. If your home is Contemporary, you can still go for English Country, you'll just have to make a bigger stretch to achieve the style. If your home is Victorian, you'll probably be drawn to a style that complements its detailing.

What kind of "feel" does a room have — is it cosy and enclosed or dramatic and open? What is its scale? Does it get much light? Does it have weird and wonderful angles?

A group of framed prints is the focal point in this small, stylized bedroom belonging to designer Gary Zanner.

Elegant mouldings? A rough plank floor? A fireplace? The answers to these questions may prove to be the inspiration you need to plunge into a style.

Don't be restricted by your space. Perhaps a big skylight will supply the wash of light you need. Perhaps removing a wall or building in a shelf unit will enhance the room's potential. Your design approach, if accomplished with sufficient flair and enthusiasm, may overcome a room's inherent problems.

As style preferences form in your mind, pursue them enthusiastically. Gather together a collection of your favourite things — a dish, a lamp, a piece of fabric, a book, even flowers or fruit — and examine them for clues of colours, textures, details, and design that appeal strongly to you. Take the same approach with magazine pictures: clip photographs of rooms that you find particularly attractive, and spread them out on the floor or on a table-top, searching for the elements that consistently draw you to a room. Consider whether the features that attract you are achievable in your space. If you like vaulted ceilings, but your ceilings are of average height, you may have to reconsider your objectives.

Many of the most successful rooms are a combination of styles. Eclecticism is championed by many interior designers who regard a slavish approach to any one style as too confining for modern tastes. Luckily, an eclectic look is what most of us already have: a formal Victorian sideboard sits beside a modern glass-top table; a pine cabinet inhabits a contemporary kitchen. So don't feel intimidated by any one style. Once you understand what appeals to you in a few styles, have fun mixing and matching to suit your own taste and creativity.

A curved wood cornice was adapted to form an interesting headboard in this romantic, sun-filled bedroom by designer Brad Currie. Log tables and field rocks are whimsical and unexpected.

The Five Elements of Design

THE HUNDRED AND ONE things to be considered when decorating a room can seem overwhelming. It's often difficult to know where to begin. As in so many challenges, however, a decoration or renovation project is not nearly so daunting once it is reduced to its basic elements. In planning your approach to your rooms, try to focus on one element of your design at a time.

WORKING WITH A DESIGNER

At some point in a design project — especially an extensive renovation — you may want to consider hiring a professional designer. By doing so, you stand to gain two things: time — especially if you are too busy to devote the required hours to the project — and expertise.

Many people think that hiring a designer is an extremely expensive undertaking. It doesn't have to be. A responsible designer will make careful choices within a pre-set budget and may actually save you money in the long run. Experienced in space planning, draughting, renovation, and lighting plans, an interior designer will help you avoid costly blunders. As well, interior designers have connections with reliable tradesmen and access to products that are not available in retail outlets.

A designer's style and preferences will inevitably influence the outcome of a project, but the clearer you can be about what you want, the more satisfying the results will be. Discuss the project thoroughly with a designer, making sure that your ideas, preferences, lifestyle, and budget are well understood. Remember, the best client is a well-educated one; the farther along you are in your thinking before seeking the help of a professional, the better.

1. Balance and Scale

BALANCE AND SCALE ARE very important in achieving a successful interior. Too many pieces of large furniture in a small space will only make a room feel cramped. Small pieces in a large room may seem lost. Similarly, the pattern size of wallpaper, upholstery, and drapery should be selected according to the dimensions of the room in which they will be used, and the scale of the windows or furniture to which they relate.

Of course, you can play with scale. You can consciously contradict standard practice to create a dramatic or humorous effect. For instance, a huge, open loft with only three beautifully arranged pieces of furniture has the effect of artfully created minimalism. A towering cactus in a small living room becomes a sculptural focal point.

2. Colour

COLOUR IS A VITAL PART OF your design scheme and is your most inexpensive decorating tool. You may have to work with a colour scheme that has already been established by your current furniture upholstery or by architectural details — green Victorian tiles around a fireplace, for instance. But if you are in a position to start from scratch, here are some ways to approach your colour scheme.

- Colours affect our sense of space. To make a room feel larger, use pale or cool colours. These colours — whites, greys, blues, greens, or lilacs — are called "receding colours" because they make the walls appear to move away from us. To make a large room seem smaller, use deep or warm colours. Reds, pinks, burgundies, golds, terracotta are called "advancing colours" because they bring the walls closer. If, for example, you have a long, narrow room, you can improve its proportions by painting the end walls a deep red and the side walls a creamy white.

  Using many colours in one room chops up the space visually, making the room seem smaller. Subtle variations of the same tone expand and unify the space, making it seem larger.

- Colour is affected by light. A paint sample in the paint store will not look the same when you get it home and see it under different lighting

The drama of this eclectic space designed by Wise Kalan and Associates is heightened by the choice of Empire furniture in a contemporary warehouse setting.

THE COLOUR WHEEL

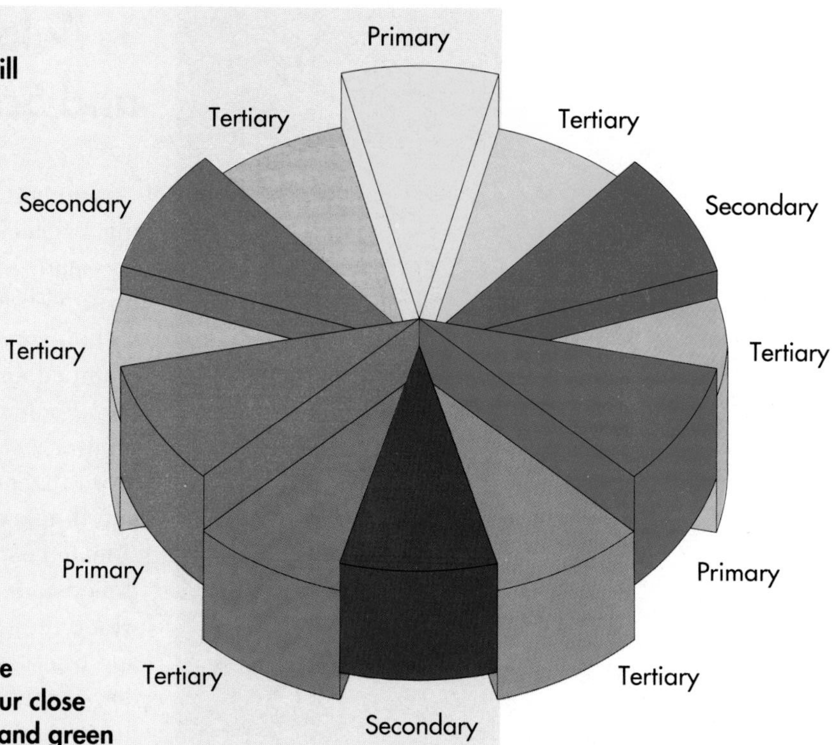

Knowing the principles of the colour wheel will help you work out your colour scheme. Its three main colours are the primaries — red, yellow, and blue. Combinations of these three can create all other colours. Mix two of them in equal parts and you'll get the secondary colours. Blue and yellow make green. Yellow and red make orange. Red and blue make purple. Tertiary colours are made by combining equal parts of a primary colour with a secondary. For example, blue and green will make turquoise.

Colours next to each other on the colour wheel are called adjacent or harmonious. They are in the same colour range, and blend into the same visual family.

Colour affects us physically. Sit down in a completely red room, and your eyes will crave something green — so much so that when your close your eyes you will actually "see" green. Red and green are complementary colours. This means they are found directly opposite one another on the colour wheel. A direct complement gives the most vibrant play of colour, but you can use a colour near or adjacent to a complement if you don't want quite so lively a combination.

Complements are completions. A green dining room, for instance, with deep turquoise and blue in the carpet and upholstery, but with no complementary reds, will feel very moody, cool, even unsettling. However, if you introduce red accents — the richness of wood finish, even a bouquet of roses — this will give the warm hues and complementary colours the eye craves.

There are a few other terms you should be aware of when working with colour.
Tone: The amount of lightness or darkness in a colour determines its tone. Blue, for example, might go from an almost white light blue to an almost black dark blue. Each time you add or subtract white or black from a colour, you are changing its tone.

Hue: Hue means colour and is often confused with tone. If you add a little red to blue, you are adjusting its hue. We often talk of a warm blue or a cool blue, a mauve blue or a green blue. Adding just a little of another colour to blue will not change it from being blue, but it will change the hue. This also means that the colour will shift its position on the colour wheel in the direction of the colour that is added.

Monochromatic colours: Colours that are similar in hue but vary in tone are monochromatic. A monochromatic colour scheme might range from pale pinks to red.

Neutrals: The neutral colours are white, black, and the greys in between. White contains all colours, and black is the absence of colour. Neutrals can be matched equally with any other colour. Today, neutral is often used to refer to any low-key, easily harmonized colour, such as beige, tan, or cream.

conditions. Be sure to look at your sample in both artificial light and daylight. Look at it in the room you intend to paint and consider it at different times of day.

The depth and intensity of colour is also affected by the size of the area painted; the tiny paint chip can't possibly convey the intensity of colour you will see on your wall. When you think you've settled on a choice, buy a small amount and cover a sizeable part of one wall. Let it dry, give it a second coat, then have a look before going full-steam ahead. This step can save a lot of time, effort, and expense. That soft dove grey that you admired so much in the paint store can pale to white on a large wall. That warm terracotta that was so radiant in daytime can be muddy at night. Now — before you paint the whole room — is the time to find these things out.

- Colour is affected by the colours around it. A red wall will look deeper and brighter next to a crisp white trim. It will be more vibrant when placed beside green, which is its "complementary" colour (see colour wheel diagram), and it will appear softer when used next to another warm colour, such as purple, which is adjacent to it on the colour wheel.

Colour can be used to camouflage or heighten specific details. A green radiator will disappear against a green wall, while a red one will have a significant visual impact.

- Colour can suggest and reinforce different historical styles or geographic settings. For example, Taos blue, the colour of natural turquoise, set against tans and whites immediately conjures a Southwest look.

Heritage colours that resemble those made from natural dyes or from milk paint recall early Canadian homes or country cottages. The nineteenth-century English loved mauve; Napoleon's France was crazy about yellow. With a little research, you can reinforce your design style with the appropriate colour choices. Use your contemporary eye to play with these palettes and give them a new interpretation.

If you don't know where to begin with your colours, look at a piece of fabric or a beautiful object that might be the starting point for your scheme, and build from there. Remember, it is easier to match paint to a colour in your upholstery than the other way around.

Keep in mind colour continuity from room to room. This doesn't mean you can't have a little mauve powder room off a lemon hall. The contrast is part of the beauty. But rooms and hallways are visible from one to another, and these views should be harmonious and pleasing.

A small bedroom dazzles with a palette of deep vibrant colours. The high-gloss lacquer reflects light and creates a dimension of depth.

3. Texture

THE MOOD OF YOUR ROOM will be affected by the materials and finishes you choose. In general, polished or shiny surfaces seem formal, matt surfaces more casual. Marble, glass, polished wood, and lustrous wall paints are often used to give an air of formality. In country or cottage homes, or anywhere that is relaxed and casual in appearance, textures will have less sheen and be less smooth. Surfaces will have a more natural patina.

This distinction also holds for fabrics. Silks, satins, glazed cottons, and brocade will suggest a formality that is not found in homespuns, linens, and unpolished cottons.

You will, of course, want some contrast of textures. The most successful rooms contain a subtle mix.

4. Lighting

LIGHT CAN BE A WONDERfully effective design tool. It can accentuate the aspects of a room you want to emphasize, or eliminate, or play down negative qualities. It can also create a mood and emphasize a focal point. But to use it well, there are several things to consider about lighting.

Keep in mind the three basic ways that light is used, and then consider how to balance your use of each method.

- The first is "general" lighting. In the absence of any daylight, general lighting creates a basic level of light in the room without focusing it on specific areas. Overheads, chandeliers, track, and spotlights are the most common.
- Next is "task" lighting, which illuminates specific areas, providing light for specific tasks — bedside lamps for reading, spotlights on wall art, pot lights over the dining-room table, counter lights for food preparation. Without appropriate task lights, a room will not function, so consider what you will be doing and where in the room you want to do it.
- Finally, there is "mood" lighting. Its purpose is to create the magic and drama you're seeking. A small spotlight shining up through a leafy palm can create wonderful shadows across a ceiling. Lamps can create intimate circles of warmth. Chandeliers or wall sconces can make a dining room sparkle with elegance.

LEFT: A rich play of textures is achieved by combining basket-weave wallpaper, distressed walls, deep wood mouldings, and antique cornice brackets. RIGHT: Two torchière lamps flank a Contemporary fireplace to create a dramatic mood.

WHICH LIGHT WHERE?

Incandescent Light: **The common light bulb. Used in standard table lamps, chandeliers, and wall sconces, the incandescent light bulb gives a warm light, and its warmth increases as it is dimmed.**

Fluorescent Light: **Fluorescent tubes give off a cool, diffuse light that decreases shadows but does not have the feeling of natural light. Ideally, fluorescents should be used in functional situations and be concealed under kitchen cabinets or other work areas.**

Halogen**: These small bulbs give a long-lasting, bright light that resembles natural light. They can be focused in very precise beams. Halogen is excellent for spotlighting art or giving pools of specific light for tasks such as reading or writing.**

When deciding where to place your lights, here are some tips you should keep in mind.

- Dark matt surfaces will absorb light, while shiny pale ones reflect it. If you don't want your deep red dining room to seem overly dark, wall sconces might supplement a central chandelier. If you have a large, light living room and want it to seem warm and cosy in the evenings, don't focus light on the ceilings. Use table lamps and floor lamps to create lower, warmer pools of light.
- Light shining directly at a surface will flatten any textures or shapes, while light shining from an angle will emphasize them by creating shadows. If your wall plaster is in rough shape, you can visually eliminate the imperfections by shining a light directly on the wall. If, however, your walls are a rich stucco, or you have hung a collection of interesting objects, light placed above, below, or to the side will add a depth and richness.

Consider what your light fixtures will look like — lit and unlit. A change of lamp shade can often make a dramatic difference. An opaque shade casts a more intense light pool immediately below it. Cloth and other transparent lamp shades will give a softer glow to a larger

surrounding area. Your lights and lamps should always be an integral part of your room's design and visual appeal. Think of them as accessories as well as practical elements.

Turning a favourite urn, vase, or silver candlestick into a lamp is a popular trick. A lighting specialist will add the necessary hardware and wire it, ready to take your shade.

Don't finalize your lighting plan until you have a clear idea of your furniture arrangements and your specific lighting needs. For example, if your sofa doesn't sit against the wall, you will need to have floor outlets installed to accommodate your table lamps. Lights should be added to your floor plan. They are an important element in building your finished scheme.

5. Fabric

FABRIC IS EXTREMELY VERsatile and can be used in many ways to express your design vision. Different colours, patterns, and textures reflect different tastes and styles. Little floral prints, checks, and ginghams suit country and cottage styles; silks and velvets can give an aura of grandeur; chintz adds an English look. Many fabric and wallpaper companies reproduce authentic period patterns.

Inspired use of fabric can make the most boring window into a room's most beautiful feature. Long curtains that puddle along the floor are elegant and luxurious, and elongate the apparent size of the window. Café curtains, which often begin halfway down the window and stop at the sill, are informal and give a clear view of the outdoors while still providing the necessary privacy. There are feminine window coverings such as ruffled tie-backs and puffy Austrian blinds. There is the masculine simplicity of Roman blinds or a simple, solid drape. In Victorian England, windows were often treated like a lady going to a ball — draped in layer after layer of interesting fabrics and textures, ruffles and bows, swags and fringes. Today a piece of translucent parachute silk held to a window frame by two industrial clamps can seem a perfectly acceptable option.

Wacky upholstery fabric can dramatically update a tired old chair, and a neutral fabric used consistently can unify an eclectic mish-mash of furniture pieces.

Interesting cushions are an easy way to introduce new accent colours into your scheme.

Laura Ashley cotton prints and solid glazed chintzes brighten a casual country kitchen.

HOW TO MIX PRINTS

By mixing printed fabrics, you can create a dazzling interior, rich in colour and pattern, enhance your palette, and set the mood of your rooms. Combining prints need not be intimidating. Here are some easy-to-use, basic principles that will help you combine colours and patterns.

The Positive and Negative of One Print: **Combine the positive and the negative version of the same pattern. In this case, one fabric is the reverse of the other; for example, the pattern colour in one is the background in the other, and vice versa.**

The Same Print in Two Palettes: **Select two different-coloured versions of the same printed fabric. The colours must work well together.**

One Floral Print and Simple Geometrics: **A complicated or busy floral print can be matched with simple geometric patterns in colours pulled from the floral print.**

Same Theme, Different Scale: **You can combine two or more versions of the same pattern that vary only in scale. The patterns must be of the same colours or contain colours that work well together.**

Two Similar Complicated Prints: **If you mix two bold, complicated prints, they must be similar in scale, the colours should be the same, and the proportions of colours within each print should be similar.**

Mix of Several Patterns: **Mix several different patterns only if their scale is either very different or very similar. There must be a colour relationship among the patterns (that is, the colours must match exactly or work well together).**

Building a Workbook

YOUR DREAM IS ABOUT TO become reality! Now it's time to organize your decorating project.

Everyone approaches projects in different ways, but one of the most common tips passed on by designers and decorators is the importance of organization. To plan and execute a successful decorating scheme, you need to break it down into manageable parts and to keep records. The tool that allows you to do all this is a reliable workbook.

Your workbook will contain everything from the photographs that originally inspired you to records, samples, floor plans, phone numbers, and invoices. In the end, it will be a complete catalogue of all your choices and purchases. Should you want to order an extra bolt of wallpaper or refer to an invoice for a particular antique, you have only to look in your workbook. The more organized your workbook is, the more manageable your project will be.

1. The Tools

YOU WILL NEED A FEW basic tools to set up your workbook. Most of them are probably already in your possession. Take a few minutes to gather them together.

- *A three-ring binder* — the regular school-size will easily accommodate your information
- *Dividers*
- *Grid paper* (three-hole)
- *Clear plastic self-closing envelopes* or some manila envelopes punched with three holes and marked, "Swatches," "Receipts," etc.
- *Pens and pencils*
- *A retractable tape measure*
- *A ruler*
- *Scissors*
- *A three-ring pencil case* to hold pens, pencils, tape measure, ruler, and scissors.

2. Clippings for Inspiration

TO KEEP YOUR EYE ON THE prize, clip the magazine photographs that inspired you in the first place and put them in your workbook. You might also include notes on rooms you've seen and ideas you've noticed. Think of this as a scrapbook. Include bits of fabric, snips of wallpaper, or a page from an auction catalogue. These are not elements that you necessarily intend to use. They're simply to remind you of what you're trying to achieve.

PHONE NUMBERS
CONTACT
RECOMMEDED BY
NOTES
CALL CAROL HERBERT
LYNDA
ROUGH !! ELEVATION
BATHROOM SECOND FLOOR
ANTIQUE DOORS
NORTH
MIRROR
BUILD IN
TILES
TOWELS
BUDGET A.
ITEM
DRAWINGS
Kitchen Shelving Unit Detail
FLOOR PLANS
SPEC SHEETS
RECEIPTS
THE PORT DALHOUSIE
15651
Kitchen
Bath
Rental Apt.
Living Area
My Studio
Caroline's Room
First Floor
Second Floor
ORDER DOORS
RUBBISH REMOVAL
ORDER MIRROR
CARPET QUOTES
CARPET LAID 2ND FLOOR
CONCERT: 8:00 MOZART
PLUMBER
SEARCH
MODE
ENTER

3. Room Scheme Pages

YOUR ROOMS WILL EVOLVE as your ideas become clearer. Assign one page of your workbook to every room you are doing. On it, write or draw a description of what you intend to achieve. Use these sketches as starting points for each room and to remind you of each room's use and the feel you want to create. Include your basic decisions on colour, furniture, lighting, window treatments — allowing yourself space to change or refine your decisions as you build each picture. Colour samples and fabric swatches should be stapled on. Reminders to yourself — such as, "Don't forget to tell the electrician about the wide, Victorian baseboards before he installs outlets" — are useful.

To show a client how a room will take shape, an interior decorator will often make a sample board — a collage of paint chips, fabric swatches, photographs of furniture, carpet samples, wallpaper, ceramic tile, and even a piece of hardwood flooring. Grouped together on a single card, these items convey an accurate sense of the look of a room.

You can make your own sample boards. Collect swatches of the fabrics and wallpapers that contain your desired palette, and staple them to each room's scheme page. Pull colours from them and match these to paint chips. Attach these to your page. Add a Polaroid photo of a furniture piece you want to buy, a picture of the lamps you are looking for, and so on.

If you are developing a colour scheme for the entire

house, keep the wallpaper samples, fabric swatches, and paint chips for each room separate. But remember that the view from one room to another should be harmonious. Making a room scheme for each room will help you develop compatible groupings of colour, style, and furniture styles.

Room schemes will also enable you to catch errors before it's too late. If the paint you've chosen for your walls clashes with the stain you want for your hardwood floor, it's best to find out before you start. With these pages, not only will you solve problems and correct mistakes, you'll begin to see your achievements as well, and your excitement will grow as your plans come together.

4. Before Shots

IT'S FUN TO TAKE PHOTOgraphs of your rooms before your work begins. They'll help you appreciate your achievements once the work is over. Before shots are also a tool. Seeing your rooms in a photograph often gives you a fresh look at their possibilities and their problems. The two-dimensional quality removes a room's familiarity and emphasizes its strengths and weaknesses. It's also helpful to have a reference shot when you're out shopping. A photograph will keep architectural details in mind and remind you of the scale in which you're working.

5. Names and Phone Numbers

AS YOU PLAN AND PROCEED with your project, you will compile a list of tradespeople, suppliers, retailers, and resources. Keeping these organized on a sheet in your workbook is a great convenience. Its arrangement is a matter of personal preference, but you might consider the following column headings: Trade; Company Name; Phone Number; Contact (the name of the person you've dealt with); Address; Recommended By; Comments.

6. Calendar

A MONTH-BY-MONTH GRID calendar with big boxes for each day's activities will help you keep track of deliveries, installations, and when orders were placed. Use your calendar to schedule tradespeople, to keep track of their work, and to remind yourself of what you need to do, check, confirm, order, or pick up.

7. Floor Plans

A FLOOR PLAN IS INVALUable. This bird's-eye view of each room will help you make basic decisions about the size and shape of your furniture, and about what goes where and how much space there is for it. It's no use falling in love with a wonderful sofa and discovering later that your wall space is too short to accomodate it. On pages 196-198 of this book, you will find grid paper and templates for standard sizes of furniture and fixtures. Use them to create a model of your room.

Measure each room and draw the outline of your walls to scale. Mark the locations of windows, doors, fireplaces, and built-ins. Use templates (the ones provided or ones you make yourself) to play with possible furniture arrangements. Include your lighting ideas, your area rugs, and even your big plants.

8. Simple Elevations

AN ELEVATION IS A TWO-dimensional view of a wall in your room. It indicates the distances between critical edges such as the mantel and the ceiling, or a side wall and a window. It will help you decide everything from how much fabric you need for your drapes to which mirror will go above the fireplace. Elevations allow you to shop with all your dimensions at hand.

9. Shop Drawings

IF YOU ARE GOING TO HAVE cupboards or furniture custom built, you will need to do a simple line drawing of each piece with dimensions. Sometimes an upholsterer or a custom furniture maker can work from this, or from a picture and some basic dimensions. However, for built-ins that require an accurate fit, have the supplier take his or her own measurements. For large or elaborate projects, it is advisable to have detailed "shop drawings" done by a professional — either a designer, architect, or draughtsman.

10. The Budget

THE ONLY THING YOU CAN be absolutely sure of, whether embarking on an extensive renovation or a more modest redecoration, is that things will cost more than you hope. If you are fortunate enough to have a large budget and very definite tastes, you may be able to accomplish all your decorating goals in one phase. However, most of us inevitably have to scale down our plans or at least break the over-all scheme into phases. Approaching a project in phases is not necessarily a disadvantage. As well as addressing budgetary concerns, it may help your ideas evolve.

Phase One will always be the essentials. In an artist's terms, this stage fills in the background and the basic elements of your composition: paint, wallpaper, built-ins, flooring, lighting, and major furniture pieces.

Phase Two will include secondary furniture pieces, area rugs, and major accessories.

Phase Three will include smaller accessories, ongoing collections, and replacement pieces.

Approaching the project in phases will help you keep your master plan in mind. You might, for instance, buy a magnificent sofa in Phase One, knowing that two inexpensive director's chairs will

have to substitute for your matching custom-made armchairs until Phase Two.

Always hide a percentage of your budget (10 percent to 15 percent) in a contingency fund. This might seem overly cautious; in fact, it's a very realistic step. There are always unforeseen expenses — extra steps in the preparation of walls for paint; the discovery of dry rot; finding antiquated wiring or structural problems that were hidden behind old drywall; the cost of disposing of garbage. And then there are those little oversights, changes of mind, and miscalculations that affect cash flow. You may also decide you want to spend "just a little bit extra" to get exactly what you want. For example, you may have budgeted a certain amount for a stove and then, in the appliance store, you set eyes on the stove of your dreams. Naturally, it's more than you anticipated. Call on the contingency fund.

To organize your budget, there are two charts that will prove invaluable. The first is the Budget Breakdown. On a sheet, draw three columns labelled Work to Be Done/ Items to Be Purchased (list everything individually); Estimated Cost; Cost to Date. This is especially necessary for big projects. When work is underway, listing costs beside your items and jobs will show you which ones are going over budget and which aren't. If you are lucky, you'll be able to rob Peter to pay Paul. If you aren't lucky, you'll know that you have to adjust your plans or be prepared to go over budget.

The second budget chart is a Running Tally of what is spent, when, on what, and to whom. The column headings might be as follows: Date; Trade, Company, or Store; Item; Amount; Subtotal. If payments become misplaced or confused, or are questioned at any point, a quick look at this sheet can provide you with answers. It also lets you know how much you've spent at every step of your project.

11. Spec Sheets

BEFORE YOU DECIDE WHAT type of appliances, furniture, hardware, and other items you want, collect the manufacturers' specification sheets. File these in your workbook to remind you of appearance, dimensions, features, and options. Add your own notes to the spec sheets, including your thoughts, the salesperson's comments, and the current price.

12. Purchase Orders, Contracts, Receipts, Warranties

ALL THESE IMPORTANT papers should find their way into your workbook.

Contracts will record exactly what is being done, on what terms, when, and for how much. Keeping them well-ordered and easily accessible can avoid unpleasant misunderstandings. Keep them up to date, and record and date any changes or adjustments to the original estimates.

Purchase orders and receipts will be invaluable should you later need to re-order items such as tiles, fabrics, carpet, and paint. These documents will serve as a useful record of the decisions you have made along the way: styles, patterns, model numbers, quantities, prices, fabric dye lots and widths. Should you need to insure fine pieces of furniture and antiques, or should you ever want to sell them, their value will be readily available.

It is important to keep track of payments. If you are ordering custom-made pieces, 50 percent of the cost will usually be expected up-front and the balance upon completion. If your decorating project involves a renovation, you will generally pay your tradespeople in instalments. To know how much you have paid, it is essential to keep a well-organized file of receipts. Be sure to record and date your various payments.

When new appliances arrive, it is easy to lose warranties. Get out your three-hole punch and file the warranties carefully in your workbook.

13. After Shots

IF YOU TOOK BEFORE SHOTS of your work in progress, why not let yourself have the pleasure of a few after shots? It will be fun to compare them with your before shots! In fact, comparing "what is" with "what was" might be the first thing you want to do in your new French Country kitchen, English Country sitting room, or chic, Contemporary bedroom. Sit down, flip through your workbook, and remind yourself of the stages of your project. Then look around and congratulate yourself.

ENGLISH COUNTRY

HOW-TO

IT'S NO SURPRISE THAT English Country is the best-loved design style in Canada. It's familiar to most of us because of this country's strong Anglo-Saxon heritage. It's comfortable, which in our often too-busy and too-hurried age, is a much longed-for quality. And because of its warmth and cosiness, it's particularly well-suited to our climate.

English Country is also a very personal style. It allows you to display your enthusiasms and tastes. In fact, your enthusiasms and tastes are its essential ingredients. If you happen to be a collector, it's probably the style for you. You can bring your toy soldiers out of the attic. You can hang your straw hats front and centre. You can reserve an entire wall for the botanical prints you've picked up at flea markets over the years. Or, if your most prized collection is simply all the photographs of your family that you don't quite know what to do with, you can put them in stand-up frames of various shapes and sizes and spread them across your mantelpiece and side tables without restraint.

English Country's charm is its accumulated, layered look. Unlike Contemporary design, in which every element of a room is considered carefully before being put in place, English Country can be added to as you go along. After all, that's what the English have been doing for generations. So, if you feel drawn to English Country, the best and the most enjoyable way to begin building your own English Country look is to immerse yourself in the elements you'll be accumulating. Wander through fabric stores and acquaint yourself with English chintzes. Visit antique shops and flea markets. Look at old oriental rugs and browse through used bookstores. Read what you can about the country gardens and famous homes of England. Look at pictures. Scavenge magazines for ideas. Gradually, a picture of the colours, textures, and furnishings of English Country will begin to take shape in your imagination. You'll start to see where they'll fit into your house or apartment. Then the real fun can begin.

THE ELEMENTS

The Palette

YOU DON'T NEED TO PULL your colour scheme out of thin air. Think of a country garden, a favourite piece of English porcelain, or a bowl of fruit. These will all provide you with a suitable range of shade and tone. But perhaps the best way to establish an English Country palette is to select a multi-coloured chintz — one that you want to use for your drapes, your sofa, or your slipcovers — and "pull" the colours from the fabric's pattern.

The light, more traditionally feminine colours — such as sage green, lavender, violet, mint green, periwinkle blue, cream, canary yellow, rose, and Chinese blue — will provide you with the airy tones you will want in bedrooms, bathrooms, kitchen, and in your living room. The darker, more dramatic, and traditionally masculine shades — cinnamon, oxblood, carmine, and deep rust — are suitable for rooms you want to feel enclosed and cosy, such as the dining room, the study, or the library. How you use these two colour groupings, and how you balance the contrast of lights and darks, will give your rooms their harmony.

Let's imagine you've fallen in love with a chintz with a cream background and with sage green, rose, pink, yellow, and blue in the floral. Buy a sample, and take it to a paint store. Pick out the paint chips that match the colours of the chintz. This selection will be the key to your colour scheme.

Begin with your background colours. What do you want on your walls? A multi-coloured chintz will provide you with any number of choices, but the easiest approach is a light colour scheme. Frequently, in English Country style, the walls are soft white, buttery cream, yellow, blue, violet, mushroom colour, or mauve. Perhaps you'll select the cream of the chintz for the background.

Think of the cream as the blank canvas against which you'll place the complementary colours and accents, the contrasts and highlights. Now you can compose your room, selecting other colours from the chintz. The chintz itself, of course, will appear prominently: as drapes perhaps, or on a large, comfortable sofa. But the blue could be used in a wide, vertical stripe on a loveseat. The yellow might appear in an all-over pin-dot covering a wing chair. Another sofa might be done in a diagonal lattice work, using the sage green of the chintz in the lattice and its cream in the background. For throw cushions, you might use a fabric that reverses the original chintz, using the identical pattern but with cream as the floral and green or rose in the background. A kilim carpet on the floor will echo the chintz's colours, but it will be a geometric that, compared to the floral of the chintz, is a pattern of much larger scale.

In each of these examples, either the style, the scale, or the pattern has been altered from that of the original chintz. This variety will bring your room to life. But the continuity of the room's colours — all drawn from the chintz — will hold its elements together.

LEFT: The dining room of this Ontario country cottage by designer Trudie Nelson is a whimsical mix of chintz, botanical prints, and cane-and-rattan furniture. ABOVE: Botanicals are quintessentially English. Frame your prints identically, and hang them in two or more layers about eye level.

If you are looking for a more dramatic background than the cream, the chintz can still provide you with your colour. If the sage green is the second most dominant colour, you could select it for your walls. A word of caution: what you probably liked about the chintz in the first place was, in part, the proportion of colour to colour. If you pull colours from the chintz to use throughout your room, you'll generally want them to appear in the same proportions as they appear in the material. When cream is the predominant colour of the chintz, we say the fabric "reads cream." If you

"A room consists of many layers. The most basic is the arrangement of furniture and the positioning of lighting. But on top of this there is the co-ordination of a whole variety of material and texture: wood, crystal, fabrics, leather, paper, china, marble. These layers have to embellish and enhance the basic layer – not work against it."

ROBERT DIRSTEIN, DIRSTEIN ROBERTSON LIMITED

want a room that "reads cream" — that gives the over-all effect of cream even though other darker, more vibrant colours are also present — aim for the same colour balance found in the fabric. Of course, you can alter the proportions if you choose. Sage green walls, for instance, can provide a contrast to the cream chintz drapes. This effect can be particularly pleasing, but it is a punchier and riskier approach than the more conventional matching. If you depart from the colour proportions of the chintz, make sure the over-all effect is one you'll enjoy.

After the choice of your background colour, the next step is almost automatic. Trims, in English Country style, are almost always white. Cornice moulding, window frames, door trims, and baseboards are rich, and painted with many coats of white. Remember that the addition of white borders and trims will tend to crispen your background colour.

Floors

PLAIN WOODEN FLOORS ARE wonderful in an English Country look. If you're going to install a new floor, wide, random-plank flooring would be the most appropriate, although more regular hardwood is perfectly fine. Stains should be medium nut brown to dark brown in colour.

Pompeiian red walls and soft warm rosy tones in this sitting room by Edward Welker Interiors, mix subtly with the many pink shades found in the fabrics and patterned carpet.

Although not a traditional approach, a painted or lightly rubbed floor blends with the light feminine colours of the English Country bedroom. In general, you will want a satin finish, and not a high-polished shine, on your wooden floors.

Broadloom is absolutely at home in an English Country room. It provides the warm, comfortable look the style celebrates. If the pile is low, plush, and tight, oriental area carpets, kilims, or needlepoint rugs can be placed over the wall-to-wall as a way of achieving a deep, layered effect. Berber, Wilton, and Saxony carpets are the most traditional. And although purists might insist on 100 percent wool, there are some sound practical reasons for choosing the new blends.

Brick floors or tobacco-coloured terracotta tiles are particularly appropriate for the kitchen and foyer. Bathrooms often use white ceramic tiles with accents in darker tile. And marble, particularly distressed, old-looking stone, can look magnificent in bathrooms and in hallways. But too much marble or too much white, new-looking stone can counter the effect you are trying to achieve. Rather than appearing grand and palatial, it can look cold and formal.

Matting is a quintessentially English floor covering. Matting, woven from natural sisal (a fibre made from leaves) comes in a continuous length, and is the forerunner of broadloom. It's ideal for any interior. Rush matting is a less expensive version and comes in squares. Laid loosely over a stone floor, it's perfect in a screened-in porch or a garden room. It's what we see most often in English Country homes. Persian carpets, Indo-Persians, kilims, or needlepoint rugs scattered over sisal matting are immediately and unmistakably English Country.

Walls

FOUR BASIC OPTIONS ARE open to you in choosing the wall treatments for your English Country look: paint, special painting finishes, paper, and panelling. If you choose paint, your walls don't have to be flawless before

PROJECT: SPONGE PAINTING

Amid the profusion of chintz, cushions, rugs, flowers, and *objets d'art* that is English Country, walls have a tendency to become mere background. One way to keep your walls lively and to echo subtly the rich palette you've chosen for your rooms is to sponge paint them. Sponge painting produces a very rich and expensive effect at a fraction of the cost of wallpapering. Sponged surfaces quickly take on a life of their own, emulating lacy cotton fabric, cool marble, or a colourful garden.

Here, paint-master David Bermann creates a custom collage, using four colours of equal intensity in top-quality latex paint. You can base your colour choices on your upholstery or drapery fabric, a favourite vase or painting. For easy-to-follow instructions, see page 206.

you begin. In fact, since age is part of the English Country look, it's better if they have the odd crack or chip or imperfection. You can even paint over old wallpaper if you want. But you shouldn't be skimpy with your paint: two coats are an absolute minimum. You want the room to look as if your family had been been plastering and painting it for three hundred years. A low-lustre is preferable to a dead flat.

Distressed wall finishes — marbleizing, sponging, ragging, and dragging — have recently come back into vogue. These finishes are fun to do and are well-suited to the English Country look. They can look stunning, especially when set off by a crisp, white trim. *Faux* finishes and *trompe-l'oeil* effects in particular bring just the right touch of whimsy. If, for instance, you imagine your bathroom or kitchen with ivy crawling up a trellis, why not paint it!

If you are using dark and dramatic tones — burgundy, emerald green, deep red, or indigo — in your dining room, you might want to select a glazed wall treatment (see page 181). This rich and elegant technique adds depth to the colour of the paint. The light from candles, the fireplace, or a dimmed chandelier will be reflected in your walls.

Wallpaper is perfectly appropriate to English Country — delicate Laura Ashley florals in your bedrooms and bathrooms, and larger, more dramatic patterns in the principal rooms. Vertical stripes are a popular English Country look. Remember, though, that wider, darker stripes should be used only in large rooms, and

Exposed beams and ceiling are painted white to emphasize the country cottage feeling of this comfortable sitting room.

Elaborate swags, trimmed and tasselled, draw attention to the windows of this traditional sitting room by designer Robert Wilson. The swags draw the eye up and highlight the beautiful cornice moulding.

more slender pinstripes in smaller spaces. And putting stripes on imperfect walls and awkward angles is a paper-hanger's nightmare. They draw attention to every flaw. If you've been drawn to the English Country look because it suits your older house, you might want to think twice about treating your walls with striped paper.

Worth remembering, as well, is that wallpaper, like paint, can look dramatically different on a wall than on a tiny sample in the store. A delicate floral pattern might read as cream up close. Its effect in an entirely papered room might be a rather claustrophobic mauve, not quite what you had in mind. Before you commit yourself to a wallpaper, tape a large piece to the wall you intend to cover, stand well back, and take a careful look.

Wood panelling is a definitively English look. Its warm, rich tones are perfect for a study or library or television room. Panelling tends to create an enclosed, masculine effect. Fruitwood, oak, English pine, and even mahogany are the traditional choices, but these, in addition to the labour of a carpenter, are expensive. It is possible to use less expensive veneer, or stain a less expensive wood.

Window Treatments and Fabrics

WINDOWS ARE OFTEN THE focal point of an English Country room. They tend to be tall and elegant, and in an ideal world they overlook the splendours of an English country garden. Lavish treatments are in order here — sumptuous and often multi-layered curtains that reach the floor or even puddle at the bottom. Rich, solid fabrics can be used, although an ideal choice for curtains would be the chintz from which you built your English Country palette. It could be echoed throughout the room with throw cushions, the drapery on a skirted table, piping, trims, tassels, and valences.

Although glazed and unglazed chintz are staples of English Country style, cotton broadcloth, velvet, damask, lace, and ticking will also provide appropriate touches in your sitting room. Eyelet and linen are perfect in the bedroom.

An ugly, uncomfortable, old card-table chair may seem an unlikely addition to your English Country decorating scheme. But a little padding and some wonderful fabric can create the perfect effect for your English Country bathroom, bedroom, or boudoir. Most pattern companies offer patterns for covering standard folding chairs.

"When looking for a quality chintz, look first at the drawing on the fabric's pattern. Is it beautifully rendered? Are its details clear? Is the scale appropriate? Then consider the depth of the fabric's colour. A really good chintz may use twenty colour screenings to give the material its richness."

CHARLOTTE AMBRIDGE, DIRSTEIN ROBERTSON LIMITED

Furniture

THINK OF ENGLISH COUNTRY furniture and you'll think large: a big, traditional sofa with loose back and seat cushions; an overstuffed armchair; a wing chair; a massive ottoman. Uniformity of height and scale, however, should be avoided. A mahogany or walnut sideboard, a breakfront, and a couple of side tables can be used to vary the shapes and heights in your rooms.

In the library, leather wing chairs are ideal. In the bedroom, vast four-posters and canopied beds with upholstered headboards perfectly establish the English Country mood. In general, beds should be higher than usual. Everything should be big and welcoming. Down-filled cushions will invite you to sink in. And the wood surfaces— whether of a modern reproduction or of a fine piece of Chippendale — should glow with a warm, rich patina.

In English Country style, furniture is arranged in clusters. A three-seater sofa and two armchairs could be placed in front of the fireplace as an inviting spot for conversation or reading. In another corner of the sitting room, a games table might be set up, or a writing desk. End tables, butler's tray tables, sofa tables (long tables that fit behind sofas), drop-leaf tables, and needlepoint footstools fill the gaps between

A playful alternative to real bookcases — this is actually wallpaper from Brunschwig & Fils. It fools the eye and lends an English "bookish" appeal to a small space.

the sofas and chairs. Tables covered with one underskirt draped to the floor and a shorter one cut squarely and placed on the diagonal across the table top are popular. These surfaces can all be filled with the books, pictures, magazines, tea sets, reading lamps, and silver collections that give the room its cluttered, comfortable charm. They also, of course, allow people to use them: readers have tables for their books, tea drinkers for their tea, games players for their games.

Today, we don't use our dining rooms as much as we'd like to, and many of us don't have a separate library. English Country style allows us a happy compromise. A dining room can be made into a combination dining room and library. Picture a book-lined room with a central dining table and chairs, but also with small wing chairs and a round reading table in front of a bay window. This arrangement not only provides the room with a function when you're not entertaining, it creates a particularly romantic and striking setting for your dinner parties.

Accessories

ONE OF THE KEYS TO THE English Country look is the presence of collections. Almost anything that catches your fancy will work. Silver pieces and porcelain are particularly appropriate. Often there is a certain whimsy to English collectibles, and the collections tend to be repeated versions of the same kind of object — cigarette cases, for example — rather than an array of dissimilar pieces. Pictures of botanical or architectural subjects, of hunting scenes, or of animals are treated as collections as well and are usually hung together, creating a grouping on a wall. Prints, paintings, and drawings can be framed with anything from simple dark to heavily carved, gold-painted wood. Traditionally, they were hung from picture rails with their wires left visible; you may want to recreate this authentic detail, or you can replace the wire with ribbons and bows.

Books, of course, are the quintessential English collection, stored in free-standing or built-in bookcases. In

PROJECT: ENGLISH COUNTRY CUSHIONS

An unmistakable signature of the English Country look is an abundance of throw cushions. Scattered over sofas, settees, and beds, they create an immediate aura of comfort and luxury. The fabric you use to cover your cushions is crucial, but you may already have the ideal solution in your own drawers. Be inspired by your favourite designer and sew up your scarves (or even your napkins or placemats) with our step-by-step instructions, beginning on page 206.

"Although an English Country sitting room might give the impression of haphazard clutter, a well put-together room is actually a careful arrangement of texture, colour, and shapes. It's not only your furniture, fabrics, colour, and objects that create the mood you want, it's also their organization and juxtaposition."

ROBERT DIRSTEIN,
DIRSTEIN ROBERTSON
LIMITED

a living room or study, built-in cases typically flank the fireplace. Nothing could be more English Country than bookcases on either side of a roaring fire, with a large mirror above the mantel.

English Country homes usually had little empty or unused space. Vacant spots can be filled with potted palms, clusters of ivy, vases of cut flowers, and porcelain urns. Bowls of pot-pourri, decorative plates on plate stands, crystal decanters, clocks, and framed photographs can cover every available surface. Lamps also add to the look. Overhead lighting should be used with caution and preference given to the softer, localized light of table lamps, standing floor lamps, wall sconces, and

A table-top grouping of accessories in the English Country style.

beautiful chandeliers. Plain and pleated silk shades and crystal, porcelain, and ceramic lamp bases will add colour and texture.

Architectural Elements

IF YOU HAVE THE OPTION OF renovating, a few additions will add greatly to the authenticity of your scheme. Baseboards should be tall and moulded. Decorative cornice moulding and ceiling medallions are relatively easy to install and can transform a room. Wainscotting, deep window trims, French doors, and bay windows — all will take you far towards achieving your English Country look. But if you had to choose a single, absolutely essential element, it would have to be a fireplace. Old or reproduced mantels and chimney pieces are easy to find. If you have the option of installing one, or better yet, a few, don't hesitate. They'll provide your rooms with a cosiness, a warmth, and a focal point around which you can arrange your furnishings.

The live-in bath complete with fireplace and family pictures in silver frames. Chairs invite reading and relaxation.

PULLING IT ALL TOGETHER

Deep cornices are accentuated in a cream that ties in with the background of the floral chintz.

An English cotton chintz provides the inspiration and the colour scheme.

This Chippendale armchair is upholstered in a royal blue damask found in the palette of the drapery chintz.

Two pedestals with a glass top make a beautiful desk that's light, yet "important," in scale and design.

A small Persian rug anchors the furniture grouping.

Pompeiian red walls add subtle texture.

A fine antique bookcase houses leather-bound books.

Blue pulled from the chintz, sponged on with white, creates a whimsical sky effect on the ceiling.

Much more interesting than placing the sofa against a wall, a black screen is a dramatic backdrop for a strong painting.

A pair of candlestick lamps with bright white shades reinforce this corner as the room's focal point.

Stripes on stripes fill empty corners.

A rich striped sofa in the chosen colour palette is formal and elegant.

The Queen Anne table is high — for tea, English style!

ail
carott
3104-54
3104-84

FRENCH COUNTRY

HOW-TO

AS THE COSY SITTING room is to English Country, and expansive living and dining areas are to Contemporary, so is the kitchen to French Country style. It is this room that spreads its honest, natural charm throughout your house, touching everything with the generous, friendly spirit that is the essence of French Country. The sunny print you use for the curtains in your bedroom might be the same pattern as the place-mats on your laden harvest table. The armoire in the living room, now housing your stereo, might just as easily be standing beside your stove, stocked with herbs and preserves. The antique, hand-painted *banquette à trois places* that serves as a sofa in your study could, if needed, provide three extra places at the dinner table.

French Country has an unpolished look and a casual friendliness that celebrates food and hospitality. But it's not for everyone. Interestingly enough, it is your kitchen — and how you use it — that provides the clues to whether you are a French Country person. If, for instance, you are still preparing a meal when your guests arrive and — apologizing profusely — you seat them in the living room with a drink and a bowl of peanuts while you tend to the last-minute cooking, French Country might not be right for you. If you go to the door in your apron, welcome your guests into the kitchen without a second thought, pour them glasses of wine, and start serving the hors d'oeuvres as you carry on, stirring, straining, tasting, and talking, then your kitchen — and probably your home — has already got the most important ingredient of French Country: the spirit. All you have to do now is add the details.

Today, many shops specialize in the French Country look. Almost anything you need to acquaint yourself with the mood, colours, fabrics, textures, accessories, and even fragrances of French Country can be found in stores such as Toronto's En Provence or Pierre Deux. Magazines and books are full of French Country. Antique dealers, as well as the manufacturers of reproductions, have tuned in to the French Country look, and many reputable showrooms now feature French Country armoires, commodes, banquettes, and harvest-style dining tables on display.

So, take a good look in the shops and showrooms. Then open a bottle of Beaujolais, cut into a wedge of ripe Camembert, and consider the possibilities.

THE ELEMENTS

The Palette

A FRENCH COUNTRY ROOM begins with the calm, pale background of its walls. You might choose a white or a cream or a grey. Or, for a style that has so much to do with the pleasure of sunshine, you might select a French Country favourite, butter yellow. Trims are often modest and are usually nut brown, terracotta, or simply a darker shade of the colour on the walls.

Then comes the fun. The joy of French Country style is the array of bright accents. A useful basis for your choice of accent colours might be a piece of French Country decorative pottery — a flower vase, for instance, that you love and want to make central to your room. Its bright colours will help you build your palette. Use the colours for accents — for the curtains, throw cushions, and upholstery, and in the florals, stripes, checks, and borders of your fabrics. If these colours are used in too solid a manner, the effect can be oppressive.

You can base your palette on a piece of fabric, as well. The bright, happy cotton prints — Souleiado or Les Olivades — that are used so prominently in French Country style present a broad array of colours. Spend some time lingering in fabric shops and boutiques that specialize in French Country imports to familiarize yourself with the wide variety of colours and prints. Once you choose a fabric that captures the mood you're looking for, its full-spectrum colours will give you the accents you'll need to bring your room to life. A fabric's bright floral pattern of red, blue, yellow, and creamy white might, for instance, provide you with a red for the upholstery of a chair and the blue for its cushions. The yellow and white might find echoes in other fabrics — in drapes or tablecloths or bedspreads.

Floors

FLOORS CAN BE STONE, slate, or their less-expensive synthetic counterparts. Or they can be wide-planked, natural-finished wood. Dark, rustic stains are popular — stains that give the impression of a patina of age. In bedrooms, wooden floors can be painted lighter shades of soft blue, turquoise, and green to give an airier, more feminine effect.

In kitchens, hallways, and living rooms, terracotta tiles are a favourite. The use of continuous flooring, with no boundaries between the kitchen, the dining area, and the living room, is well suited to the openness of the French Country look.

Although they can be expensive to purchase and install, tiles — abundantly produced in Provence — bring an authentic touch of rural

LEFT: A single chair upholstered in plaid gives a French Country feeling to this small, simple bath. BELOW: The natural textures of brick, iron, and terracotta combine in a French Country kitchen. Painted wrought iron adds colour and drama.

RIGHT: Designer Norma King turned this tiny room into a charming sitting room that doubles as a great bedroom. The French day bed is draped in soft white cotton. BELOW: This highly personal, eclectic mix by designer Gary Zanner, gains its French Country feeling from the mirror above the mantel and the toile de Jouy fabric on a French Country chair.

France to any room. The use of tiles need not be restricted to your floors. They come in many shapes and sizes, some prettily decorated, some perfectly plain. They look wonderful around a fireplace, on a table-top, a kitchen counter, or as counter backsplashes. Leftover tiles, or tiles bought specially, can be used here and there throughout your house, echoing your French

Country theme. Use them as coasters or heat pads or, propped on a mantel or window sill, simply as decorations. (Less expensive alternatives — Mexican and Canadian tiles, for instance — are available and offer a fine choice.)

Wooden, tile, and stone floors can be made warmer and more comfortable with area rugs, needlepoint or the thin woven oriental rugs called kilims, or even rush mats. Try to avoid broadloom in a French Country room.

Walls

"NATURAL." THE WORD crops up frequently in French Country style, and nowhere more frequently than in the treatment of walls. Often they look as though they have been weathered by nature and time. Cracks and irregularities are perfectly acceptable. Although your cracks and bumps may not be the same as those in a three-hundred-year-old French cottage, they still possess an honest charm.

The natural look of French Country walls — the deep sills, the plaster, the unapologetic patches — makes French Country ideal for older homes and for lofts.

Plain walls, or walls painted with a low-lustre finish, are the most common in French Country kitchens, dining rooms, and living rooms. Usually they are unencumbered

PROJECT: MAKING NEW WALLS OLD

An old, thick, plaster wall has a textural beauty that seems worlds away from the pristine flawlessness of modern drywall. The cracks, uneven surfaces, and trowel swirls of a barn or farmhouse wall are so full of character they seem the perfect backdrop for a beautiful armoire or a china-filled sideboard. The effect is absolutely French Country, yet it's not a particularly difficult one to achieve.

To transform your flat, perfect walls into ancient stone and plaster, you can use two basic methods. Both require some practice before you embark on a complete room.

Faux Treatment

A *faux* treatment will give the illusion of texture while keeping the actual surface of your walls exactly as it was.

Apply several coats of a pale, semi-gloss, off-white, cream, or soft yellow background paint. Once your background is dry, paint the same walls with a slightly darker version of the same colour. While this topcoat is still wet, "sponge" the paint (see page 119) so that the pressure of the sponge reveals the background surface. If you use oil-based paint, the drying time will be longer, giving you more time to create the desired effect.

Plaster

A somewhat more authentic look can be created by actually trowelling a plaster-based compound, such as Dramex, on your walls. Mix the compound with water, and spread it on your walls exactly as a plasterer would — use trowels, knives, paint scrapers. Apply the compound to a thickness of 2 to 6 mm (1/16" to 1/4"). The effect can be as smooth or rough as you wish.

If you have shiny enamel walls, sand and then seal them with an oil-based primer to ensure bonding before applying plaster.

"We've found that using the colours of French Country prints in bold ways gives the fabric a very contemporary punch. Les Olivades cotton is wide and strong enough to upholster loose-cushioned furniture. It can also be lined for extra strength and used on more fitted pieces."

JEFFREY MURTAGH, EN PROVENCE

with trim and architectural detailing. If beams are visible, or if you want to install the convincing Styrofoam version, your French Country look will be greatly enhanced.

Your approach to bedroom and bathroom walls can be more decorative. Wallpapers based on the patterns of traditional French Country prints can be used for dainty trims as well as more expansive wall treatments.

Window Treatments and Fabrics

DAZZLING PRINTS — whether used as curtains, throw cushions, placemats, napkins, teacosies, or upholstery — give French Country

Les Olivades cotton upholstery by En Provence on an iron sofa is quintessentially French Country.

rooms an aura of warmth and comfort. Although wools and linens are popular fabrics, glazed and unglazed cotton prints make the most direct French Country statement. Since French Country is a natural, down-to-earth style, you'll probably want to avoid the rich textures of velvets, brocades, and satins.

French Country prints are ideal for curtains and upholstery in any room. In selecting them, try not to be too timid. Mix and match freely. Mixing patterns is a typical French Country decorating technique. (See How To Mix Prints, page 107.) You might, for instance, match the negative and positive versions of the same print: white flowers on a rust-red background alongside rust-red flowers on a white background. Or you might use patterns of differing scales and designs in fabrics that have the same colour palette. Or — and this is very French Country — you might use several versions of the same print, each with different colours.

Don't be timid — but do be cautious. French Country prints can be busy and their colours overwhelming. Always bring a swatch of fabric home and consider it carefully before you commit yourself to drapes or

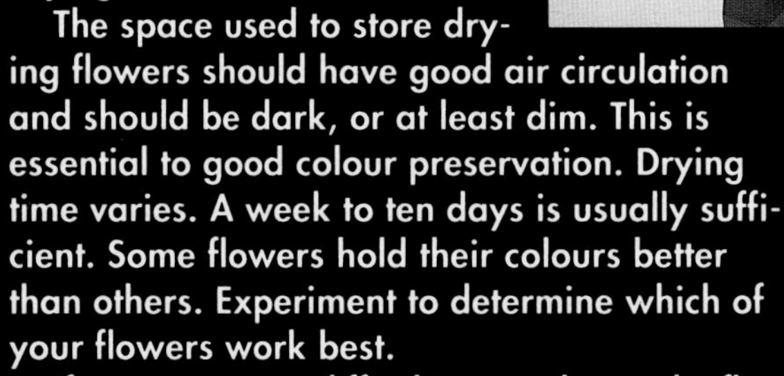

PROJECT: DRYING FLOWERS

Dried flowers bring a natural beauty to any room. With a little trial and error, you can achieve excellent results at home. Here are a few tips to get you started. Fresh herbs can also be dried in this way.

Choose the most perfect blossoms. Cut flowers from your florist may be suitable for drying, but they are not always fresh enough to ensure good results. It's best to pick your own just as they reach maturity. Noon on a hot sunny day is the ideal time to pick flowers for drying. Their moisture content will be low but they won't be wilting.

Once the flowers are picked, don't put them in water. Hang them upside down immediately. To prevent mildew, hang large-stemmed flowers individually and smaller ones in bunches of less than a dozen. The bigger the bunch, the longer the drying time. Elastic bands are ideal for holding stems together for hanging because the elastic shrinks along with the stems during the drying process. Bunches can be hung from hangers, from a clothes-line, or from a drying rack.

The space used to store drying flowers should have good air circulation and should be dark, or at least dim. This is essential to good colour preservation. Drying time varies. A week to ten days is usually sufficient. Some flowers hold their colours better than others. Experiment to determine which of your flowers work best.

If you encounter difficulties, try drying the flowers in silica gel. This sand-like powder, available from florists and nurseries, will dry flowers in a few days, and they will retain their bright colours. (You can re-use the gel many times. Do not, however, use silica gel with herbs that will be eaten.) Leaving flowers in the gel for too long will result in brittleness. Check your flowers daily.

upholstery or even to a cluster of cushions.

Lace is a wonderful way to soften a French Country room. It is especially effective as a romantic but simple window dressing. Hung from small rings on a rod or with a casing and rod insert, a half-curtain, or café curtain, is the perfect French touch.

Wooden shutters can create a comfortable, pleasant effect. Often shutters are painted, as are the window trims and sills, in the bright accent colours — a sky blue, for instance — that you found in your pottery or choice of prints.

Modern window treatments — blinds and sheers — should be avoided.

Furniture

YOU CAN BUILD AN ENTIRE room around one great piece of furniture — a classic French Country armoire, for instance. An armoire can go almost anywhere: in a bedroom or hall for linens and clothing; in the dining room for china; or in the living room for the television set, the stereo, or the bar. This one piece will lead you to the next. Once French Country is established, you'll notice that some things — highly varnished surfaces, overstuffed sofas, and large armchairs — simply look out of place. Other pieces, while not truly French Country (a Canadian pine harvest table, for example) will fit right in. In general, French Country is a much more spartan look than many traditional styles. Even in bedrooms, furniture tends to be simple and uncluttered, with pillows, curtains, coverlets, and linens adding touches of comfort.

A day bed and tall, straight-backed side chairs with rush seats are perfect additions to a French Country living room. What is more, they can be used in the dining area as well. This free-flowing use of furniture is typically French Country. One room opens into the next: sitting, dining, and kitchen areas tend simply to run into one another. As a result, there are few dramatic distinctions between each room's furniture. Pieces do not have to be restricted to only one room.

This French Country bedroom by designer Leo LaFerme is dominated by a magnificent carved bed dressed in layers of blue-and-white country prints.

PROJECT: PAINT A FRENCH COUNTRY CHEST

A plain, ordinary pine chest of drawers can be easily transformed into a French Country classic. All it takes is a little imagination, a little work, an inexpensive chest with strong lines and a gentle arc above the top drawer, and – *voilà!* On page 210 you'll find complete instructions for this *trompe-l'oeil* chest and for a pickled pine version, as well.

PULLING IT ALL TOGETHER

Drapes are simple tie-backs in cream for contrast against terracotta walls. Plaid lining, which echoes the plaid chair upholstery, is an important detail.

A French floral cotton print provides the room's colour scheme.

Terracotta "pulled" from the fabric's palette is perfect for the walls.

An open-arm Bergère chair in traditional plaid co-ordinates with the floral chintz.

A fine-patterned Persian rug echoes the room's palette but doesn't fight with the floral fabric.

A torchière lamp in a corner adds mood lighting.

The classic French Country armoire makes the biggest statement. Soft greys and golds against the terracotta walls are dramatic and provide a strong focal point. A practical place to hide away the television and stereo.

A simple iron table with glass top allows the rug to show through.

SOUTHWEST HOW-TO

WHEN YOU DAYDREAM about the interiors you want to create, you probably see yourself in them and imagine the pastimes and pleasures your rooms will encourage. Perhaps you see yourself listening to music while cooking. Maybe you're curled up on a sofa with a good book. You may see friends coming to call and relaxing in a home that has an effortless, calm, spacious atmosphere that puts people immediately at their ease.

If, in your daydreams, you imagine rooms that are as relaxed and as inviting as a holiday in the South, you are already on your way to choosing a style. That quality of easy-going comfort and casual elegance is the great appeal of Southwest style. It takes its inspiration from those simple elements that draw us to the Southwest: the vast sky, the white of sun-bleached walls, the sparse, expansive desert. It's a style that blurs the distinctions between indoors and outdoors: verandas run into hallways, gardens merge with garden rooms. Even its accessories — a single cactus in a terracotta pot, a giant ficus tree, the bleached bone of an animal skull — tend to bring the outdoors into our interiors.

Southwest style has been featured prominently in decorating magazines and books in the past several years, and an afternoon in your public library will provide you with a quick introduction and plenty of ideas. There are stores that specialize in the Southwest look, and a day of browsing will start the wheels turning.

In the end, though, the elements that you use to create the Southwest look you want will come from the souvenirs and images of the Southwest that you've collected all your life: whether driving across the deserts of New Mexico, or watching western movies, or perhaps just flipping through *National Geographic*.

THE ELEMENTS

The Palette

THE BASIC SOUTHWEST palette is drawn from the colours of nature: the soft tan of sand, the blue of the sky, the reddish brown of terracotta, the salmon pink of a sunset. White, of course, is a popular background colour, and although it doesn't come from nature exactly, the white of a hot, sun-drenched wall is typically southern.

Southwest accents are the bright, playful, vibrant colours of folk art, the deep reds of Navajo blankets, the jewel tones of native dolls, or the rich Taos blue of Indian turquoise. These accents are usually kept to a minimum and should never be allowed to accumulate to the point that they overwhelm the soft wash of the background colours.

Wood also plays a prominent role in the Southwest style. In general, it occurs — whether in furniture or in beams — in dark tones.

Floors

THE IDEAL FLOORS FOR A Southwest look are wide wooden planking, hardwood, terracotta tile, and stone. The more natural

A lower level family room features the soft desert palette of sun-washed sand and cactus green, and the relaxed ease of simple seating mixed with Canadiana furniture.

your floor's appearance, the better. Neutral colours are preferable.

One of the charms of Southwest style is the absence of a rigid boundary between various living areas: dining rooms merge with kitchens, and hallways blend with verandas. To create this look, your flooring should flow freely from room to room. Before making a choice, therefore, take the over-all look of your home or apartment into account, not just the specific requirements of individual rooms.

Your floors should suggest a light, airy look. Hardwoods can be bleached, stained a light, natural tone, or tinted with one of the new pastel colours: pink, sand, taupe, pale grey, or soft blue. Whether tile or wood, your floors can be softened with the addition of Navajo rugs, kilims, or oriental area rugs.

In bathrooms, light-coloured ceramic tile is ideal. Terracotta tile, stone, natural tiles, or the one-piece flooring that simulates clay brick are wonderful in a Southwest kitchen.

If you already have low-pile wall-to-wall carpeting in a light, neutral colour, don't worry. It's fine. Southwest style doesn't really need the warmth of wall-to-wall, however, and if you have a choice, you should avoid extensive carpeting. Remember that the texture you want for your floors is solid and bare. Your floors should give the impression of the ground underfoot.

This is an eclectic mix of English, French, and California influences. The overriding feeling, however, is relaxed Southwest style.

"Southwest style mixes well with all kinds of styles – with English and French Country, even Contemporary. Put a Navajo blanket on a modern leather sofa and a drum coffee table in front of it. If you surround yourself with what you like, you'll find your own style."

SUE BURGER,
TAOS DESIGN

The handmade texture and vibrant colours of accent cushions punctuate an otherwise neutral room — proof that accessories can greatly influence the mood of the room.

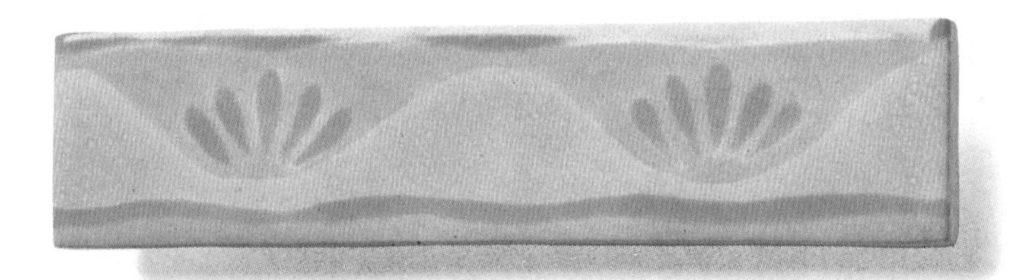

Walls

PERFECTLY SQUARED, FLAWLESS drywall is not required for Southwest style. Inspiration comes from the rough adobe walls of the missions in New Mexico and California and the thick stone and plaster walls of Indian dwellings. None of these is noted for its smooth, unblemished surface. Cracks, flaws, and patches need not be corrected.

Your walls will be light — beige, cream, white, tan, salmon, taupe, maize. Think of them as the canvas against which you will set the woods of your furniture and the bright accents of your cushions and Navajo blankets. Their lightness should also be used to emphasize the spaciousness of the Southwest look. And if you decide that a wall isn't necessary, you might consider taking the spacious look to its logical conclusion and remove the wall entirely in order to open up your interior.

Window Treatments and Fabrics

WINDOWS ARE GENERALLY treated simply in the Southwest style. Wide louvred plantation shutters are ideal. Shutters can be painted — as can your window trims and sills — in the same colour as your walls or in a vibrant contrasting colour, or their natural wood can be stained a soft shade. Cotton drapes can be hung from a simple wooden or iron rod, or, for a more dramatic and interesting effect, from a branch or twig. In general, your drapery should be unstructured and free-flowing with no elaborate sewing details.

The easiest way to choose the fabrics throughout your home is to start with a geometric cotton print in the Southwest palette. Manufacturers have many lines of fabric that feature the desert colours. These lively geometric patterns or co-ordinated solid coloured cottons, linens, and canvas can then be used for drapery, bed covers, and upholstery. Throw cushions, area rugs, and accessories can draw their colours from the brightest shades of the pattern.

Furniture

SIMPLE FURNITURE arrangements best create the open and spacious Southwest look. Sofas and chairs should be large and upholstered in natural fabrics. Unbleached whites are lovely, but in places where you can expect a good deal of wear and dirt, opt for a more practical solution.

PROJECT: PLANTS

Nothing conjures the grandeur of the outdoors, and brings it to your interiors more naturally, than a large, dramatically positioned houseplant. *Ficus benjamina* — or, as it is also known, weeping fig — parlour palms, oleander, lemon and orange trees can make the kind of bold, exotic statement that is the hallmark of the Southwest style. If the desert look has captured your imagination, a cactus is probably the plant you'll choose.

Plants that store available water to be used during droughts are called succulents, and cacti are the best-known members of this family. There are more than two thousand varieties of cactus — ranging in size from the little aloe that sits on a window sill to the giant desert cacti, some as tall as twelve metres (forty feet).

The specific needs of cacti differ from variety to variety. When buying one, ask exactly how you should care for it. With the proper attention, many varieties of cacti bloom annually.

In general, the cacti you grow indoors will prefer a bright room with a south or west exposure. Since central heating can often cause problems — a dry, cool winter is often required for summer growth and summer flowering — you might consider a plant rotation: the ficus or lemon tree you bring in from the patio for the winter can take the place of the cactus. The cactus can be kept in a cooler room.

Cacti should be watered during the summer growing period whenever the soil is clearly dry. During the dormant winter months, they require very little water. Cacti that are always indoors, however, need to be watered on a slightly more regular basis.

The desert palette geometric design might be perfect.

The combination of comfortable and uncluttered can be tricky to achieve. Your furniture will have to be selected with care. You may find that the shapes and sizes you require can be best achieved with custom-made pieces. A good custom furniture maker and upholsterer can often copy a style from a photograph clipped from a magazine.

With the new popularity of the Southwest look, there is an array of furniture available in this style. Canadian manufacturers now produce many lines of sofas and chairs with roll arms and loose back and seat cushions in solid, neutral colours.

In your living room, the few, carefully chosen chairs and sofas will probably be arranged around a fireplace and a low, expansive coffee table. This arrangement works well with sectional sofas, L-shapes, and banquettes. The coffee table is a central element; its size invites plates of hors d'oeuvres, trays of drinks, or simply the pile of books or magazines that you intend to browse through on a lazy Saturday. A slab of granite, *faux* stone, or a thick glass top are great on a base of iron or wood. A tree trunk or a chunk of rock or *faux* stone could also be used, as can a low, rough pine box.

You can highlight Southwest's celebration of Native crafts with the use of pigskin and cedar Mexican Equipale chairs and colourful drum tables. Solid New Mexican armoires, side tables,

The extensive windows add drama to this sitting room, and the choice of one huge sectional in simple cotton, angled in the centre of the room, is a bold focal point.

and bookcases are part of the Southwest's Spanish heritage. Authentic, antique New Mexican furniture is often magnificent but expensive. Its dark tones and solemn weight can provide a dramatic contrast to the light airiness of your background. Convincing reproductions are readily available.

Southwest furniture doesn't have to be dark and heavy. Bleached, modern wood finishes, or even whimsical hand-painted surfaces can blend perfectly with your desert tones. Twig furniture, Canadian pine, and even French Country pieces provide the right rustic touch.

PROJECT: A STENCILLED TERRACOTTA POT

You can add beautiful accents to your terracotta pots with the use of stencils. It's easy to do and can create a stunning effect; even the most ordinary pot can be turned into a colourful artifact. Stencils can be purchased at hobby and craft shops. The stencil used here is Ancient Navajo Rug Pattern by Norma Clarke Designs. **See directions on page 212.**

"Cushions are so noticeable, they really have to be special. The strong, bold colours of Navajo designs, for instance, can give quite a zing to an otherwise quiet room. You can change the entire look of a room with your cushions. They make a very personal statement."

BONNIE BICKEL,
B.B.BARGOON'S

Accessories

IF YOUR SOUTHWEST LOOK is to remain uncluttered, your accessories should be chosen as carefully and as sparingly as your furniture. Your selections — terracotta urns, Navajo blankets, animal bones, folk dolls — should be displayed dramatically.

BELOW: Joan Eiley's Toronto showroom was the setting for these New Mexican baskets, pottery, and hand-carved furniture.

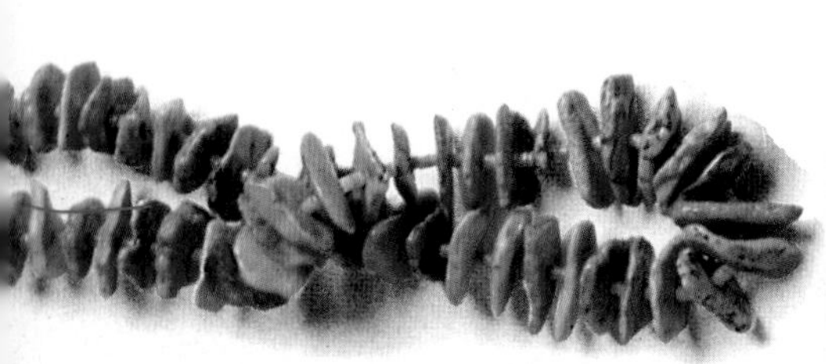

Left: Handmade cushions in the Southwest theme. Cushions can be made of old kilims and blankets, or other lightweight carpets and weavings.

Much of the style's drama is created by bringing elements inside from outdoors: floors that look like stone or sand, wooden beams and heavy trims that suggest trees, and houseplants that look like transplanted trees or succulents. Use plants sparingly but dramatically. Think of the isolated bursts of green in the desert, or a tropical island with a single palm tree, and you'll have the right horticultural picture in mind. Don't go overboard and end up with a greenhouse.

Lighting plays an important role in Southwest style. Daylight is essential, and whatever you can do to increase the effect of the shifting angles of sunlight in your interiors will help immensely. At night, your light should either be dramatic — a spotlight on a horse's skull or a single Pueblo pot — or soft and mysterious, reminiscent of moonlight. Pot lights and other invisible sources of light are ideal.

Architectural Elements

DAYLIGHT. MOONLIGHT. THE light of sunsets. The light of wide-open spaces. Skylights and big windows are invaluable, and if you have the option of installing them, don't hesitate.

The effect that light creates in your rooms should be reinforced by the easy, fluid transition from one room to the next. Open, spacious, calm — these are the qualities you want to achieve, and they are simply impossible in a warren of dark rooms. If you can, remove unnecessary walls. If not, let your palette blend one living area into the next.

PROJECT: STENCILLING A FLOORCLOTH

The lively accent colours of a Navajo rug can brighten the dark wood or tile of a Southwest floor. The same effect can be achieved with a *tromp-l'oeil* stencilled floorcloth. With paint brush, paint, and stencil, you can match your room's colours perfectly and create your own Southwest designs. **For instructions see page 212.**

PULLING IT ALL TOGETHER

Cotton striped fabric echoes native blankets and gives a strong frame to the neutral grey doors.

A milk-painted corner cabinet is a rustic touch.

White cotton is informal and cool. The sofa is deep and the loose back cushions are casual and inviting.

A tan-and-white easy chair co-ordinates with the sofa.

Cacti in terracotta pots remind us of the desert.

A faux *stone table looks real but is light and easy to move.*

Market baskets on a pine armoire add height and interest.

A faux stone lamp is California casual and its scale lends importance.

A twig accent chair with pony-skin fabric feels very Western.

Pottery on a woven throw makes a dramatic tablescape.

FOLK

HOW-TO

CHEERFUL, EASYGOING, and undemanding, Folk style has enjoyed a huge and astonishing revival in recent years. Everywhere you look there are examples of Peruvian, Scandinavian, Russian, Southeast Asian, and North American folk art — in stores, in design magazines and books, and in interiors across the country. In fact, because folk art is, by definition, a creation of people for their own use and amusement, it has as many variations as there are communities.

Folk style's popularity also has a lot to do with its adaptability. It depends less on the demands of space than on the personality of the person who chooses it. A quaint Victorian cottage and a modern high-rise, a four-bedroom house and a student's apartment — all welcome the cheerful touch of colour, antiquity, and down-to-earth furnishing that are the hallmarks of Folk style.

Folk style also lends itself to vastly different approaches in decoration and design. You can turn your house into a treasure trove of artifacts and rugs, antique furniture and quilts, curios and knick-knacks without overdoing it. You can be a purist and research the authentic colours of milk paint, strip every door and window trim in sight, and select only genuine heritage cotton prints for the seat cushions of your Shaker chairs. Or you can take a more modest approach. You can place a collection of loved domestic bric-à-brac in a plain kitchen. You can have fun with a few carefully chosen pieces: carved farm animals, beautiful quilts, Grandma's baking tins, and a pressed back chair painted cherry red.

THE ELEMENTS

The Palette

THE SOFT, MIDDLE TONES OF paints once made from the natural dyes of berries, roots, and animal blood, and then mixed with a combination of milk and lime are the origins of Folk's palette. This restrained, muted quality is a distinctive part of the Folk look today. The heritage colours that we associate with milk paint are the soft tones of dusty rose, cornflower blue, moss green, poppy red, buttermilk, teal blue, and lavender — the colours of the countryside. The soft chalkiness is either retained or brightened a little for modern tastes. Colour sensibilities are a little more adventurous today than they were a hundred years ago, so don't feel you need to keep your rooms duller than you'd like simply because you think they'll

Whimsical hand-painted furniture and accessories in bright colours are elements of the strong folk art revival.

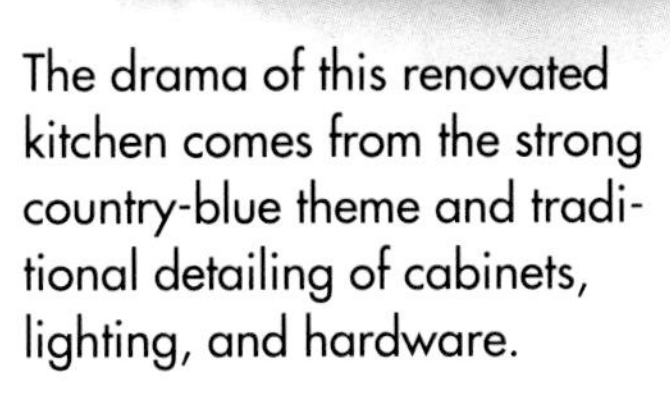

The drama of this renovated kitchen comes from the strong country-blue theme and traditional detailing of cabinets, lighting, and hardware.

be more authentic. The colours we see today in antiques and that we associate with the Folk palette are colours that have been toned down by a century of wear.

White, off-white, and soft cream can be used as background colours. These light shades contrast well with wood, and keep smaller rooms from feeling too closed in and too dark.

Accent colours should be bright and lively. If you think of your backgrounds as the quiet, soft-spoken tones of the countryside, it might be useful to think of your accents as the lively, irresistible notes of a fiddle at a barn dance. Your accents will give your rooms the touch of friendliness and simple charm that is such an important part of Folk style.

In large part, accent colours are drawn from the gingham and calico prints that were traditionally used in patchwork quilts and throws. These quilts provided warmth and comfort, and you should let your accent colours do exactly the same thing. Bright reds, vibrant greens, and sunshine yellows will bring your rooms to life. The lively colours of hand-painted toys, dolls, curios, and board games add a cheerful touch.

In Folk style, the palette tends to remain consistent from room to room. Colour distinctions between masculine and feminine rooms, and between the rooms of children and those of adults, are not very clear, if they exist at all. Nor does the palette change significantly in mood from living room to kitchen to bedroom to bathroom. Your colours should unify your house or apartment into a single style statement. Folk's traditional emphasis on family life encourages a palette that doesn't mark certain rooms only for certain functions or for use by certain people. A child will feel perfectly at home doing homework at the dining-room table. And, should adult guests ever spend the night in a child's room, they won't wake up feeling as if they fell asleep inside a crayon box.

Floors

WOOD IS AN IMPORTANT element of Folk style, and its role is particularly apparent in flooring. Wide-planked, natural-finished floors are ideal. They're beautiful in their own right — their colour and texture are definitively Folk — but they're also the perfect canvas against which to spread hooked and rag rugs, kilims, needlepoint, and oriental area rugs. Ordinary hardwood floors are also

"I prefer working freehand to stencilling, and when I'm doing a floor I approach it as I would a canvas except that I'm on my hands and knees. I chalk in the design first and then work over the chalk with oil paints. The beauty of freehand is you can let the design grow."

RAYMOND ARCHER,
DECORATIVE ARTIST

Plenty of wicker and cotton chintz against candy-floss pink walls add charm in a country cottage.

appropriate, although you might take a slightly more colourful approach to their treatment. Tinted stains or even paint — in light blues, greens, or flesh tones — can give any wooden floor a pleasant, countrified feel. Stencilled garlands of flowers and berries painted directly on the floors of kitchens and bedrooms (and then protected by coats of urethane) can add a folksy, whimsical touch.

New wooden floors can be made to look old and more suitable to Folk style. Simply coat your floors with a dark, natural wood stain, then after the stain is dry, paint it with several coats of milk paint. Sand the floor along heavy traffic routes to let the underlying stain show through. Seal with urethane, and — presto — instant country floors.

Brick flooring and its various imitations suit entrances and hallways. Tile, either ceramic or terracotta, go well in both the kitchen and bathroom. Broadloom, imitation slate, even linoleum can also be used, if necessary. Keep their colours neutral and try to prevent these floors from calling attention to themselves. The less suitable your floor is, the more you can rely on scatter rugs.

Window Treatments and Fabrics

IN THE FOLK STYLE BOOKS, windows are often shown with no treatment whatsoever. This look is fine for photographers, and for houses that are far away from the nearest neighbour. It is not quite so suitable for anyone who lives less than a field away from a street or another building. Still, the image of the curtainless, shutterless window

PROJECT: A STENCILLED TABLE

The adaptability of Folk style is one of its greatest attractions: a patchwork quilt on a bed, a collection of hand-painted dolls on a table top instantly set a cheery, folksy mood. Here, a nondescript table is transformed into a folk artifact with stencil, paint, and a little imagination. Have a look around your house for pieces of furniture waiting to be brought to life with some artfully applied pattern and colour. For instructions, see page 213.

This renovated kitchen had a fresh cosmetic "lift" with lattice, paint, and colourful country linens and accessories.

TOP: In this Folk style kitchen in an Ontario heritage home, fine Canadiana antiques are simply displayed for their primitive beauty. BOTTOM: Ruffles, gingham, and plaid cushions accent a Vancouver country interior by Josette Whist.

is worth keeping in mind.

In Folk, the simpler the window treatment, the better. Short, lace curtains and plain cotton curtains work well. Simple gingham tie-back curtains and heritage prints — small florals or animal motifs — are appropriate, although modest checks and quiet stripes can also be used. Wooden shutters — plantation shutters or wide-louvred shutters — can be left their natural wood colour, but if you feel a contrast is necessary between the shutters and the window trim, they can be painted.

Folk style is a celebration of materials and textiles, and your choice of fabrics will go a long way towards establishing a comfortable, homespun look. In general, natural fabrics should be your choice. Cotton, linen, lace, and wool can be used throughout the house. Their colours should be muted. Nothing should look too "store-bought." For instance, the sharp contrast between the red-and-white checks of gingham — a wonderfully folksy material — might be toned down with a few washings or a bath in tea before being used.

Woven throws and blankets add great colour and texture. And patchwork, of course, is a Folk classic. Use it almost anywhere — pillows, throws, bedspreads, upholstery. Particularly beautiful quilts should be thought of as folk art. They are as wonderful hung on a wall as covering a bed.

Furniture

SIMPLE, STURDY, HANDmade, functional. Keep these four qualities in mind, and you can happily follow your own inclinations. For nowhere else is the easy-going openness of Folk style so apparent as in the choice of furniture. You can remain true to a period and a region. Or you can pick and choose, swinging from Shaker to rural Ontario to West Coast to

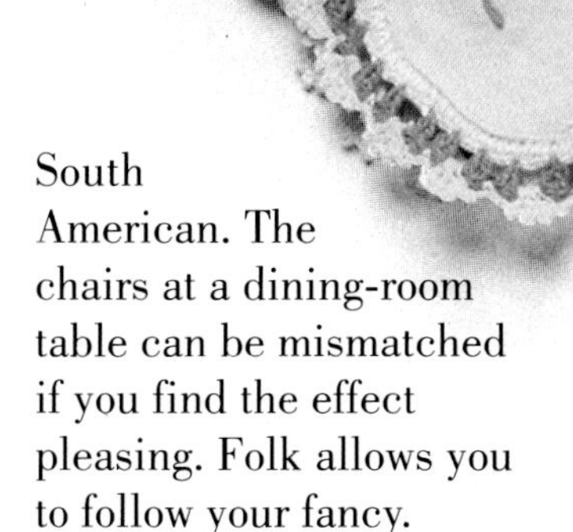

South American. The chairs at a dining-room table can be mismatched if you find the effect pleasing. Folk allows you to follow your fancy.

Bentwood or straight-backed wooden chairs, often with rush seats, gathered around a harvest table, are a traditional choice. Their clean simple lines and sturdy design make them Folk classics that add a down-home flavour to the most formal setting. Patchwork has the same effect, and the simple addition of a patchwork quilt — or even an old-fashioned, embossed white-on-white cotton slipcover — will convert any sofa or armchair to country casual.

Side tables, coffee tables, and end tables can be pulled together with a trip to a flea market and a little imagination. A well-scarred wooden bench can become a side table; packing crates and blanket boxes can become coffee tables; barrels, baskets, wire-spools, and butter churns can be put to new and charming uses. Look for twig or wicker furniture and add a patchwork cushion for comfort and colour.

PROJECT: MILK PAINT

The beautiful soft, chalky colours of authentic milk paint, with traces of fine old wood showing through the well-worn surface, are certain signs of a venerable and expensive antique. Right? Well, actually, it ain't necessarily so. You can achieve the "wear" of age in a few fleeting hours with milk paint, stain, steel wool, and a little elbow grease. For instructions, see page 213.

PROJECT: A TWIG PLANTER

Do-it-yourselfers are drawn to Folk because it is, by definition, a homegrown style. Hobbyists and amateurs find that their own creations fit perfectly with the unpretentious creations of generations gone by. You can learn to weave, carve, or make pottery — or, if you don't have quite the leisure time you'd like to have, you can spend an afternoon making a twig planter.

Alluring in their natural simplicity, twig-covered planters are an easy and inexpensive way to add a touch of woodland whimsy to your porch, patio, or garden. Directions on page 214.

High-posted beds, spool beds, sleigh beds, brass beds, iron beds, and cannonball beds — all can turn an ordinary bedroom into a charming, eiderdown-covered, comforter-strewn retreat. Or just throw a quilt over your futon. A blanket box at the foot of the bed can be put to precisely the use for which it was made — the storage of linen and blankets — while looking beautifully rustic. Pine tables, chests of drawers, rocking chairs, and even an antique cradle add the colour and texture of natural wood. In the kitchen, open wooden shelves held up by decorative wooden brackets can display your collection of preserves or china. Soften the shelves by pinning a lace border along the edge, and hang your cups and utensils from cup hooks.

Although wicker furniture can be used throughout your house, in the bedroom you might want to lighten its effect by painting it white or a soft pastel. Try a sky blue for a lively effect.

Most provinces have craftspeople who carry on the art of twig furniture making, currently enjoying a tremendous revival. This corner combines other examples of Canadian folk art, as well.

Accessories

IT IS YOUR USE AND CELEBRATION of accessories that make Folk style so varied and personal. Whether their age suits the age of your house or whether they create an interesting contrast with a more modern environment, they say Folk loud and clear.

Your accessories can create a cheerful, cluttered look, or they can evoke the mood of a more austere, serious collector. That decision is yours. Once it is made, the whole range of folk art, objects, and curios is open to you. Folk's emphasis on family life means that many of your accessories will be relics of traditional family life: toys, games, hand-carved animals, hobby-horses or even carousel horses, and dolls. Kitchen utensils are popular: baking tins, old crockery, wooden spoons and spatulas, baskets, china, candles, preserving jars. And outdoor implements and decorative pieces can bring a lively sense of history into your rooms: weather vanes, farm tools, old signs, decoys, rifles.

After you have taken the trouble to pull your collection of accessories together, don't drown them in a wash of modern lighting. Lighting should be soft and subdued, reminiscent of candle-light or the glow of an oil lamp.

Architectural Elements

FOLK IS WONDERFULLY adaptable to a wide variety of architectural styles. (A Toronto accountant has decorated his modern, high-rise office entirely in Folk style, and the effect seems perfectly natural.) However, a Victorian farmhouse with arrow-head latches on the doors and large, black hinges is the folk ideal. Beams are wonderful. Brick and stone hearths and simple pine mantels are perfect. The addition of a Franklin stove suddenly makes any room as friendly as a cup of warm cocoa.

"Folk" can mean a clean contemporary renovation where hand-painted tiles and country accessories provide pure country charm as shown in this room by designers Marshall Cummings.

PROJECT: A QUILT

"Even people who have sewn for years are hesitant to tackle a quilt," remarks Mary Lew Montague, the owner of Wooden Hill Quilts in Guelph, Ontario. "But no more." The pattern created by Mary Lew for beginners — and for lovers of Folk style — is called Rail Fence. It will keep your winters warm and cosy, and your room bright and happy. See instructions on page 214.

PULLING IT ALL TOGETHER

Dramatic yellow and blue "art" draws the eye up to the soaring ceiling.

This day bed allows the sitting room to double as a guest room.

A small light wicker trunk doesn't weigh down the centre of the room or block the view. A glass top is very practical.

A handwoven rug was the inspiration for the room's colour scheme.

An antique painted cupboard fills a corner with colour and wit.

Windows are left bare for a clean line and lots of sunshine.

A milk-painted harvest table makes a great desk.

A lively, bold plaid updates and lightens a heavy traditional wing chair.

Jaunty yellow painted floors are fresh and contrast sharply with light cotton fabrics.

TRUE NORTH
HOW-TO

TRUE NORTH STYLE IS about escape and relaxation, simple pleasures and quiet luxuries. It's about the outdoors. It's about days without clocks and evenings with no obligations other than keeping the fire stoked. It's a look that reflects the way you feel when you haven't seen your briefcase for days and the only shoes you've had on are a pair of moccasins. It's where you might want to warm up at the end of a day of skiing. It's where you pour the wine, sit back, and relax after a sun-drenched afternoon on the dock.

Most of us have an instinctive understanding of what True North style is. We know that the bright colours of Indian blankets look attractive on log walls. We know the look should be comfy, simple, and warm. Wicker, rattan, plain wood, and twig furniture are perfect. And the accessories — the oil lamps and cast-iron frying pans and old skis — are not exotic items that have to be hunted down in expensive boutiques. We can find them easily, or perhaps we already have them in attics, garages, and basements. Outfitting your house in True North style involves collecting — you'll find yourself spending a lot of time at flea markets and crafts stores. But it also involves some imagination — knowing that a pair of old skates or a paddle, when hung on a wall, are exactly suited to the style.

Because True North style is so popular now, it is possible to obtain wonderful ideas from magazines and books, restaurant interiors and advertisements. The Ralph Lauren log cabin look has been the style's most obvious promoter. Specialty stores such as Heartland in Calgary, Up Country and Pack-Rat in Toronto, Beaver Canoe, Roots, and J.J. Farmer are excellent places to begin envisioning the retreat you want to establish. Northern inns and mountain lodges are often goldmines of decorating possibilities. There are dozens of beautiful photography books that document the Adirondack, Georgian Bay, and Rocky Mountain look. Local and rural museums will show you the style's origins.

But perhaps the best way to begin is to think of what it is you enjoy doing when you get away from the city and away from work: skiing, swimming, hiking, canoeing, birdwatching, or simply relaxing. Think of the forest, the lake, the trails, a perfect day of powder snow. Then imagine the kind of place that would best suit your reasons for heading to the mountains, getting out to the country, or throwing your briefcase in the back seat and driving north.

THE ELEMENTS

The Palette

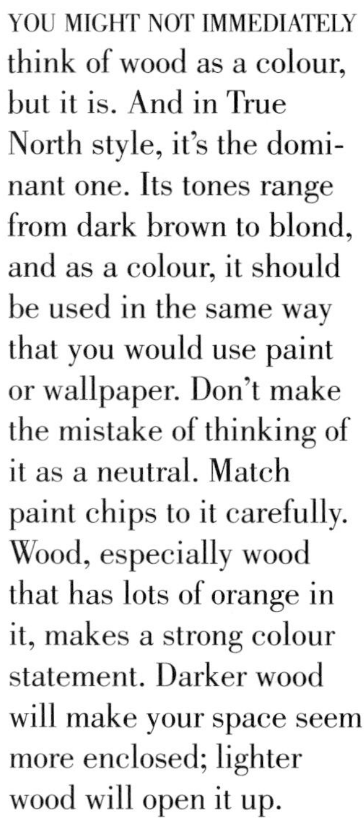

YOU MIGHT NOT IMMEDIATELY think of wood as a colour, but it is. And in True North style, it's the dominant one. Its tones range from dark brown to blond, and as a colour, it should be used in the same way that you would use paint or wallpaper. Don't make the mistake of thinking of it as a neutral. Match paint chips to it carefully. Wood, especially wood that has lots of orange in it, makes a strong colour statement. Darker wood will make your space seem more enclosed; lighter wood will open it up.

Wood is a given in the True North palette. So is the grey of rock and stone. And grey is the perfect complement to your wood tones. Wherever you use it — hearths, chimneys, floors, even walls — it will hold its own with the dominant natural browns.

Accents should be bright. They have to be, in an interior where browns and greys are everywhere. Think of Indian blankets, headdresses, and beadwork. Think of the paintings of Norval Morrisseau. Think of the red, green, and black check of a lumberjack jacket and the bold yellow, green, and red stripes on the cream background of a Hudson's Bay blanket. Think of the indigo of a dark sky or the rich black of a bearskin. Your accent colours are crucial to establishing the warmth and comfort that are so important to True North style.

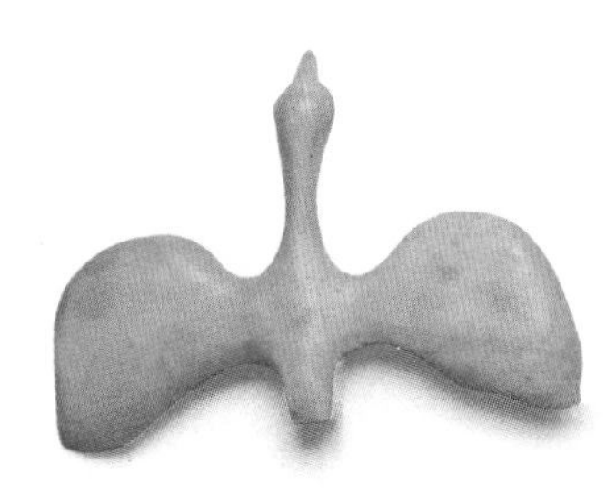

Floors

WOOD — THE ROUGHER, the wider, the more weathered, the better. If you're installing a floor and it's possible to find them, wide reclaimed planks are ideal. Colourful area rugs, such as Navajos and kilims, will brighten your floors and add a touch of warmth. If your environmental politics allow it, you may want to scatter skins and fur rugs on a wooden floor to create authenticity. They are a handsome, practical part of the northern tradition, and if you happen to have them already, they should be treasured.

If you want the comfort and warmth of broadloom, use a colour that doesn't draw attention to itself

Antique snowshoes become interesting art when hung on a log wall. Light walls and a dark ceiling highlight the lines of the log construction.

but blends into the wood and stone colours.

A painted runner is a practical and witty addition to a wide plank floor.

Walls

LOGS. PLAIN TIMBER PLANKS. Wood, wood, and more wood. If the expanse of wood is broken by a flat painted wall, use it as an opportunity to introduce a lightness with white, cream, or yellow. Alternatively, to maintain continuity and warmth, you could use deep rich earth tones. Beams can always be painted white, of course, to liven up the browns, but this is an irreversible decision and

An open hutch or Welsh dresser displays antique pewter. The patina of wood gives this vacation retreat a warm welcoming glow.

should be made carefully.

Ceremonial blankets and Indian rugs can add splashes of colour. Curios such as snowshoes, rifles, skates, mounted fish, and trophies, when displayed on your walls, will give them a quaint, whimsical flavour. These decorations can also reflect your passions and interests, easily mixing your own personality into the elements of your design.

Furniture

IN GENERAL, YOUR FURNITURE will be rugged, simple but well-made, and solid. It will tend towards the traditional and the masculine, and its decorative ornamentation will be minimal. Wood, again, will be everywhere: wide-armed Adirondack chairs, pine tables, twig sofas, settees, and even the

headboards of beds. Armchairs, barrel chairs, dining chairs, coffee tables, and end tables can be made of log. You should see as many wood-knots in a room done in True North, as you would curlicues and curves in a formal French salon.

Chair seats can be made of rattan, rush, wicker, and twig. Rawhide, leather, and traditional woollen blankets are ideal materials for upholstery. Of course, you don't have to stick rigidly to sparse pioneer roots — and the addition of big, overscale sofas and armchairs, usually clustered around the absolutely fundamental fireplace, creates a luxurious sense of comfort and adds a dash of contemporary flair to rustic surroundings. Throw cushions, blankets, comforters, and deep, down-filled cushions can accentuate this look.

There is nothing formal about True North. Mismatching furniture — even the chairs around a dining table — is fine. In fact, it helps emphasize the style's serendipitous charm. Twig beside pine beside wicker; Victorian beside Shaker beside garage sale, will only say that life is easy-going here, and everyone's too busy relaxing to worry about matching furniture.

Even bathrooms can be done in True North style. Victorian fixtures fit into the over-all look; pedestal sinks and claw-foot tubs are perfect. A bathroom sink can be built into a pine dry-sink, a magazine holder can be made of twig or log.

In the bedroom, simple wooden dressers and twig bedside tables are practical additions. Twig headboards can be extraordinary, and a log four-poster bed is quintessentially True North.

The kind of

PROJECT: A PAINTED STAIRCASE

The brilliant accents of True North — the bright colours of Indian blankets, quillwork, beading, and the solid hues of pioneer weaves — can be put to use in all kinds of places. They can brighten dark corners, reduce the over-abundance of wood colour, and add a touch of playful whimsy. Here, two plain wooden staircases have been made over with hand-painted designs.

If your staircase has been painted or urethaned, you will need to lightly sand the area you wish to paint. Be sure the surface is clean and dust-free. Using acrylic paints and artist's brushes in various sizes, paint a freehand design.

It will be helpful to have your source of inspiration close at hand — whether it be our examples or a discovery of your own. You can use stencils if you don't wish to paint freehand.

It is always easier to paint on a flat surface so you may wish to have a carpenter make you an extra set of risers. Once these have been painted you can attach them with finishing nails. To protect your design, seal it with one or two coats of urethane.

"Twig furniture can also be urbanized; I love the extremes of putting silk cushions on twig chairs. Put two of them in a room with a chintz sofa, and it looks fantastic."

MICHELLE CROWLEY, PACK-RAT

Lumberjack black-and-red plaid on twig furniture is quintessential Canadian True North style.

rustic, natural kitchen associated with French Country style is well suited to True North. Both styles are enhanced by plain wooden counters, butcher blocks, hanging pots, and antique cupboards. Microwaves and refrigerators should be down-played, or disguised if possible. New, updated versions of classic stoves and cooking ranges such as the Aga cooker are available.

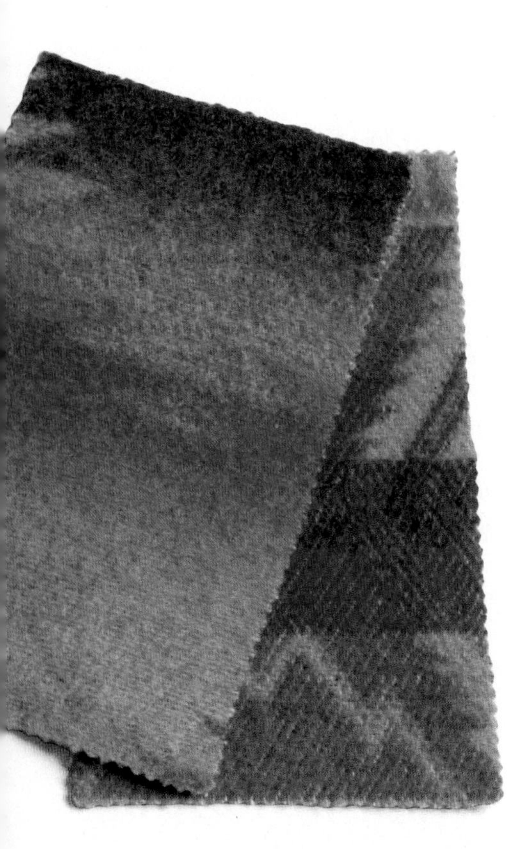

Window Treatments and Fabrics

SIMPLE, HOMESPUN FABRICS work best with True North style. Avoid glazes, sheens, exotic patterns, or heavy, sumptuous materials such as velvet or brocade. Gingham, plaid, weaves, wool, canvas, leather, and khaki are perfect. These fabrics will contrast nicely with your wood, and their colours can be as bright as Indian beadwork or as bold as the check of a lumberjack's shirt. Decorative touches such as fringe, beads, or leather thonging can add a western or Native Canadian feel.

Window treatments, in the rooms that require them, should be simple. Curtains are usually short centre-splits and range from cotton plaid, gingham, and denim to wool tartan, unbleached linen, and woven Navajo prints. They can provide walls with splashes of colour.

Wooden shutters, painted or stained, are an excellent choice.

Accessories

IN TRUE NORTH, THE ACCESSORIES are the icing on the cake. Use them playfully. They'll add a sense of the past and a delightful touch of whimsy to your interiors.

How you outfit your rooms will depend on your activities and what objects attract, amuse, and interest you. Fishing gear, snowshoes, Indian quill boxes, western art, antlers, silver buckles, Pendleton blankets, serapes, hooked rugs, coal-oil lamps, fire irons, old trunks, farm implements, head-dresses, buckskin bags, milk cans, eiderdowns, creamware, cow troughs for planters, work benches for coffee tables — the list goes on. You'll find an abundance of accessories at flea markets, junk stores, and auctions. Accumulating your chosen collectibles

A light palette of soft pastels, ruffles, and rugged log furniture is a more feminine version of rustic ease.

"Quill boxes are made of birchbark and are usually round or oval in shape. The colours of their quilled lids can be extremely beautiful. In the early part of this century, cottagers often purchased them from local Indians. Today, quill boxes can be bought at craft stores and native centres."

KEN LISTER,
ROYAL ONTARIO MUSEUM

can be enormous fun.

Lighting should mimic the soft effect of coal-oil lamps and candle-light. Task lighting — small lamps, standing floor lamps, and simple iron chandeliers — are preferable to general lighting. But you'll want lots of lights. Wood tends to absorb light, and you don't want your rooms to seem dark and dreary. Cheerfulness and warmth are important, and your lighting will help provide these qualities.

Architectural Elements

FOR ALL ITS SIMPLICITY, TRUE North is dependent on its architecture. It's not a look that can be easily achieved in a modern urban environment. You may not absolutely have to have authentic wide-planked wood floors, walls of hand-hewn log or plain timber, a stone hearth and chimney, thick-trunked ceiling beams, simple, old-fashioned windows, and a view of the forest. But they certainly help. If you don't have the architectural elements that add up to a rustic, outdoors, north-woods effect, the addition of pot-bellied stoves and a few pairs of artfully hung snowshoes won't create a completely satisfying True North look. Victorian homes are adaptable, but you should carefully consider the basic suitability of your home before committing yourself to True North.

A hearth and chimney of river rock is common in Canadian log homes. Traditional wing chairs are reminders of an English heritage.

PROJECT: A TWIG TABLE

The classic twig table hearkens back not only to pioneer days but also to the hey-day of northern retreats — to the grand lake-side resorts, majestic mountain lodges, and rambling cottages of days gone by. It's hard to imagine anything that so gracefully combines rustic simplicity and fashionable sophistication — and that is so easy to make. Instructions on page 217.

PULLING IT ALL TOGETHER

Painting window frames white adds crispness to log walls.

White candles are dramatic against the dark log walls.

An antique dry-sink is charming and practical.

Dried flowers in a big basket and a decoy lend interest and charm to this corner.

This Oriental runner adds warmth and picks up the colours in the quilt.

Simple plaid curtains in strong navy and white complement the room's rustic style.

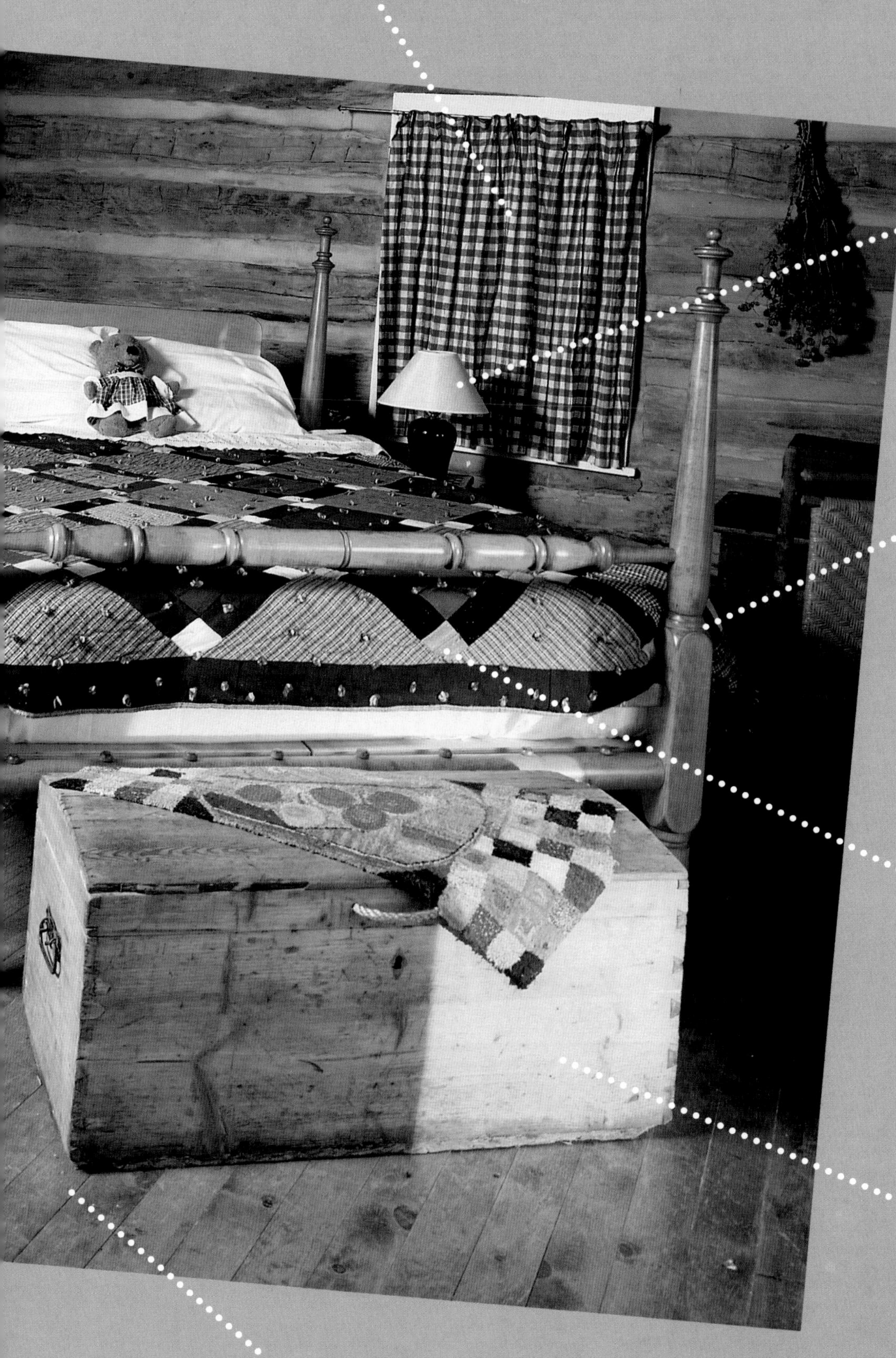

White sheets and a white lampshade punctuate all that brown behind.

A Canadiana four-poster bed can be set on an interesting angle — much better than blocking a window sill.

This country quilt was the inspiration for a palette of navy, red, white, and tan.

A pine blanket box adds extra storage.

Bare wood floors add to the rustic beauty.

SHARP
Metric Converter
TO METRIC
FROM METRIC
ELSI MATE EL-344A
R·CM
M+
ON
CA
C·CE

CONTEMPORARY HOW-TO

LESS IS MORE. IT'S ONE of the century's most famous statements, and, within the context of Contemporary style, one of the most useful to remember. Whether your plans include Art Deco, Bauhaus, Fifties style, or Post-Modernism, Mies van der Rohe's dictum probably applies to what you have in mind.

Contemporary style is restrained, unadorned, and functional. It has clean lines, streamlined surfaces, and smooth textures. It reduces clutter and includes only what's necessary. It celebrates space as much as it does the objects that fill it.

"Designing your space" — as opposed to "decorating a room" — is an expression often used in Contemporary style. The distinction is worth remembering. "Space" implies an openness, an area reserved for human activity, and Contemporary style, at its most basic, is simply an elegant and efficient accommodation of the way we live our lives.

Unlike the traditional styles, Contemporary cannot be built gradually or added to whenever inspiration strikes. Because your rooms will be more like single creations than collections of objects, you have to construct them as if they were pieces of sculpture.

Contemporary style is ideally suited to both older homes and to the most modern condominiums or apartments. In older buildings, its simple lines and smooth surfaces often provide a pleasing contrast to the more traditional architecture that surrounds it. In more modern homes, where it blends naturally with the style of architecture, it tends to make spaces seem larger than they really are.

A Contemporary look is sophisticated and stylish. At its most successful, it achieves a balanced arrangement of colour, texture, and form. If all this sounds a little intimidating, it shouldn't. Of all the popular design styles, Contemporary is the one with the most straightforward first steps.

To begin your planning, all you have to do is consider how you live. Do you watch television in the living room? Do you like to listen to music in the study? Do you work out on your rowing machine in the bedroom? Do family and friends gather in the kitchen while dinner is being prepared? Whether your study is primarily for working at home, reading, or playing chess, whether your living room is for listening to opera, displaying art, or entertaining friends, Contemporary style will help you design a space in which nothing else gets in the way.

THE ELEMENTS

The Palette

THERE IS NO SINGLE PALETTE for Contemporary style, for the simple reason that there is no single Contemporary style. The colours range from Syrie Maugham's white-on-white to the comic-book primaries of the Memphis Group. The spectrum is as wide as the one you would see if you were standing on a beautiful beach: the calm expanse of sand and blue sky, the vivid turquoise of the water, and the brilliant accent colours of beach balls, umbrellas, and towels.

As with the other styles, however, it's a good idea to acquaint yourself with the range of Contemporary colours. Look at pictures of Contemporary rooms. Visit furniture showrooms, and pay attention to the displays in the trendiest clothing-store windows. If you can bear it, watch rock videos — they are often a useful indicator of the latest and most popular combinations of design elements and colours.

There are, however, three basic approaches to the palette that will help you pick your way through the Contemporary rainbow. A monochromatic colour scheme is ideally suited to styles such as Art Deco, Bauhaus, or Minimalism (see pages 82 and 90). A balanced scheme of three or four harmonious colours suits Fifties style and Post-Modernism. And brilliant splashes of colour are typical of the Memphis Group and New Wave. Perhaps the best way to keep these three categories in mind is to think once again of our beautiful beach.

A monochromatic colour scheme is achieved with "step-colouring." If you think of the sand on a beach, you'll have a good image of what this means. All the sand is basically the same colour, but depending on whether it is wet or dry, in sun or in shade, it will have different shades and tones.

OPPOSITE: A clean, contemporary sitting room by designer Norma King achieves strong impact with a monotone palette. Interest comes from the unusual grouping of framed prints and the pointed folding screen. LEFT: Strong colour in a tiny kitchen. The combination of deep red and chrome industrial shelving gives electric impact.

> ***"To establish a colour theme you can choose a paint colour and 'step' it – use it in five, six, seven different tones throughout your home. What you want is for people to feel the differences in the mood as the colour intensity changes from room to room."***
>
> DOROTHY AMES, DOROTHY AMES DESIGN STUDIO LIMITED

To step-colour, begin with a base colour — let's say the deep green-grey of natural slate. At a paint store, collect paint chips of the varying depths of this colour. Sometimes, they'll be found on a single colour card. When used together in a room, the varying intensities of shade — from dark to light — will produce a harmonious, calm, and distinctly modern effect. The deep green-grey that you chose first might be used as a solid for the fabric on your sofa; a much lighter variation, the colour of your walls; somewhere between the two, you might find the right colour for the venetian blinds.

Now, go back to the beach, but widen your view. You've seen the sand. Now add the ocean and sky. The colours are equally balanced and have a soft, friendly relationship to each other; there are no hard edges or dramatic contrasts between them. An armchair, covered with aqua-coloured leather, might sit against a tan wall, beside a window draped with sky-blue parachute silk. This is the kind of palette favoured by Post-Modernism. You may remember that a few years ago people called it the "Miami Vice look." Pink, aqua, tan, turquoise, burnt yellow, and olive green work well in this scheme — but it's their fresh, delicate contrasts that give them their Contemporary feel.

Black lacquer on bare wood floors surrounded by walls of glass create a bold setting for dining.

Back at the beach, a beach ball is tossed into view, beside a black-and-white checked towel. It's bright, fun, and hard to ignore. Its colours are the brilliant primaries of a box of crayons. These are the colours of the Memphis Group and Post-Modern designers — used largely as a reaction against the sometimes austere tones of Bauhaus — and choosing them will involve a certain sense of daring and humour. These splashes of colour, when used as accents, enliven a room and, in broader strokes, make an entirely modern statement. But remember: a fire-engine red loveseat flanked by two yellow end tables isn't going to fade into the background. Be prepared for drama. Make sure your colour combinations are ones you'll be happy with for more than a short while.

Floors

THINK CLEAN, FUNCTIONAL, and unfussy. After that, almost anything goes. A neutral-coloured broadloom is perfect in most living rooms, the study, the halls, and in bedrooms. It can provide warmth and comfort to a modern room without interrupting the over-all design. In the kitchen, there are no rules, but bleached wood, black-and-white tile, one-piece flooring, natural slate, or many of the new synthetic materials are perfect. In the bathroom, classics such as marble or ceramic tile are great. And they don't have to be modern! Even Victorian tile — set against Contemporary bathroom furnishings — can give you the look you want.

PROJECT: GLAZING A WALL

The most common misconception about glaze is that it is something you spread on a surface simply to give it a shine, like glazing a ham. In fact, a glaze doesn't have to be shiny at all. Glazing is a method of providing a richness and depth to a colour that even the glossiest high-gloss paint would never achieve on its own. It's an unmistakable effect. A room finished with a glazed paint treatment has a formal, modern splendour that cries out for extravagant folds of drapery and dramatic furnishings.

First, paint your walls with an enamel gloss or semi-gloss paint in your chosen colour. Then, mix some tint (also called paint colourizer) or acrylic artists' colours — available at most paint stores and art supply stores — of the same shade into a clear varnish and apply that over your background colour. The combination of the tinted, translucent varnish and the background paint will create a new, richer version of the colour with which you began. The layers of the coats of varnish will create the colour's depth. The more coats, the deeper your walls will appear. And the sheen of the varnish — it can range from low lustre to high gloss — will give you anything from a flat to a "wet" surface.

Commercial glazing liquid is available as well. It appears milky in the can, but dries clear and can be mixed with tints or artists' paints. The advantage of commercial glazing liquids is that they can be more easily "manipulated" than varnish. Spread over a background colour, they can be ragged or sponged (see page 119) to produce a deep, textured effect.

A sun-filled loft by Taffi Rosen shows that contemporary chic can be achieved using inexpensive simple fabric slipcovers, painted finishes, a soft, washed palette, as well as a deft eye for mixing interesting shapes and eclectic accessories.

Walls

PAINTING YOUR WALLS WITH matt-finish neutrals such as pale creams and greys will create a simple and adaptable background. Light and unobtrusive colours will help create the illusion of more space — a quality that is particularly important to Contemporary styles, and particularly welcome in modern apartments. A light-coloured ceiling, especially if painted with a high-gloss paint, will "lift" your rooms. Mirrors can also make a room feel bigger and can give a room a wonderfully Contemporary gleam. Full-mirrored walls are an integral part of many modern interiors. By manipulating small spaces such as foyers or bathrooms with mirrored walls, you can achieve a playfully elegant effect. When using a mirror, however, think carefully about where it will begin and end, and what it will be reflecting.

Painted finishes such as marbleizing, dragging, sponging, and "pickling," are well suited to the Contemporary look. Wallpapers can be a less labour-intensive way to achieve a *faux* finish. Draping or covering your walls with fabric can create a look that is sumptuous and luxurious, but that doesn't contradict the simplicity of Contemporary style.

Window Treatments and Fabrics

THERE ARE TWO BASIC approaches to window treatments in Contemporary style. The first is to play down your windows, to let them blend coolly into the background. Simple, discreet coverings such as vertical or horizontal blinds, painted shutters, and roman fabric blinds can be as unobtrusive as the eggshell or soft grey you've used on your walls. Light, floor-length curtains, made of fabric the colour of your walls, can add a slightly softer touch.

The second approach is to go for drama: tumbles of glossy *faux* silks, sculpted folds of polished cotton, generous cascades of luminous parachute silk that trail casually along the floor. Vibrant colours, echoed elsewhere in the room, can be exciting. In Contemporary style, there is almost no such thing as too vibrant a colour. You should, however, avoid sheers and valances and the "party frock" approach to window dressing — unless they can be executed with a sense of whimsy.

"Thirty years ago, when we first introduced Bauhaus pieces, people didn't know what to make of them. Since then, consumers have become more informed and more sophisticated. People know the difference between beautiful, well-made chairs and tables and cheap reproductions. People know how to look for high quality."

KLAUS NIENKAMPER, NIENKAMPER

Whether for window treatments, upholstery, or for accents, patterned fabrics should be chosen carefully. In general, plain silks, cottons, wools, or synthetics are serene and elegant, and are the easiest to use. If you want the zip of patterns, however, go for the Post-Modern amoeba-like squiggles, the small "tie" patterns, the computer grids and graphics, or the tongue-in-cheek fun of *faux* animal prints: leopard dining-room chair seats or zebra sofa cushions.

Furniture

FURNITURE IS ONE OF THE foundations of a Contemporary look. Keep in mind that Contemporary pieces can blend with other furnishings, but only if used with care and restraint. A carefully chosen antique can add warmth or a touch of humour to a modern room, but the wrong combination can ruin the balance you're trying to achieve. If you haven't inherited a large number of hard-to-ignore antique pieces or are starting from scratch,

Designers Marshall Cummings created an oasis of Contemporary calm with soft lighting and an eclectic mix of furniture and textures.

Contemporary style is an ideal choice.

When planning a room, a floor plan is always useful; in Contemporary style, it's essential. It will help you think through your rooms. What is the best arrangement of furniture? How does the traffic flow? What distance do you want to maintain between chairs and the stereo speakers, or the sofa and the television? What are the room's focal points? This simple "block" plan is the basis of your designed space. It will keep your furniture arranged around your chosen focal points — the fireplace, a magnificent view of the skyline, a painting, or a media centre. It will also help you overcome any design problems inherent in your room. For instance, a living room with many doors and windows might lend itself best to an L-shaped or U-shaped seating arrangement. Your floor plan will suggest this solution before you buy any furniture.

Then with your floor plan in hand, you will be able to maintain the integrity of your design. If a sofa is too big — no matter how wonderful it looks in a furniture showroom — you'll know it can't work in your home: it will interrupt the traffic flow; it will block one of your speakers; it won't leave enough space for your elegant Italian standing lamp. If you happen to see a nice armchair in a store, you'll be able to resist the temptation. A glance at your floor plan will tell you not only that there's no place for it, but also — if you've thought your floor plan through carefully — that there's no need for an extra chair.

The array of Contemporary furniture can be overwhelming. After all, the modern era of design covers almost a hundred years and includes dozens of trends and styles. In the end, your choices will be based on your own aesthetic judgement. The best way to select furniture is to look but don't buy for a while. Visit showrooms, retail stores, and shops that specialize in Art Deco, Fifties style, or Post-Modern style. You should think of these excursions as being similar to outings to art galleries, for, in Contemporary style, your furniture will be pieces of art. Remember, "less is more." The few pieces you do buy will command a good deal more attention than they would in a more crowded environment. A beautiful piece of Contemporary furniture — let's say a Barcelona chair — will be central to your design scheme, and because your rooms are not going to be filled with clutter, it will be as much

PROJECT: PAINTING A CHAIR

Just because your gleaming, ultra-modern Contemporary look has left your old furniture behind, don't relegate everything to the garage sale. A little paint and an appropriately modern sense of fun can transport anything — even the simplest wooden kitchen chair — out of the past and into the day after tomorrow. **Directions on page 218.**

"I take issue with the appellation 'accessories.' The word implies that once the main part of an interior is done, you simply fill the empty spaces. Accessories really have to be part and parcel of any layout, and they should be chosen as carefully as furnishings, lighting, even basic architecture."

PAUL PAPINEAU,
TRIEDE DESIGN
INCORPORATED

the focus of a room as a piece of sculpture.

There are classics of Contemporary furniture design — the Barcelona chair, the Chesca chair, the Wassally chair — that, in their original form, are serious investments. They are costly but timeless and if your budget allows such a purchase, you will be acquiring an extraordinary combination of design, engineering, materials, and craftsmanship. If you can't afford one of these, there are cheaper reproductions available. Or you can be daring. One of the pleasures of the Contemporary look is making discoveries and decisions on your own. In every city in Canada, young, talented furniture designers are doing exciting and innovative work. Often they are represented in group shows — the annual Virtu exhibition in Toronto is a good example. Take the time to see what your own local cabinet makers and furniture designers are creating:

This hall grouping features a French Country, highly carved mirror. But the manner in which it is used, above a contemporary table, and the interesting mix of topiary trees and accessories make a modern statement.

you may be astute enough to buy a future "classic."

You may find, as you browse through magazines and clip photographs of Contemporary rooms, that the effect that appeals to you is created by custom-made, built-in units. No amount of arranging and re-arranging furniture will give you the same clean lines and uncluttered simplicity. Built-in closets in the bedroom, kitchen cupboards, bookcases and media units, banquettes, window seats, and pot lighting can require draughtsmen, carpenters, architects, and electricians, and that can be expensive. But they can provide ideal solutions to difficult space problems. And the results can be stunningly simple.

Accessories

BECAUSE THERE IS LESS visual clutter in Contemporary rooms, individual accessories take on greater importance than they do in more traditional styles. Both functional objects — telephones, kettles, lamps, stereos — and decorative ones should be co-ordinated with the colours, textures, and over-all look of a room. Choose your accessories carefully, but trust yourself: be bold in what you choose and daring in your presentation. Without these expressions of your personal style, the wonderful dramatics of a Contemporary look might be lost. A fabulous "tablescape" of spot-lit marble eggs, displayed on a glass table in a stark minimalist room, has a more dramatic effect than the same collection would have, lost amid the clutter of an English Country library.

Contemporary style is perfect for the art lover and collector. Its openness and calm sense of order allows attention to be drawn to well-placed *objets d'art*, sculpture, paintings, drawings, or prints.

Contemporary style also does away with unnecessary or clumsily designed hardware. Hinges, fasteners, and latches are invisible. In general, wherever something can be made cleaner, or simpler, or more efficient, that is the option you should take. Touch-latch cupboard doors are the most notable example of this shift.

But, thanks to High Tech, we have also grown accustomed to seeing how things work. If something can't be neatly and gracefully tucked away, don't feel you need to resort to elaborate disguises (remember your parents' hi-fi consoles). Be willing to call a knob a knob and a cord a cord. Throughout the modern house, chrome, porcelain, stainless steel, plexiglass, and the new plastic composites are not only kept visible, they're celebrated.

Electric blue leather chairs are a dynamic approach, made even more interesting by the addition of a "retro" lamp.

Nowhere is this more apparent than in the kitchen. If an appliance is frequently used and is also well-designed and engineered, it can be an integral part of the room's design. In Contemporary style, some of the most beautiful objects in the house are the most functional. The place to store your gleaming European juicer may well be on your kitchen counter.

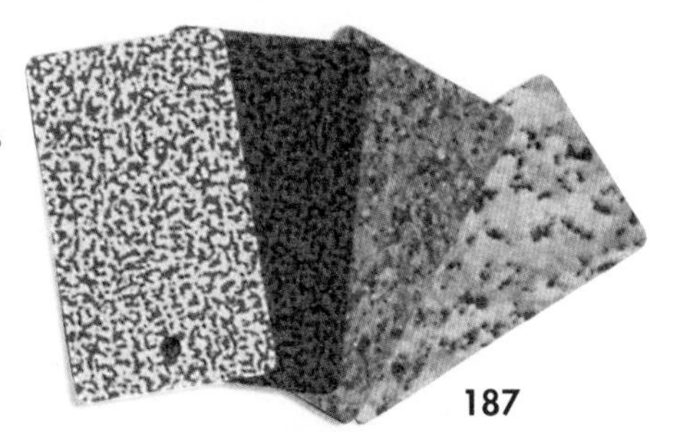

PULLING IT ALL TOGETHER

A monotone grey palette starts with matt grey walls.

Peach flowers are cool and fresh against all that grey.

A pair of simple tables in black gives weight to the centre of the grouping.

A strong print creates a focal point. Leaning, instead of hung, is unexpected and more casual.

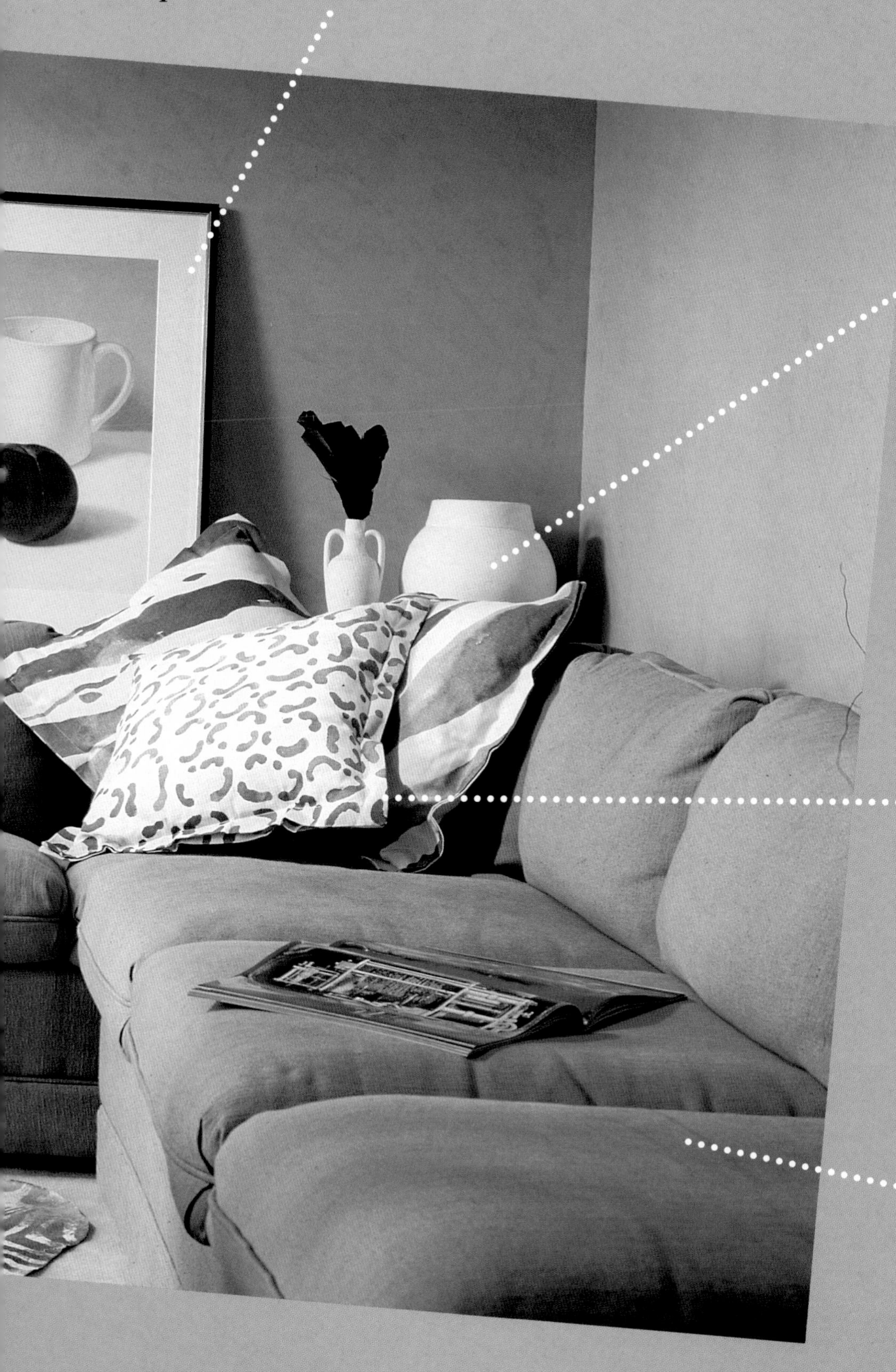

White accessories create a dramatic corner and echo the painting's still life.

Simple cushions in three patterns of grey, white, and cream break up the expanse of grey.

A sectional sofa provides plenty of seating. The taupe upholstery fabric "steps" the colour from the grey walls.

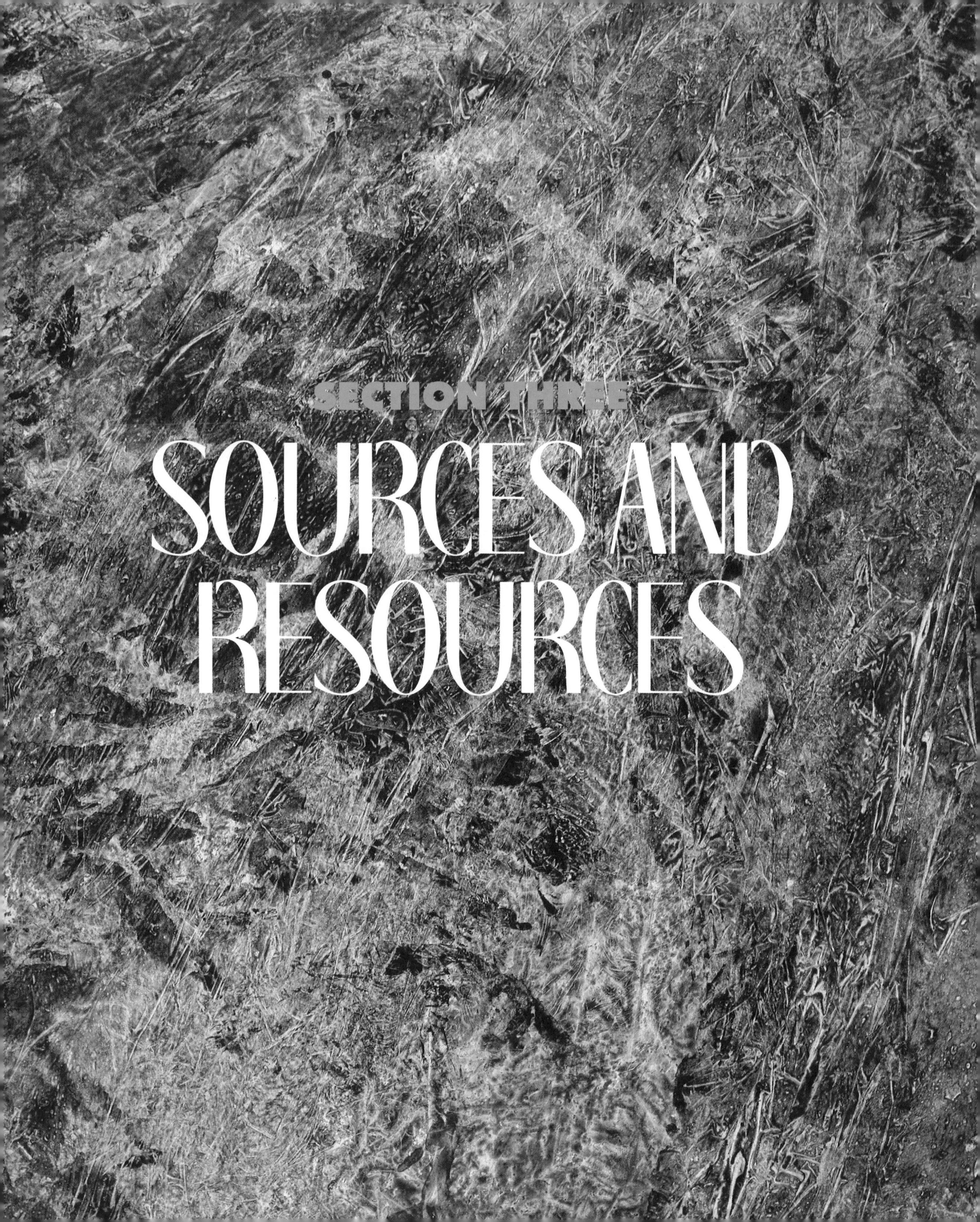

SECTION THREE

SOURCES AND RESOURCES

HOMESTEAD HOUSE PAINT
HOMESTEAD
HOMESTEAD HOUSE PAINT CO

SOURCES & RESOURCES

RULES OF THUMB AND TRICKS OF THE TRADE THAT are second nature to decorators and designers can provide much-needed practical assistance to the amateur. "Why didn't somebody tell me?" is probably the most common refrain when things go wrong in a renovation or redecoration.

One of the things we've always tried to do at *Canadian House & Home* is to be that somebody. We want to tell you what you'll need to know before you embark on a project. Why re-invent the wheel or learn through trial and error when there are accepted design standards and guidelines for specifying materials, calculating quantities, doing a simple floor plan, or measuring a window? In these pages you'll find the most commonly used and essential charts, along with great tips from the experts. Some of these charts should go directly into your workbook. We've included grid paper and templates to help you draw your own floor plans, a glossary to take the mystery out of terms you'll encounter, and an extensive directory of sources and services available across the country.

Finally, there are complete instructions for the decorating projects shown earlier in this book. Take the time and use this book to plan your approach – you'll spend less time dealing with problems that could have been avoided, and more time creating the look you want to achieve.

A Note to the Reader: The transition from imperial to metric measures has been irregular in Canada, and the home furnishing sector has not escaped the confusion. We've tried to present the following charts in both measures; however, you will find that in some cases imperial measures are given first and in other cases metric measures precede. This is to take into account the type of measure most frequently used by the manufacturers of various materials.

THE BASICS

How to Make a Floor Plan

A FLOOR PLAN IS A BIRD'S-EYE view of your room. It is an extremely useful tool in making basic decisions about your furniture — its size and shape — and about the room's composition. It will help you keep your thinking clear and realistic as you approach your project.

1. Begin by making a rough sketch of the shape of your room so that you can note measurements as you take them. In addition to the walls, you will want to note the positions of any solid fixtures — doors, windows, fireplaces, support pillars, radiators, etc.

2. Using a metal tape measure (and a friend), start in one corner and measure out the room: corner to door, door width, door to window, window to next wall, and so on. It is useful to indicate electrical outlets. Note how far your fireplace extends into the room, how deep the bay window is, and the thickness of partitions.

3. With all relevant measurements clearly marked on your rough sketch, you are ready to make a scale drawing of your floor plan. Use a sharp pencil (preferably a draughting pencil),

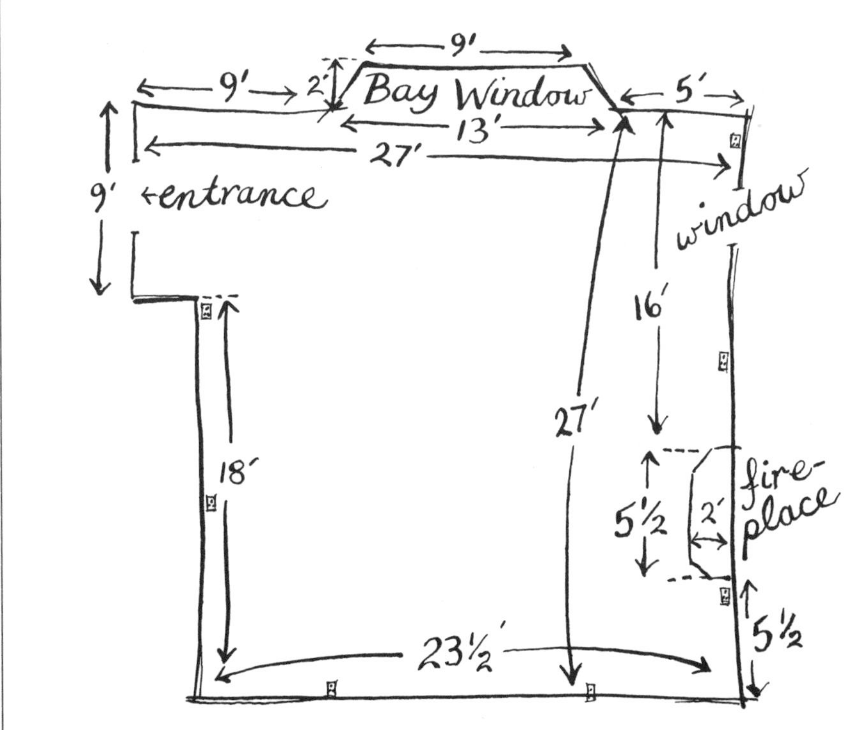

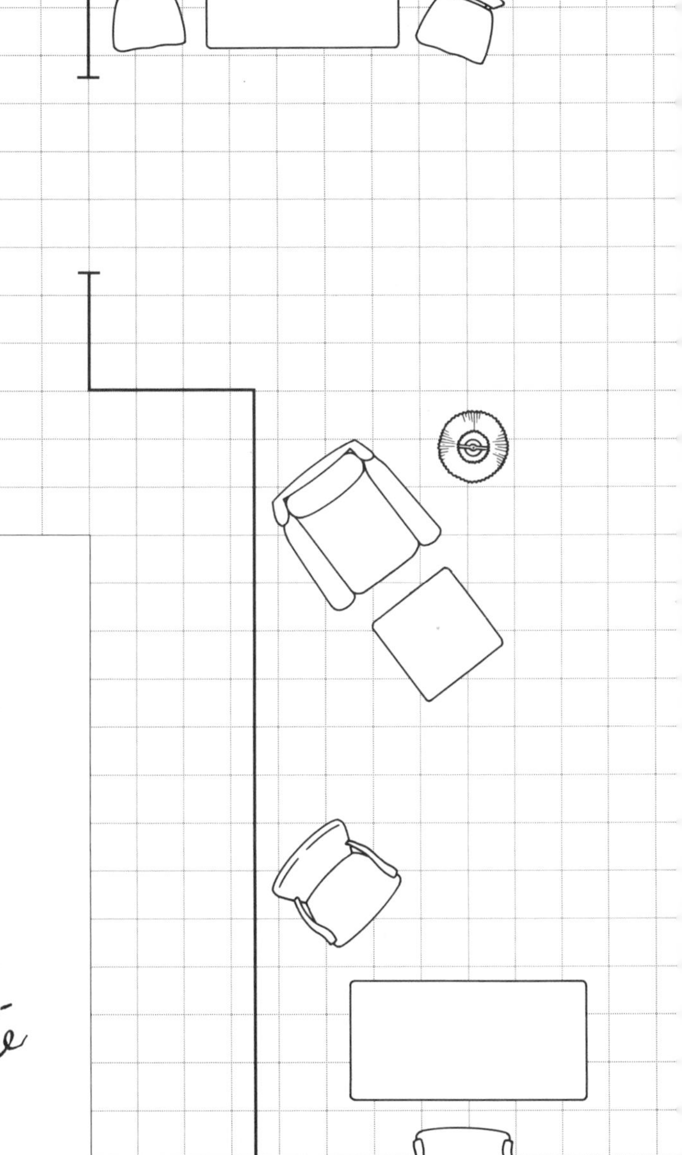

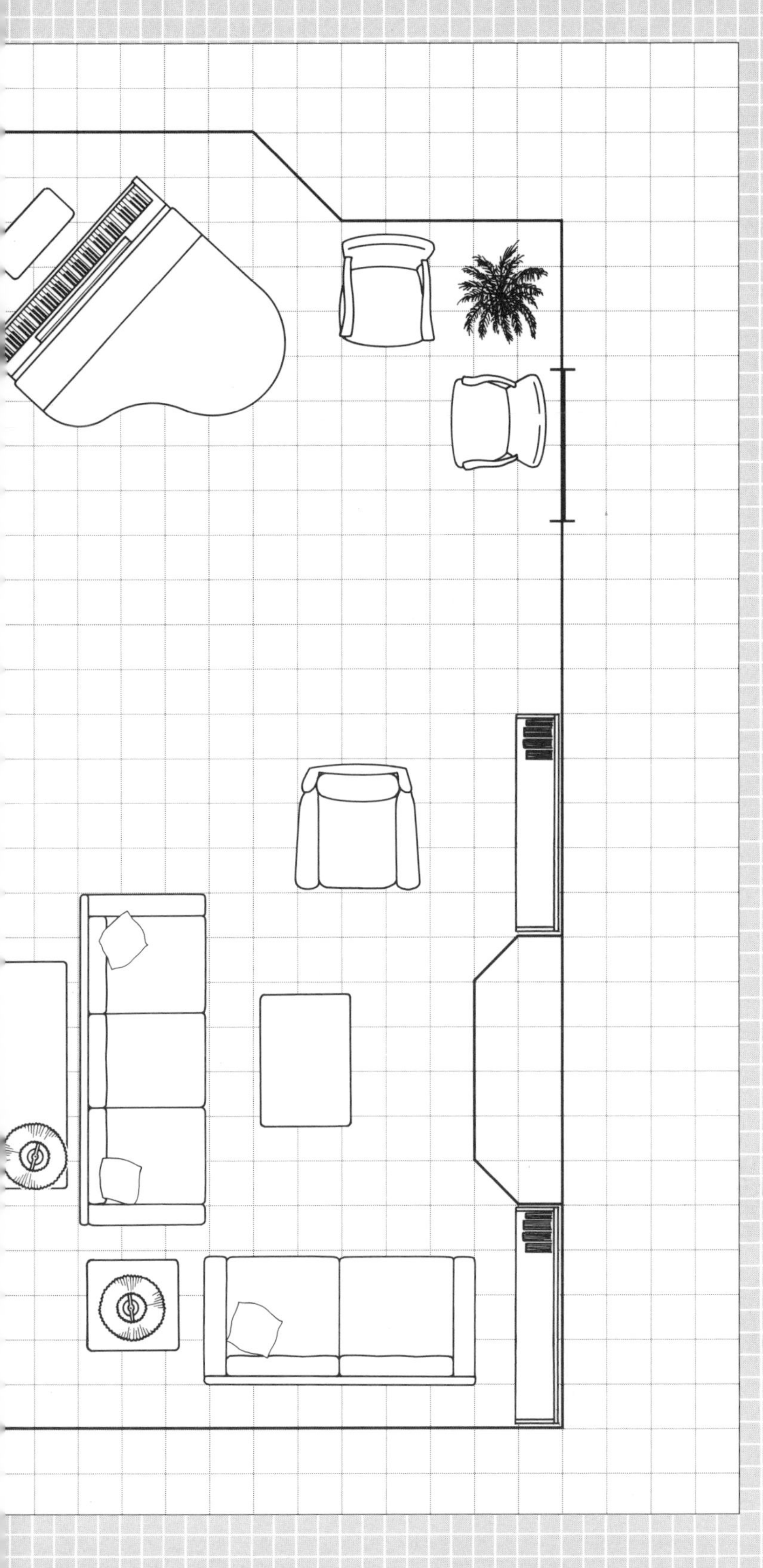

a ruler, and photocopies of the grid paper on page 198 and proceed carefully, being very exacting in all measurements.

4. You will find furniture templates on pages 196-197. Use these or prepare your own templates for your main furniture pieces using a separate sheet of grid paper. Draw simple shapes to the same scale as the floor plan (1/4" = 1'). Cut them out and move them around the plan. Think three-dimensionally. Will the armchair block the window? Will the side table fit under the sill? Think about traffic flow. Will you still be able to walk around the dining table even when the chairs are pushed out? Is the only way through the living room an interruption of the people sitting there? Move your furniture pieces around until problems such as these are solved.

5. Once you are happy with your floor plan, either fasten the pieces to the paper or trace them in position.

6. Take a copy of your floor plan and a tape measure with you when you go shopping. Make certain that your furniture will fit the space you have.

Tips

● If you are having custom built-ins made, be sure the carpenter or builder takes his or her own measurements.

● If you live in an apartment, measure the size of the elevator to be sure your furniture will fit into it. In houses, also ascertain whether what you are buying or having built will fit through your doors or windows, and whether it can be manoeuvred around the bend in the stairs.

Furniture and Fixtures

THESE TEMPLATES REPRESENT standard sizes of many of the pieces of furniture and the appliances that you will be working with as you plan your rooms; compare them to the sizes of your existing furniture and adjust them as necessary. We invite you to make photocopies of the templates, cut them out, and arrange them on the grid paper in order to see your rooms accurately. If you have pieces that are unusual sizes, measure them, reduce them to the scale of the grid paper, and create your own templates. Don't trust your memory! A few inches can mean the difference between perfection and expensive errors.

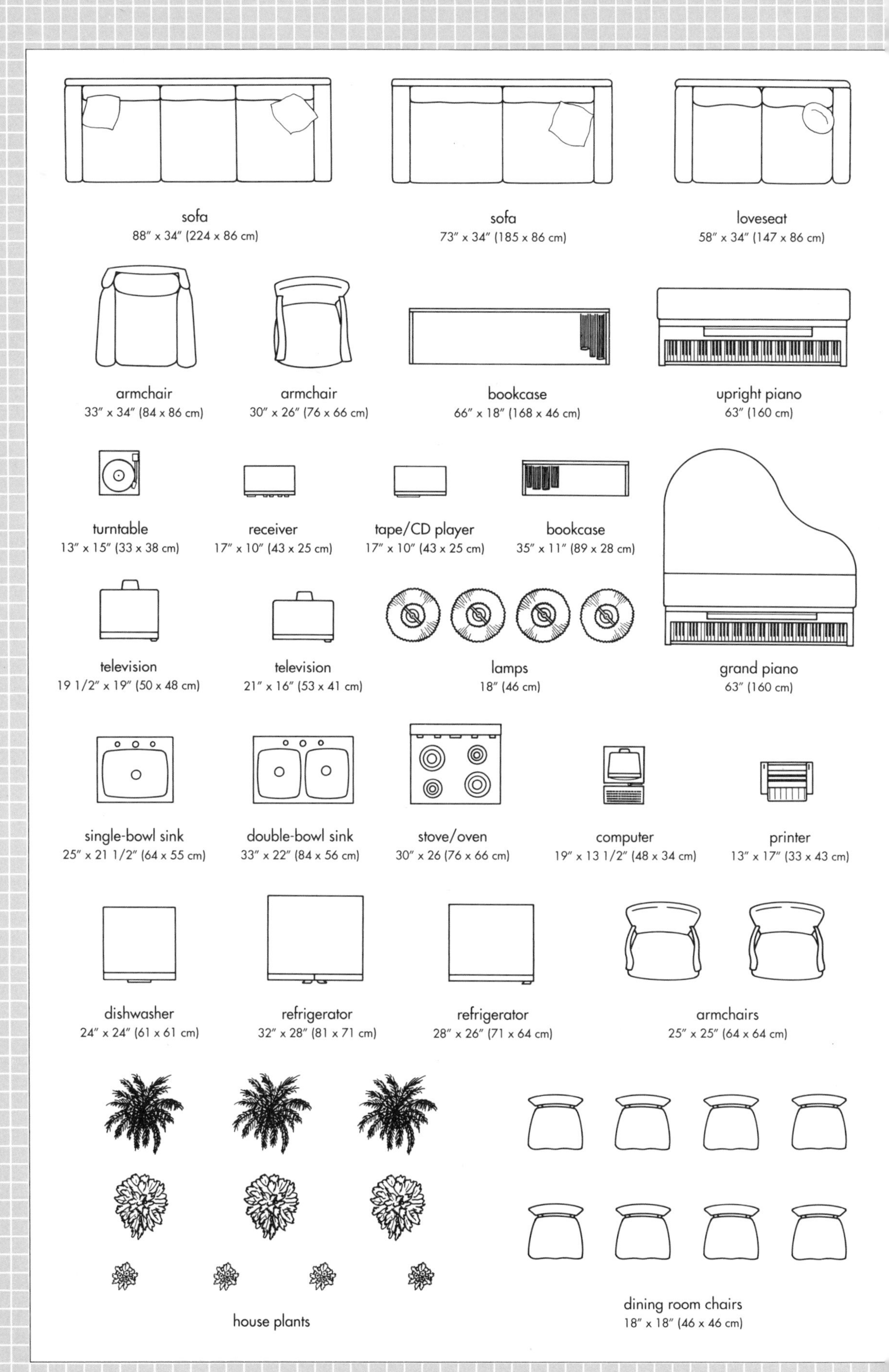

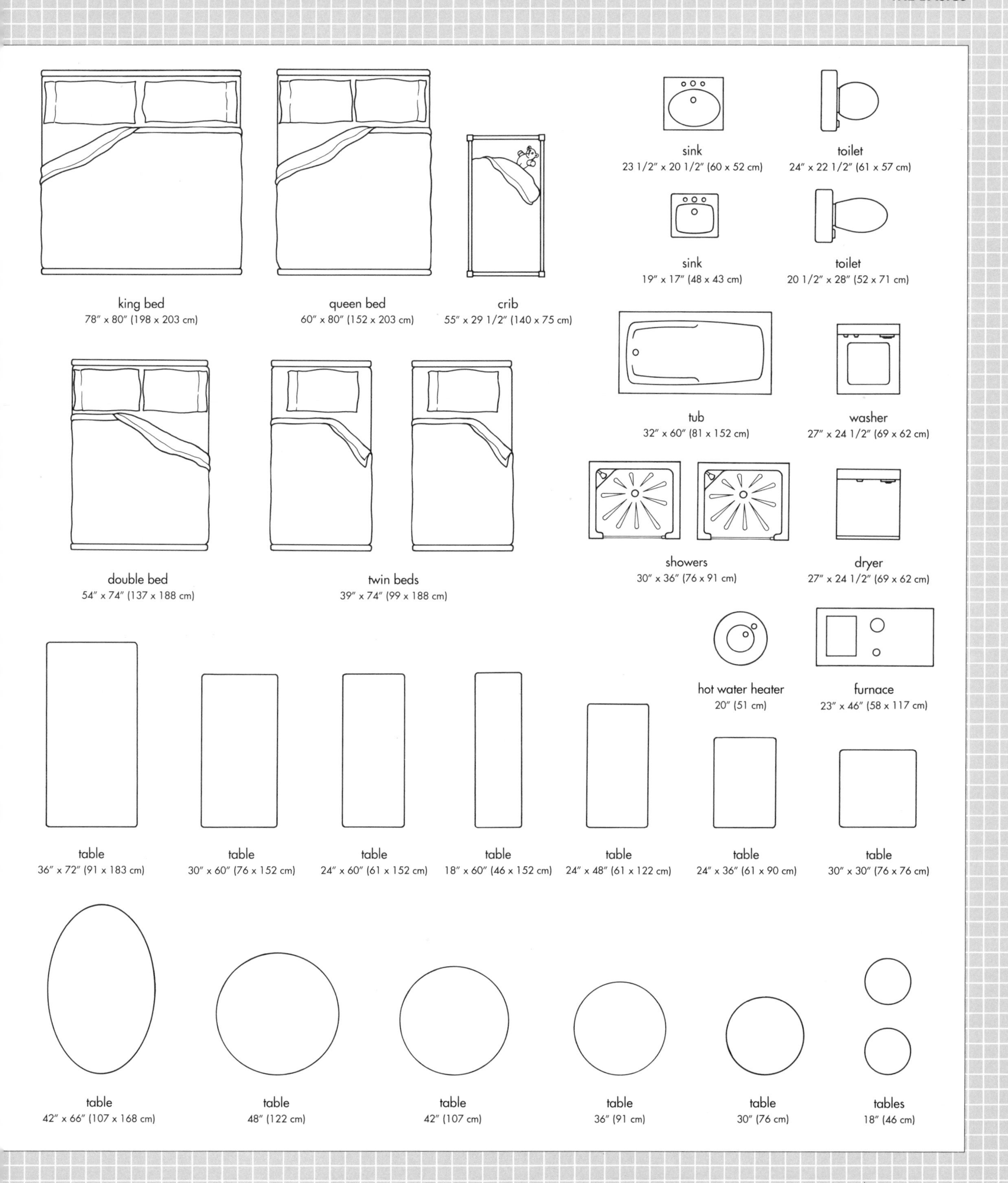

These pages may be photocopied as needed. Scale: 1/4" = 1'

This grid page may be photocopied as needed. Scale: 1/4" = 1'

How to Calculate Wallpaper Quantities

THERE ARE EFFECTS THAT CAN be achieved with wallpaper that can never be duplicated with paint however artistically it is applied. The transformation can be as sudden and dramatic as laying down a lawn of healthy sod on a patch of brown earth. Wallpaper requires some forethought, however. Take your time, and prepare carefully. The results will be worth it.

1. Check the size and origin of your wallpaper before you order it. Wallpaper is available in varying lengths and widths, depending on the country of manufacture. Wallpapers may be sold as single or double rolls, with the length of the rolls increased proportionately.

2. Measure the distance around the room, excluding major obstacles such as picture windows, built-in cupboards and bookcases, but not doors and regular windows.

3. Measure the height of the room or wall area and add a few centimetres or inches for a trimming allowance. If you are using a patterned wallpaper, add extra allowance for matching the repeat. (The repeat is the measurement between identical points in a repeated pattern. Wallpaper sample books always note the required repeat allowance and you should add this allowance onto the height of your room for the purpose of calculating required quantities.)

4. Divide the length measured in Step 3 (referred to as the "drop") into the length of the rolls in order to find out how many drops you can cut from each.

5. Divide the perimeter of the room (from Step 2) by the width of the roll. Then divide this number by the number of drops per roll. This will give you the number of rolls required. Add extra if there are irregularities in your walls or areas that will be difficult to cover. Make sure you order enough wallpaper to complete the job all at once, or note the lot number of your wallpaper and be sure it will be available later. Different lots may vary slightly in colour. Stores will often let you return unopened rolls if you do so promptly — check with your supplier. The following charts are only approximate guides to quantities.

Single American Rolls Required
(14 yards per double roll, 21″ - 21 1/2″ wide)

Distance to be covered		*Ceiling Height*		
feet	*metres*	*7′ (2.13m)*	*8′ (2.44m)*	*9′ (2.74m)*
6′	(1.83m)	2	2	2
8′	(2.44m)	2	3	3
10′	(3.05m)	3	3	3
12′	(3.66m)	3	4	4
14′	(4.27m)	4	4	5
16′	(4.88m)	4	5	5
18′	(5.49m)	5	5	5
20′	(6.10m)	5	6	6
22′	(6.71m)	6	6	7
24′	(7.31m)	6	7	8
26′	(7.92m)	7	7	8
28′	(8.53m)	7	8	9
30′	(9.14m)	7	8	9
32′	(9.75m)	8	9	10
34′	(10.36m)	8	10	11
36′	(10.97m)	9	10	11
38′	(11.58m)	9	11	12
40′	(12.19m)	10	11	12
42′	(12.80m)	10	12	13
44′	(13.41m)	11	12	14
46′	(14.02m)	11	13	14
48′	(14.63m)	12	13	15
50′	(15.24m)	12	14	15

Single Metric Rolls Required
(11 yards per double roll, approximately 20″ - 21 1/2″ wide)

Distance to be covered		*Ceiling Height*		
feet	*metres*	*7′ (2.13m)*	*8′ (2.44m)*	*9′ (2.74m)*
6′	(1.83m)	2	3	3
8′	(2.44m)	3	3	4
10′	(3.05m)	4	4	4
12′	(3.66m)	4	5	5
14′	(4.27m)	5	5	6
16′	(4.88m)	5	6	7
18′	(5.49m)	6	7	8
20′	(6.10m)	7	8	8
22′	(6.71m)	7	8	9
24′	(7.31m)	8	9	10
26′	(7.92m)	9	10	11
28′	(8.53m)	9	10	12
30′	(9.14m)	10	11	12
32′	(9.75m)	10	12	13
34′	(10.36m)	11	13	14
36′	(10.97m)	12	13	15
38′	(11.58m)	12	14	16
40′	(12.19m)	13	15	16
42′	(12.80m)	14	15	17
44′	(13.41m)	14	16	18
46′	(14.02m)	15	17	19
48′	(14.63m)	15	18	20
50′	(15.24m)	16	18	20

Deduct 1 single roll for every 2 standard-size openings (for example, 1 window and 1 door). These charts allow for repeats and loss in trimming.
Adapted from the St. Clair Wallpaper Estimating Chart

How to Calculate Paint Quantities

A GOOD PAINT JOB WILL require an undercoat and at least two topcoats. In order to calculate the amount of paint you'll need, take each wall or surface to be painted and multiply its width by its height in order to get the area. Add the total of separate walls or surfaces together, and then refer to the paint coverage chart below.

This chart is a rule of thumb only; the amount of paint needed will be affected by the nature of the surface — rough or porous areas will require extra paint and the amount will vary depending on the number of undercoats.

It is much more economical to buy a large can of paint than several smaller ones. Try to take all the rooms you are doing into consideration. For instance, you may be using the same colour for trims or ceilings throughout your house and will therefore be able to cut down on costs by purchasing in quantity.

Paint Coverage Chart

Quantity	*Area*
1 litre (.26 gallons)	9 square metres (100 square feet)
4 litres (1.06 gallons)	37 square metres (400 square feet)

How to Calculate Tile Quantities

THE FOLLOWING CHART IS A guideline for calculating tile quantities. Add 5% to your quantity as an allowance for breakage; add 10% if you are working on the diagonal or with terracotta tiles. If your room is an irregular shape, just divide it into smaller areas and calculate in sections.

How to Calculate Tile Quantities

sq m	*sq ft*	*4″ x 4″ 10 x 10 cm*	*6″ x 6″ 15 x 15 cm*	*12″ x 12″ 30 x 30 cm*
—	1	8	4	1
1	—	96	44	12

Painting Tips

COLOUR IS THE SINGLE-MOST important element of design in your home, and paint is one of the easiest ways to change your rooms. Painting is easy to do, but it requires patience and preparation. Don't rush!

- Take time to get ready — this is a very important step. Prepare your rooms. Pretending that you don't need to — that you'll be able to work around things — will only cost you time and money.
- Remove anything fragile or valuable.
- If you need to strip wallpaper, think about renting a steam machine. This machine will cut down on the time you spend on this tedious job.
- Wherever possible remove hardware — doorknobs, switches, grips, etc. Where removal is impossible, cover hardware carefully with masking tape.
- Lower ceiling light fixtures in order to thoroughly paint your ceilings.
- If you can't move all furniture out of the room (which is always the preferable option), cover your pieces carefully with dust sheets or drop cloths.
- Cover floors and hallways with plastic or drop cloths.
- Edge window panes and fixed mirrors with masking tape. Also use masking tape to protect the edge of the floor when you are painting the baseboards.
- Ensure that the walls you are painting are clean. Wash them down thoroughly using warm water and a little dish detergent or white vinegar to cut grease. Rinse with clear water.
- Try not to paint in artificial light. If you have to, use as much light as you can. Be sure to inspect your work in daylight.
- Always start with ceilings, then paint the walls, then the woodwork. (If you are wallpapering, paint all woodwork first.)
- Don't mix paint types: use an oil-based primer on wood that will be painted with an oil-based paint.
- Never apply a topcoat until the undercoat is completely dry.
- You can keep paintbrushes used for oil-based paints wrapped in tin foil and stored in the freezer between coats.
- Write the colour number and manufacturer of your paint on the back of light-switch plates so that you can easily match up colours in the future.
- The key to success in all paint jobs is to buy top-of-the-line paints and tools.

A Paint Glossary

Primer Primers can be either latex (water-soluble) or alkyd (oil-based). They are usually white, although they can be slightly tinted. Primers are used to cut down the absorption by the surface of finished coats and to prepare the surface for the finishing colour. A primer coat is an absolutely essential first step.

Latex primers are generally used for all wall and ceiling surfaces. The quality of latex increases with the amount of acrylic used in the paint. Emulsion paint is the British term for latex. Latex paint can be cleaned from brushes and hands with water.

Alkyd primers are used for preparing woodwork — trim, doors, floors, etc. — for finishing coats. Alkyd paints require mineral spirits for clean-up.

Both latex and alkyd primer can be applied with brush, roller, or spray.

Undercoat On general areas — walls and ceilings — the undercoat is usually the same paint as the finished coat. As a general rule, use an alkyd undercoat if you have used an alkyd primer, and latex undercoat if you have primed with latex. However, you can paint with alkyd over latex paints. Never use latex as an undercoat on woodwork. Both latex and alkyd surfaces can be washed.

Gloss The amount of gloss in paints ranges from zero light reflection (flat or matt) to 90% light reflection (high gloss). This range is available in both latex and alkyd paints. In both latex and alkyd paints, the term "enamel paint" refers to any paint with a gloss factor higher than flat. Enamel paints seal their surfaces, and flat paints are absorbed by their surface. The higher the shine of a paint, the more durable its surface will be.

Flat (Matt) Flat paint is commonly used in areas where no shine or light reflection is desired. It is not suitable for kitchens, bathrooms, or high-traffic areas, as it is not as durable or washable. However, matt paint will hide imperfections because of its non-reflective quality.

Eggshell This frequently misunderstood term does not refer to a pale, off-white colour. It is possible to have eggshell red, for instance. Eggshell is a gloss level in paint — a 10% light reflection — and the lowest level of shine available. It is a great all-purpose gloss level and can be used on walls, ceilings, and halls if you want a slightly more reflective effect than is possible with a flat paint.

Semi-gloss This is ideal for all woodwork — trims, doors, sills, etc. Because of its durability and the ease with which it can be washed, it is also popular in bathrooms, kitchens, and children's rooms.

High Gloss This is most frequently used for woodwork, cabinetry, and floors. It is highly durable and its light-reflective quality gives it a formal appearance. It is also used for specialty, lacquer-like wall treatments.

Artists' Paint This paint is often acrylic and is used for special decorative treatments. Because it does not have the durability of household paints, it generally requires protection with clear-coats such as varnish, urethane, or polyurethane.

Urethane, polyurethane These clear-coat, varnish-like finishes are used to protect painted or stained surfaces. They are available in various levels of gloss and are more durable than varnish.

Varnish Although not as durable as the urethanes, varnish is often preferred by traditionalists because urethanes sometimes have a slight amber colouration. Varnish is often used on fine furniture because it can be hand polished.

Exterior Paints Latex paints are now the professional's choice for exterior jobs. Latex allows the painted surface to breathe and, as a result, does not crack or blister as much as oil-based paints. Latex can be used for exterior woodwork, brick, stucco, masonry, and even metal if primed properly.

Paint Glossary courtesy of David Bermann, Scandinavian Decorating Contractors

Measuring for Bedding

THE MOOD AND PALETTE OF your bedroom will be set or reinforced by the approach you take to your bed. Inevitably it will be the room's focus. You don't want to have the perfect linens in the perfect colours, and a dust skirt that is a little too long or a duvet that seems skimpy at the sides. Follow these simple rules to measure bedding.

For comforters, covers, and duvets: Measure the bed across the top of the mattress from the top to the bottom for the length, and from side to side for the width. Add the drop length to these measurements by measuring from the upper edge of the mattress to 7.5 to 10 cm (3" or 4") below it. This is usually 23 to 30.5 cm (9" to 12"), depending on the mattress depth. This amount should be added to the width twice and to the length once to cover the bottom.

For dust skirts: Measure from the top of the box spring for regular beds (or the top of the bed frame for day beds) down to the floor. With a 5 mm (1/4") seam allowance, attach the skirt to a piece of fabric equal to the length and width of the mattress; this can be plain cotton or any inexpensive fabric. The 1 cm (1/2") that will be taken up into the seam allowance will create the necessary floor clearance for the dust skirt.

To find out how many widths of fabric you will need for your comforter or duvet cover, divide the width you have calculated (the mattress width plus the two drops) by the width of the fabric you will be using and round it off to the next highest number. For example, if your fabric is 92 cm (36") wide and your cover will be 198 cm (78") wide, you will need three widths. Multiply your length (mattress length plus drop) by the number of widths to calculate your quantity. If your cover is 2.25 m (7'6") long and requires three widths, you will need 6.75 m (22'6" or 7 1/2 yards) of fabric. If you are using the same fabric on both sides of your duvet cover, double this amount. Otherwise you will need an equal amount of another fabric for the reverse side.

If your fabric is patterned, always allow extra to match the repeats. It is also a good idea to machine wash and dry the fabric at least once before cutting it.

When sewing together your fabric, use a complete width down the centre and use equal partial widths on the sides. This makes the seams less conspicuous.

Sheets are ideal for making duvet covers. Their width eliminates the need to seam or match. The chart below will help you determine the size and quantity of sheets you will need for a duvet cover.

How to Calculate Fabric Quantity for Duvet Covers

Bed Size	*Sheets Required for Cover*	*Sheets Required for 10 cm (4") Self-Ruffle*	*Standard Duvet Sizes*
Twin (Single)	2 twin flat	1 twin flat	152 x 218 cm (60" x 86")
Double (Full)	2 full flat	1 twin flat	193 x 218 cm (76" x 86")
Queen	2 queen flat	1 twin flat	234 x 234 cm (92" x 92")
King	2 king flat	1 twin flat	274 x 234 cm (108" x 92")

How to Calculate Fabric Quantities for Drapes

A ROOM CAN BE UTTERLY transformed by its window treatments. Gone are the days of humdrum fabric dangling gracelessly from a naked aluminum rod. English chintz, French Country prints, Contemporary swags — the options are endless. Think of your windows as priceless paintings, and choose your drapery as carefully as an art collector would choose frames.

Length: First decide on the length of the drapes and how they will be hung. For example, will they end at the window sill, just below the window sill, or in a puddle on the floor? Will they hang from a track, on eyebeam hooks, or from a rod and rings? The position of the track, the type of hook, and the size of rings will affect length. Include these in your measurements.

Width: The width of your drapes is the next consideration. Measure the width of the supporting rod or track (or the combined length of the tracks if you have two that overlap in the centre). As a rule of thumb, this width is then multiplied by 2, 2.5, or 3 to get the fullness (2 will produce a flat effect; 2.5 is average; 3 is generous and full). You can be more generous with thin fabrics such as sheers. Use a lower multiplication factor with heavier fabrics, but don't skimp to the point of losing luxurious folds.

When you have multiplied your width by the factors above, divide that total by the width of your fabric and round it up to the next highest number. For example, if your rod is 137 cm (54") long and you want an average fullness, your curtain width becomes 137 (54) x 2.5 = 342.5 cm (135"). If your fabric is 122 cm (48") wide, then you divide 342.5 (135) by 122 (48) = 2.8 widths. So you need three widths; this includes allowances for turning the edges.

Multiply the number of widths by the desired curtain length. You must also add on an amount to accommodate a generous lower hem and a turned top hem or casing (usually 15 cm or 6" for lightweight or sheer fabrics and 25 cm or 10" for heavy ones), and enough to match up the pattern repeat. The repeat can be easily measured if it isn't already indicated on the edge or selvage of the fabric. As a rule, you add the length of the pattern repeat to each fabric width except one. So if you need four widths, add the length of three repeats to your total amount. It is always better to be a little generous with your allowances. It's preferable to either trim or have a wider hem than to run short.

Matching patterns: With floor-length curtains, you usually start with the full repeat at the top, or just below the heading. Short curtains or blinds start the full repeat at the bottom. Repeats should match not just on each fabric width but from window to window in a room.

It is usually necessary to match repeats even on fairly small prints, but you can check this in the store when buying your fabric. Unroll enough of the fabric to be able to see two complete repeats side by side. If you don't notice a pattern difference when they are shifted, you won't need to allow for the repeats. Working with plain fabrics usually requires less fabric because matching is not a consideration.

Tips

- Unless you want the effect of extravagant puddling, allow 10 mm (1/2") clearance between the bottom of your drapes and the sill, floor, or carpet. This helps with cleaning and allows for unevenness in the floor. Allow at least 10 cm (4") clearance above baseboard heaters for safety.
- Lower hems are usually doubled over for extra weight and body. On a full-length drape, allow 20 cm (8") for a standard 10 cm (4") hem. For sheers or lightweight fabrics, this can be increased to a 13 or 15 cm (5" or 6") finished hem width. Valences or short curtains can have from a 2.5 to 7.5 cm (1" to 3") double hem.
- The amount of fabric needed for rod pockets and headings will be the diameter of the rod plus 10 mm (1/2") to turn under and 5mm to 2.5 cm (1/4" to 1") for ease, depending on the fabric thickness — less for light fabrics and more for heavy ones. For headings, use the same calculations for the rod but add an amount that is twice the desired depth of the heading. These can be 2 to 6.5 cm (3/4" to 2 1/2"), depending on the weight of the fabric and the desired effect.
- If window heights in a room vary, use the highest one as the measuring standard and try to hang all the other drapes the same height from the floor.
- If you are using coordinating fabric and wallcovering, make sure any design patterns (repeats) match across both. If the drapes are already made, hang them in order to see where the repeat will need to fall on the wallpaper. Otherwise, paper your walls, then match the fabric before making drapes.
- If you are making an elaborately draped or swagged curtain, consider doing a mock-up or rough version first. Use an inexpensive fabric that approximates the weight of your final choice. This mock-up will save you making mistakes on your more expensive fabric and it can then be used as a pattern or guide.
- If you are hanging heavy drapes and want to avoid losing too much light when the curtains are drawn back, hang them from tracks that extend more generously beyond the window sides.

Popular Window Styles

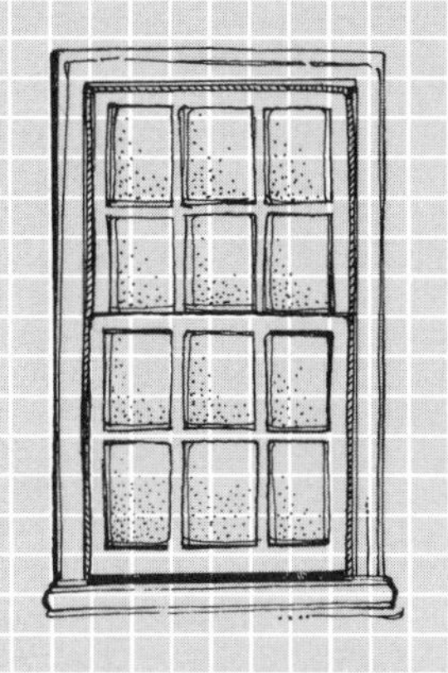

Double Hung Window
(also called Georgian Sash)

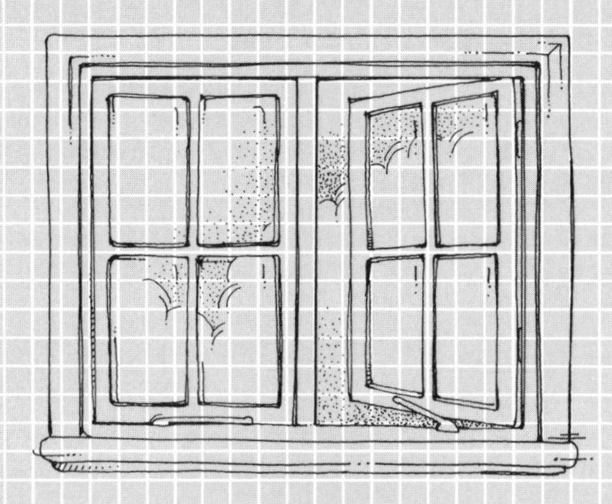

Casement Window

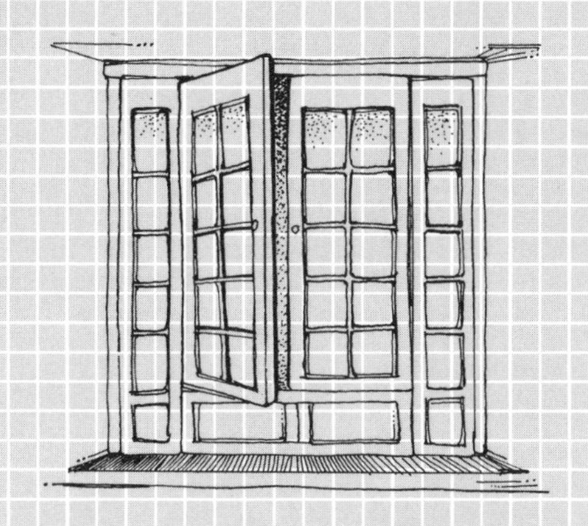

French Doors - French Windows

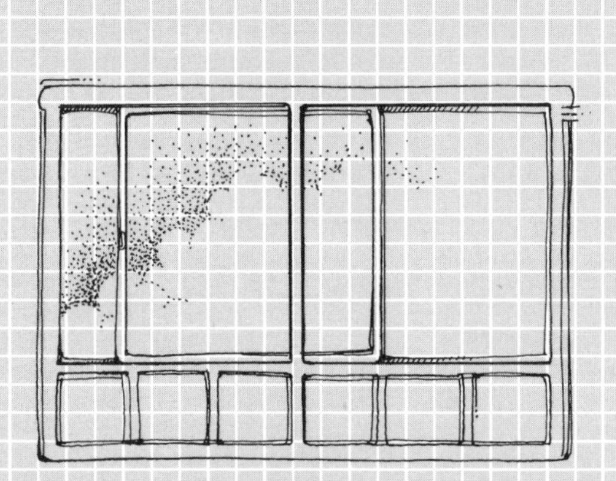

Picture Window

Palladian Window

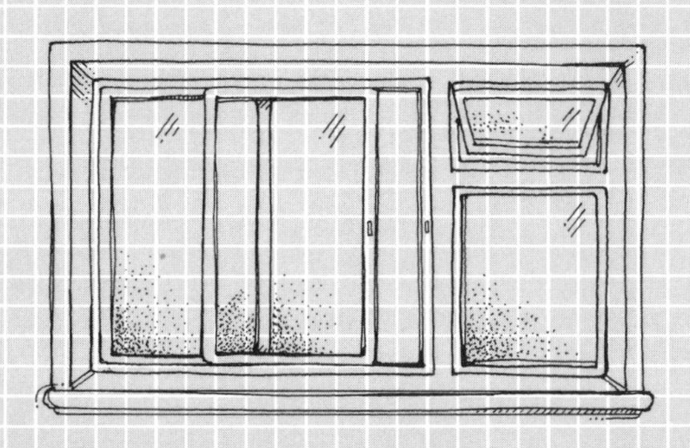

Horizontal Window

Dormer Window

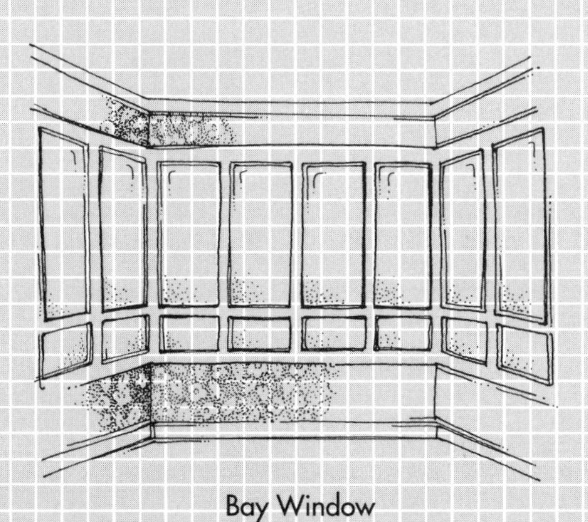

Bay Window

Favourite Window Coverings

Tie Backs

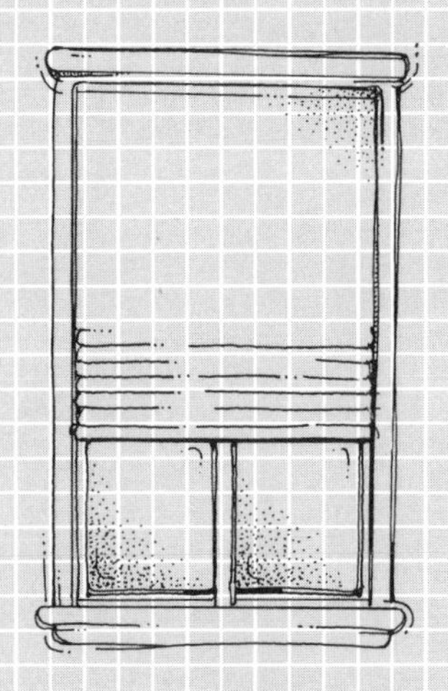

Roman Blinds

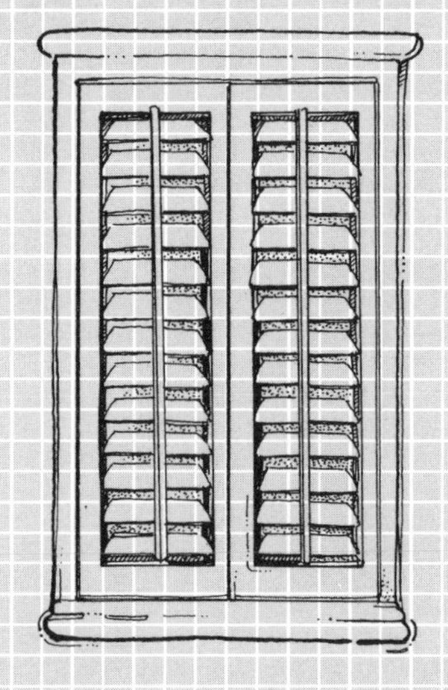

Wide-Louvered California Shutters

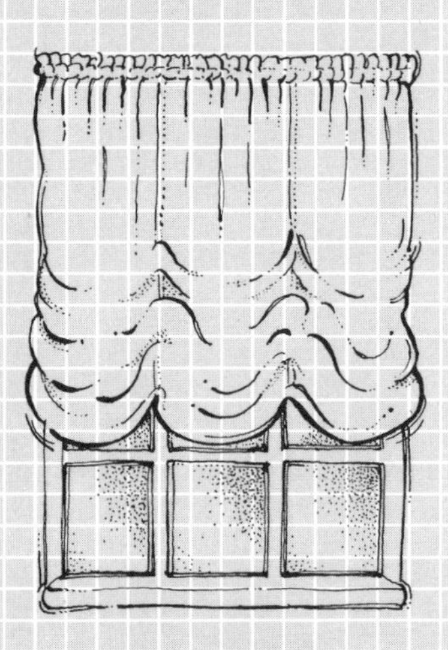

Balloon Blinds

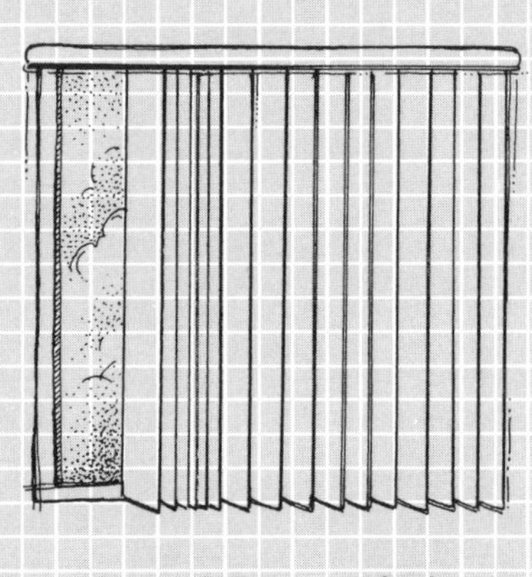

Vertical Venetian Blinds

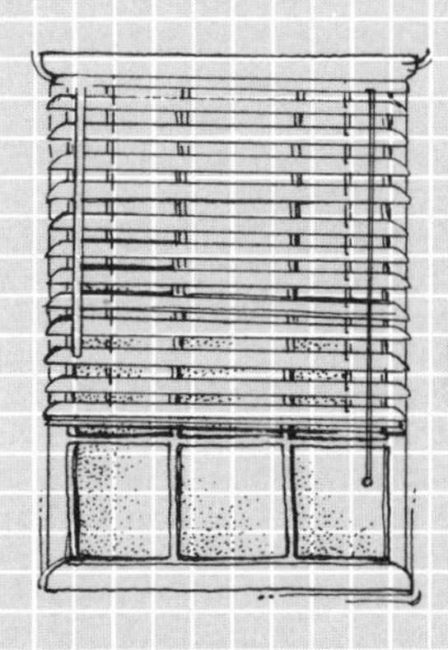

Horizontal Venetian Blinds

Swag and Jabot with Straight Side Panels

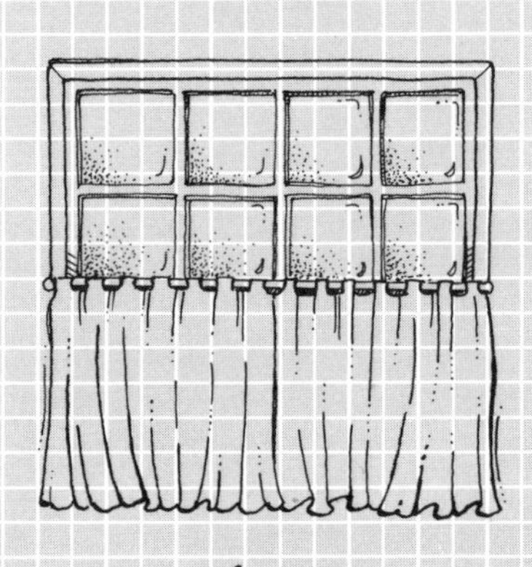

Café Curtains

Simple Centre-Split Straight Drapes

DIRECTIONS FOR PROJECTS

Sponge Painting

(shown on page 119)

Supplies:

- Top quality latex paint in four colours —
  Ground colour - Violet
  Contrast 1 - Aqua
  Contrast 2 - Pink
  Contrast 3 - Yellow
- Sponges

Directions:

1. Apply two coats of the ground colour, violet, to the walls.
2. Paint the woodwork with two coats of yellow, and allow it to dry completely.
3. Tape off the woodwork and ceiling line.
4. Sponge on contrast aqua, applying a full coat. To sponge:

a. Soak the sponge in water, then wring it dry.

b. Pour a few centimetres (about an inch) of paint into a large paint tray.

c. Dip the sponge into the paint, then dab off the excess on the upper part of the tray.

d. Apply a sponge layer by dabbing paint on randomly, approximately 10 dabs per 30 square centimetres (square foot). The sponge will now be drier. Start to fill in the areas between the darker imprints. Work an area of about two square metres (two square yards) at one time, starting in the centre of the wall, then moving down to the baseboard and finishing at the top, using a ladder if necessary.

e. Continue dipping the sponge into the paint, dabbing off drips on the upper tray. Dab the wettest (darkest) paint randomly and fill it in with drier (lighter) paint.

f. Work around the room in one-metre-wide (three-foot-wide), floor-to-ceiling panels, joining the panels together with more light dabbing.

g. Edges: In order to complete the look right down to the baseboard, take a cheap, old 2.5 cm (1") brush and dab it into the excess paint that has accumulated in the upper part of the paint tray. Dab along the area missed by the sponge.

h. Corners: Cut up an old sponge so that it has a flat side and is smaller. You will now be able to work almost to the inside line of the corner, dabbing as you did the wall. Work down one side of the corner, then the other side. To reach the innermost line, use the 2.5 cm (1") paintbrush again.

5. Sponge on the second contrast colour, pink, applying a full coat.
6. Sponge on the third contrast colour, yellow, covering only about two-thirds of the area. This is a bright colour, and you want the aqua, pink, and violet colours to show as well, so check your work constantly as you proceed.
7. Remove the tape from the woodwork and ceiling as soon as the walls are dry.

Directions courtesy of David Bermann, Scandinavian Decorating Contractors

English Country Cushions

Square Cushion with Flange Trim

(shown on page 123)

Supplies:

- Two 76 cm (30") square designer scarves
- Lightweight iron-on interfacing
- 50 cm (20") pillow form

Directions:

1. Press the interfacing to the wrong side of the scarves.
2. Make a 5 cm (2") fold on each edge of the fabric, so that the scarf is the size of the pillow with a 7.5 cm (3") border. Press.
3. Stitch the folded bands close to the edge of each fold. Stitch again, 13 mm (1/2") in from these edges, to make sure the bands are secure.

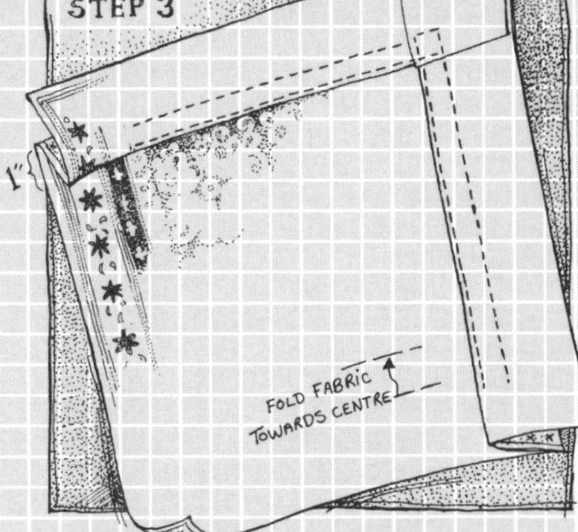

4. Repeat Steps 2 and 3 for the second scarf.
5. With the wrong sides of the scarves facing, stitch them together about 7.5 cm (3") in from the outer edge. Stitch on three edges only, leaving the fourth edge open to slip the pillow in.
6. Insert the pillow form and stitch the fourth edge.
7. Stitch the outer edges of the scarves together.

Bolster with Tassels

(shown on page 123)

Supplies:

- 122 x 25 cm (48" x 10") designer scarf
- Lightweight iron-on interfacing
- Quilt batting, 61 x at least 122 cm (24" x at least 48") long
- Fibrefill
- Tassels
- Cording, 1.3 m (4') long
- Sobo glue, optional (a white, clear-drying glue that stays flexible; available in crafts and fabric stores)

Directions:

1. Cut the scarf in half, so that you have two 61 x 25 cm (24" x 10") pieces.
2. Press interfacing to the wrong side of each piece.
3. With right sides facing, stitch the scarves together along the two long edges, leaving a 5 mm (1/4") seam allowance.
4. Fold in 5 mm (1/4") all the way around at both open ends and press.
5. Sew two rows of gathering stitches (the longest stitch on the sewing machine) on each 5 mm (1/4") fold.
6. At one end, gather the threads as tightly as possible and tie them up. Slip-stitch to close any opening.
7. Turn right side out.
8. To make the bolster, roll the quilt batting up as tightly as possible. For added firmness in the pillow, stuff wads of fibrefill inside the tube of batting.
9. Slip the bolster into the casing.
10. Pull the gathering stitches at the open end and tie off tightly. Slip-stitch any opening.
11. Stitch the tassels at each end of the bolster, using a double thread for added security.
12. Pin the cording in place around the ends of the bolster and slip-stitch in place, being sure to stitch securely where the cord ends meet.
13. Optional: Take one strand of the cord and glue it around the base of the tassels for added effect.

Gathered Rectangle

(shown on page 123)

Supplies:

- Two 76 cm (30") square designer scarves
- Lightweight iron-on interfacing
- Tracing chalk
- Standard bed pillow
- Quilt batting

Directions:

1. Press the interfacing to the wrong side of the scarves.
2. With the right side of one scarf facing you, divide it lengthwise into four equal sections. Make a chalk line along these three gathering lines.
3. Gather-stitch along these lines.
4. Repeat Steps 2 and 3 for the second scarf.
5. Gather in the thread until each gathered line measures 48 cm (19") and gathering is evenly distributed.
6. Stitch along these gathered lines with a regular stitch to secure them.
7. With right sides together, stitch along the top and bottom of the pillow casing (perpendicular to the gathered lines), leaving a 5 mm (1/4") seam allowance.
8. Turn the casing right side out.

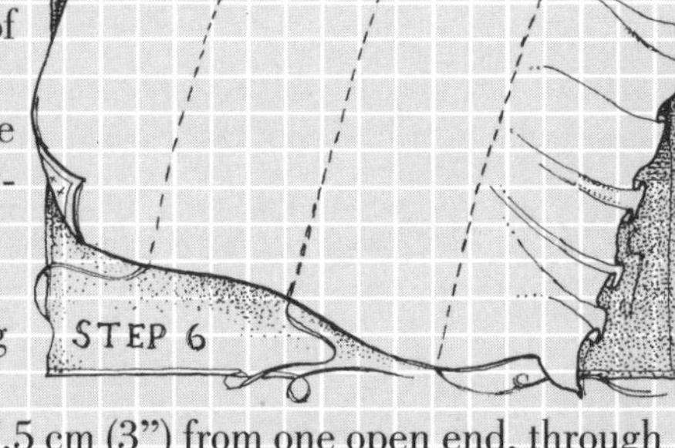

9. Gather-stitch 7.5 cm (3") from one open end, through both layers of scarf, pull to 48 cm (19"), and stitch down with a regular stitch.
10. Insert the pillow. Add quilt batting for increased firmness.
11. Gather-stitch 7.5 cm (3") from the remaining open end, through both layers of scarf, and gather to 48 cm (19").
12. Stitch again along this line with a regular machine stitch.
13. Slip-stitch the outer edges of the scarves together.

Flat Bolster with Fringe Trim

(shown on page 123)

Supplies:

- 122 x 30.5 cm (48" x 12") designer scarf
- Lightweight iron-on interfacing
- Quilt batting
- Fibrefill
- Fringe

Directions:

1. Cut the scarf in half, so you have two 61 x 12 cm (24" x 12") pieces.
2. Press the interfacing to the wrong sides.
3. With the right sides facing, stitch along the two long edges of the fabric, leaving a 5 mm (1/4") seam allowance. Turn right side out.
4. Slip-stitch one end of the casing closed.
5. Cut six pieces of quilt batting 63.5 x 30.5 cm (25" x 12").
6. These layers of quilt batting form the pillow. Tack the corners to keep them together, then stick wads of fibrefill in the middle to round out the pillow, making it as thick as you like.
7. Insert this pillow into the case and pad out with fibrefill where needed.

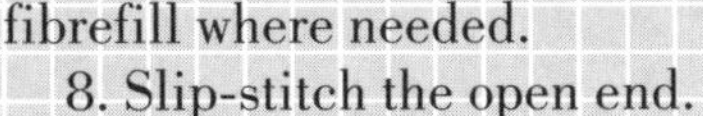

8. Slip-stitch the open end.
9. Cut the fringe to the width of the pillow ends plus 13 mm (1/2").
10. Pin the fringe to the edge and slip-stitch into place, turning the extra 5 mm (1/4") on each end.

Square Pillow with Padded Edge

(not shown)

Supplies:

- Two 68.5 cm (27") square designer scarves
- Lightweight iron-on interfacing
- Quilt batting
- 61 cm (24") pillow form

Directions:

1. Press interfacing to the wrong side of the scarves.
2. With the wrong sides facing, stitch the scarves together around three outside edges, leaving a 5 mm (1/4") seam allowance.
3. Cut four pieces of quilt batting 15 to 18 cm (6" to 7") wide and 67.5 cm (26 1/2") long.
4. Roll one piece of the batting lengthwise very tightly into a tube.
5. Place the tube of batting inside the pillow and pin the scarf down so that the batting is lodged tightly against the side of the casing. Stitch into place, taking care not to stitch into the areas where other batting will be inserted.
6. Repeat Steps 4 and 5 for the other two stitched sides, cutting the tubes of batting shorter as required.

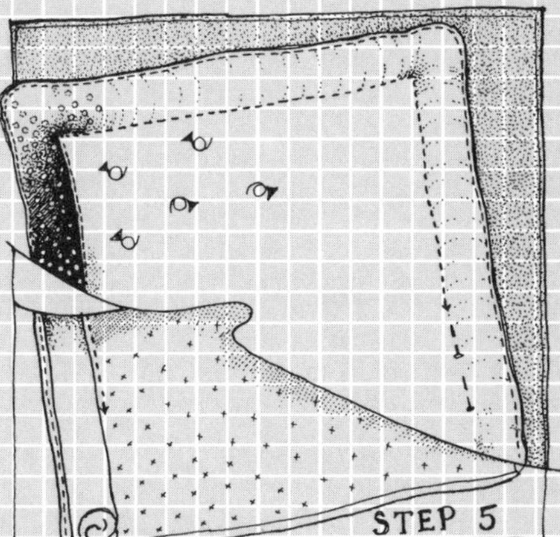

7. Insert the pillow form into the centre space, padding with layers of quilt batting for extra thickness.
8. Stitch the open edge closed, close to the pillow.
9. Insert the last tube of batting and pin together the outer edges of the scarf.
10. Slip-stitch.

Rectangular Pleated Pillow with Frilled Flange

(not shown)

Supplies:

- Two 68.5 cm (27") square designer scarves with borders
- Lightweight iron-on interfacing
- Quilt batting
- Fibrefill

Directions:

1. Press interfacing to the wrong side of the scarves.
2. Press 13 mm (1/2") pleats, at intervals along the scarves.
3. Stitch along the edges of the pleats. (Note: Do not stitch past the inner edges of the scarves' outer borders.)
4. With wrong sides facing, pin three edges of the scarf together along the inner edge of the border. Stitch.
5. Use layers of quilt batting (tacked together at the corners), with fibrefill padding inserted in the middle, to make the pillow. Insert into casing.

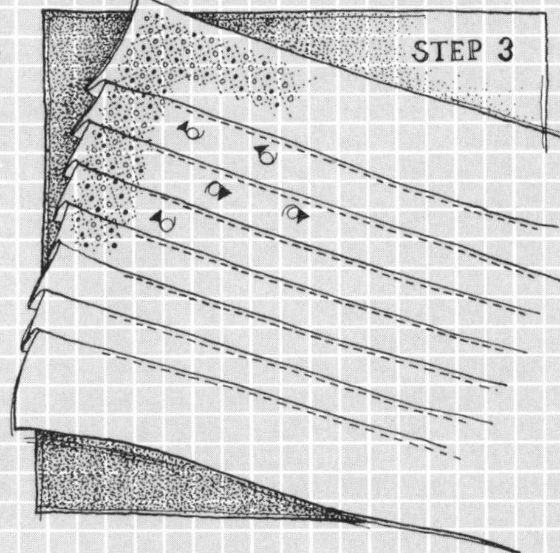

6. Stitch the fourth side closed at the inner edge of the border.
7. Slip-stitch the outer edges of the scarves together.

Square Cushions with Fringe Edges

(not shown)

Supplies:

- Two 38 cm (15") square scarves with borders
- Lightweight iron-on interfacing
- 2m (2 yards) cauliflower trim (or any thick pile fringe)
- 36.5 cm (14") pillow form
- Fibrefill

Directions:

1. Press the lightweight interfacing onto the wrong side of the scarves.

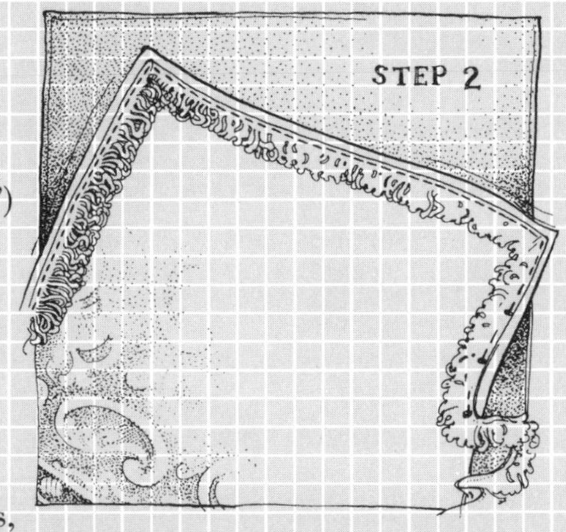

2. On the right side of one of the scarves, pin the cauliflower trim about 13 mm (1/2") from all edges.
3. Stitch with a regular machine-stitch.
4. Pin the two scarves together, right sides facing, around three edges, leaving the fourth edge open. Use the trim as a guideline.
5. Stitch the three edges.
6. Turn right side out, leaving the corners of the seams untrimmed. The extra fabric will give body to the corners of the pillow.
7. Slip the pillow form inside, tucking the corners firmly into place, and using extra fibrefill if necessary to pad it out.
8. Fold the two edges of the remaining open side inward and pin together. The trim will stand up from the pillow.
9. Slip-stitch, using a double thread, keeping stitches as small as possible.

Tufted Square with Centre Tassel

(shown on page 123)

Supplies:

- Two 76 cm (30") square scarves with 7.5 cm (3") borders
- Lightweight iron-on interfacing
- Tassels and/or fabric-covered buttons
- 46 cm (18") pillow form

Directions:

1. Press interfacing to the wrong side of the scarves.
2. Fold the scarves in half, and then in half again.
3. Cut a rounded piece out of the centre corner of each scarf creating round holes, 15 cm (6") in diameter (a 7.5 cm or 3" radius), in the centre.

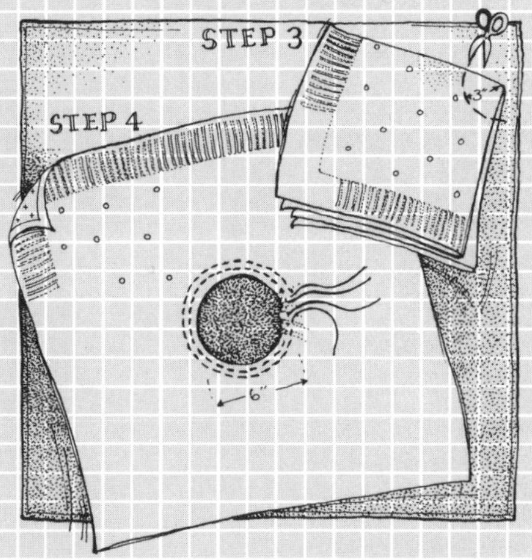

4. Stitch two rows of gathering stitches around the holes, 3 mm and 5 mm (1/8" and 1/4") from the edges.
5. Pin the scarves together, wrong sides facing, along the inner edges of the border, on three edges only.

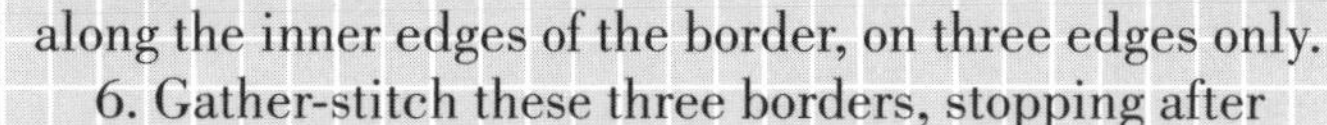

6. Gather-stitch these three borders, stopping after each edge and cutting threads.
7. Now, pull the two rows of gathering stitches at the centre holes as tightly as possible and tie them off.
8. Slip-stitch any opening, again very tightly, using a double thread.
9. Slip the pillow form inside. Adjust the gathers to fit pillow. Remove the pillow form.
10. Stitch around the three previously gathered edges with a regular machine stitch.
11. Gather-stitch the fourth edge.
12. Put the pillow form in the casing.
13. Pull the threads to gather, then sew over with a regular machine-stitch.
14. Using double thread on a darning needle, squish down the centre of the pillow and sew through the middle, tightly, at least four or five times, to secure.
15. Sew tassels or fabric-covered buttons to the centre of the pillow.
16. Slip-stitch the outer edges of the scarves together.

Square Cushions with Cross Pleats

(shown on page 123)

Supplies:

- Two 76 cm (30") square designer scarves with borders
- Lightweight iron-on interfacing
- Pillow form (size will depend upon width of scarves' borders)

Directions:

1. Press interfacing to the wrong side of the scarves.
2. Fold one scarf diagonally, wrong sides together, so that it lies in a triangular shape.
3. Pin 5 cm (2") from the fold line, and stitch edge-to-edge.
4. Unfold the scarf and press flat, creating a band across the scarf.

5. Fold the scarf in half from the other two corners, and repeat Steps 3 and 4. You now have two flat bands criss-crossing the scarf.

6. Repeat Steps 2 to 5 with the second scarf.

7. Stitch the two scarves together, wrong sides facing, along the three inner borders, taking care not to catch the bands in the stitching.

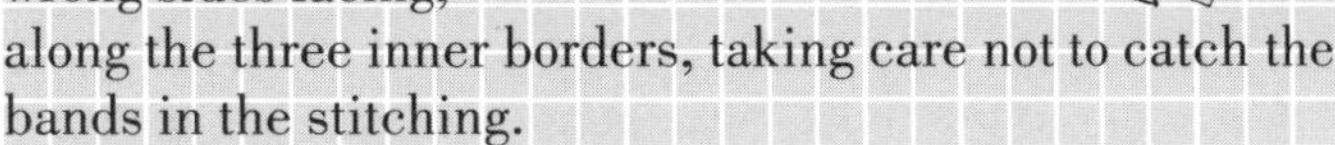

8. Slip the pillow form inside the casing.

9. Pin the remaining open edge, and stitch closed.

10. Slip-stitch the four outer edges of the scarves.

Square Cushions with Double Tassels

(shown on page 123)

Supplies:

- Two 76 cm (30") square designer scarves with 7.5 cm (3") borders
- Lightweight iron-on interfacing
- Standard bed pillow
- Cord with tassels

Directions:

1. Press interfacing to the wrong side of the scarves.

2. With right sides facing, stitch the scarves together along two opposite edges, along the inner borders of the scarves, leaving 13 mm (1/2") openings at each side for the tassels (see diagram).

3. Turn right side out.

4. Stitch along the inner edge of the border at one end of the casing.

5. Pin the tassel cord along this edge, in between the scarves; pull the tassels through the openings at the top and bottom, and stitch a final casing line to hold the tassel cords in place.

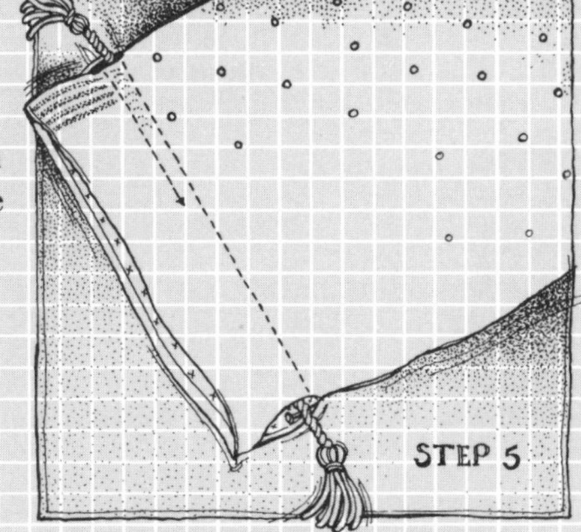

6. Put the pillow form in the case.

7. Repeat Steps 4 and 5 at the open end.

8. Slip-stitch the outer edges of the scarves together.

9. Optional: Pull the tassels to create a gathered effect at each end of the pillow. Tie to secure.

French Country Chests

Trompe-l'oeil Chest

(shown on page 137)

Supplies:

- Unfinished chest of drawers
- Wood filler
- Putty knife
- 320 sandpaper
- Sanding sealer
- Acrylic paint (mint green, white, yellow, and black)
- Mylar
- Permanent ink pen
- X-acto knife
- Masking tape
- Regular paintbrush
- Cardboard
- Simple drawer knobs

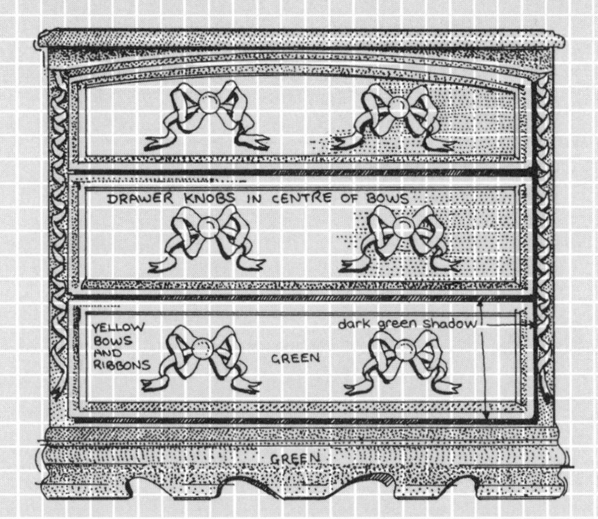

Directions:

1. Remove the hardware from the chest and fill the holes with wood filler (if your chest of drawers has knobs rather than pulls, you can leave the holes). Lightly sand the entire chest to ensure a smooth surface. (Note: Always follow the grain of the wood when you're sanding.)

2. Brush on a coat of sanding sealer so the paint won't sink into the porous surface of the wood.

3. Paint the entire chest with a base of the green acrylic paint.

4. After the base coat is completely dry, the chest must be "dry-brushed" with a slightly lighter shade of the same paint. To do this, first mix a bit of white paint into the

green, but reserve some of the original green for Steps 8 and 10. Fill the brush with the lighter paint, then wipe it on a piece of cardboard until there is just enough paint on the brush to give a streaky effect. Brush the paint on sparingly, making sure to follow the grain of the wood. Let dry.

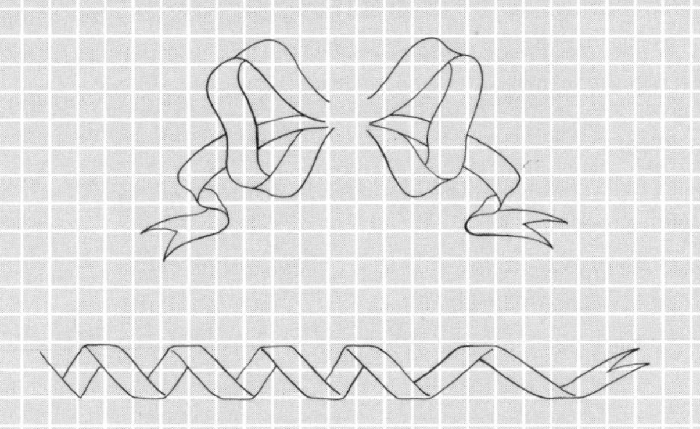

Scale: 1/4" = 1"

5. Draw the ribbon pattern to scale on the matt side of the Mylar with a permanent ink pen; continue the ribbon pattern as necessary to fit the height of your chest. To cut out the pattern, use an X-acto knife or small manicure scissors. Although Mylar is easy to cut, it is important to go slowly and carefully. Cut the entire shape without lifting the blade; it's easier if you turn the stencil continuously so that you are always cutting towards yourself. The edge will then be smooth and accurate.

6. Centre the stencil over the spots where the holes for the hardware have been filled. Tape in place.

7. Fill in the bows using yellow acrylic paint.

8. After the bows are dry, a slightly darker yellow should be used to dry-brush them, using the same technique as before. The darker yellow can be made by adding some of the background green to it, but reserve some of the original yellow for Step 9. Dry-brush the darker yellow on, using clockwise strokes for the right-hand loop of the bow and counter-clockwise strokes for the left-hand loop.

9. Once the paint is dry, use a lighter yellow (the original yellow mixed with a little white) to go over the high points of the ribbon; this highlighting adds a three-dimensional effect.

10. To create a shadow, move the stencil slightly lower and to one side (about 5 mm/ 1/4" each way). Draw the outline of the shadow, then paint it in with a slightly darker shade of the green background paint (made by mixing black with the original green).

11. This shadow effect can also be created on the bevelled edges of the drawers of the chest. Apply the darker shade of green from Step 10 in a thin line along the bottom, up one side, and between the drawers. This adds to the feeling of depth.

12. Finally, transfer the coiled ribbon pattern onto Mylar and cut a stencil. Tape in place down the vertical edge of the chest. Fill in as you did in Steps 7 to 9.

13. When your design is dry, drill holes at the centre of each bow and install drawer knobs.

Directions courtesy of Gordon Adams

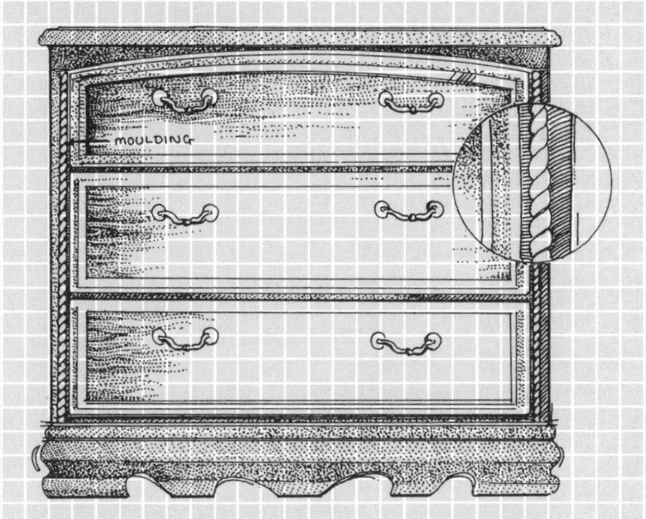

Pickled Pine Chest

(not shown)

Supplies:

- Unfinished chest of drawers
- Sanding block
- 220 sandpaper
- Pine or natural rubber putty (also called finishing surface putty)
- Putty knife
- 360 sandpaper
- Absorbent cotton cloth
- Natural colour stain
- White, fast-drying wiping stain
- 1/2-round rope-edging moulding (10 mm or 3/8" wide) available at any lumber yard
- Finishing nails
- Finishing sealer (comes in spray or liquid)
- Paintbrush
- 220 no-fill sandpaper (a finer finish paper)
- Clear satin lacquer

Directions:

1. Remove the hardware from the chest.
2. Using a sanding block, lightly sand the surface of the chest with 220 sandpaper until it is smooth. (Note: Always follow the grain of the wood when you're sanding.)
3. Fill any holes with pine or natural rubber putty.
4. When the putty has dried, give the chest another sanding with 360 sandpaper.

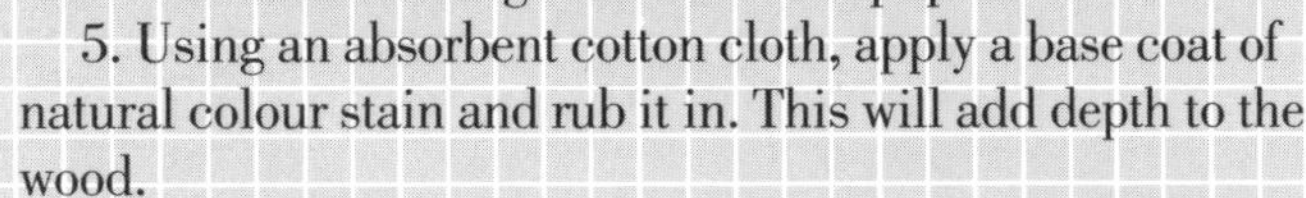

5. Using an absorbent cotton cloth, apply a base coat of natural colour stain and rub it in. This will add depth to the wood.
6. Apply a white, fast-drying wiping stain and wipe it down with a cloth until it dries. Wait twenty-four hours.
7. Repeat Steps 2 to 6 on the mouldings.
8. Using finishing nails, nail the mouldings to the front edges of the chest. Countersink the nails. To do this, place the tip of another nail on the head of a nail holding moulding in place and hammer gently until the nail head is just below the surface of the wood. Fill the depression with a small amount of putty.

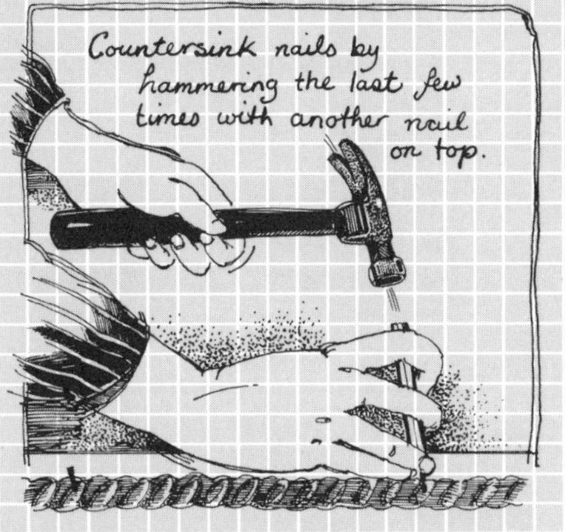

9. Brush on a coat of finishing sealer. Allow five hours to dry.
10. Give the entire surface a fine sanding with 220 no-fill sandpaper.
11. Apply a coat of clear satin lacquer. Allow twenty-four hours to dry.
12. Affix hardware.

Directions courtesy of Jeff Leuchter

A Stencilled Terracotta Pot

(shown on page 147)

Supplies:

- Terracotta pot
- Stencil (available at craft stores)
- Masking tape
- Stencil paints
- Palette
- Stencil brushes
- Paper towelling
- Tack cloth
- Paintbrush
- Urethane

Directions:

1. Secure all four sides of the stencil to the terracotta pot with masking tape.
2. Put approximately 5 mL (1 teaspoon) of each colour of stencil paint on palette.
3. Use one brush per colour. Dip the bristles of the brush in the paint and wipe excess paint off on paper towelling, using an upright and circular motion.
4. Using the same upright, circular motion, apply the paint, filling in the cut-outs of the stencil. Be sure to use a light touch. You can always apply more paint to make your colours darker.
5. Remove stencil and allow stencil paint to cure on pot for forty-eight hours.
6. Dust pot with tack cloth.
7. Apply a coat of urethane.

Stencilling a Floorcloth

(shown on page 149)

Supplies:

- #8 or #10 gauge canvas
- Masking tape
- Flat latex paint
- Paint roller
- Fabric paint (available at craft stores)
- Stencils (available at craft stores)
- Stencil brushes
- Paper towelling
- Glue gun and glue sticks
- Varnish
- Tack cloth

Directions:

1. Using either #8 or #10 gauge canvas, determine the size of your floorcloth and add 7.5 cm (3") all around before cutting. The extra canvas allows both for shrinkage after the rug is painted, and for a 2.5 to 5 cm (1" to 2") hem allowance.
2. Using long strips of masking tape, mask off 2.5 to 5 cm (1" to 2") (depending on the size of your floorcloth — the larger the cloth, the wider the hem) along all four edges of the canvas.
3. It is necessary to paint only one side of the canvas.

Two coats of paint will be needed. Using a flat latex paint for your background, apply the paint with a roller. Save some of the paint for touch-ups. When the paint is dry, remove the strips of masking tape.

4. You are now ready to stencil your design on the floorcloth. Remembering to use one brush per colour, dab your brush in a small amount of fabric paint (approximately 2.5 mL or 1/2 teaspoon), and wipe excess paint off your brush on a paper towel. Using an upright, circular motion, apply paint to stencil using a light touch. Remember, you can always apply more paint to get a darker shade, but you cannot make it lighter.

5. After your stencilling is completed, allow at least forty-eight hours for the paint to cure.

6. To complete your hem, turn the cloth upside down on a clean surface and press the unpainted edges down, making a good crease. Using a glue gun (and preferably an extra pair of hands), apply the glue under the edge and press this hem down (try using an old rolling pin) as flat as possible.

7. Once the stencilling paint has cured, apply the varnish with a roller. Allow a day's drying time between each of the coats. (Wrap your roller tightly in plastic wrap between each application.) Your floorcloth should have at least three coats of varnish. Be sure to wipe your floorcloth clean with a tack cloth before each coat of varnish.

8. The finished floorcloth may be cleaned by wiping it with a sponge or cloth and warm water and mild soap.

A Stencilled Table

(shown on page 157)

Supplies:

- Unfinished table
- Steel wool
- Stencils (available at craft stores)
- Masking tape
- Stencil brushes
- Stencil paint
- Palette
- Paper towelling
- Paintbrush
- Tack cloth
- Urethane

Directions:

1. Lightly sand the table-top, sides, and legs with fine steel wool.

2. Find the centre of the table and lightly mark with pencil.

3. Divide the table into four equal sections, marking lightly with pencil.

4. Applying stencils centrally in the four quadrants, secure all four edges of stencils with masking tape.

5. Put approximately 5 mL (1 teaspoon) of each colour of paint on the palette. Use one brush per colour.

6. Dip the bristles of the brush in the paint and wipe the excess paint off the brush onto a paper towel using an upright and circular motion.

7. Using the same upright, circular motion, apply the paint, filling in the cut-outs of the stencil. Be sure to use a light touch. You can always apply more paint to make your colours darker.

8. Allow stencil paint to cure for forty-eight hours.

9. Dust with a tack cloth.

10. Apply two or three coats of urethane, allowing each coat to dry. Remember to dust with a tack cloth before each coat.

Milk Paint Application

(shown on page 159)

Supplies:

- Wood stain (for new wood)
- Milk paint powder
- Mixing containers
- Measuring cups
- Portable mixer or electric drill with mixing attachment
- Paintbrush or roller
- Fine steel wool
- Double-boiled linseed oil
- Rags
- Paste wax

Directions:

1. Make sure surface of furniture to be painted is clean and dust-free. New wood should be stained before milk-painting process begins if you wish to create "wear" marks (see Step 7).

2. Measure 1 part milk paint powder to 1 1/2 parts water into mixing container. (For stencilling, add less water; for a wash effect, add more). Keep un-used powder in sealed milk paint bag.

3. Using a mixer, mix thoroughly at low speed for three to five minutes.

4. After mixing and before painting, wash all mixing tools.

5. Paint surface with first coat. Apply paint with a brush or roller, remembering to stir frequently to prevent paint from setting in container. Drying time may vary, but two hours should be adequate.

6. Apply a second coat. Let dry.

7. After second coat is dry, lightly rub entire surface with fine steel wool. This will produce a lustre while removing any surface particles. Evidence of "wear" is

achieved by rubbing desired areas (corners, edges, etc.) more firmly with the steel wool.

8. When you have achieved your desired "distressed" effect, rub the cabinet with a rag to clean the surface. Then brush with double-boiled linseed oil. This seals the paint into the wood.

9. Wipe off excess oil with a clean, dry rag. Rub surface with paste wax when dry.

A Twig Planter

(shown on page 159)

Supplies:

- Cedar planter, or any plastic or wooden planter (available at garden nurseries)
- Tree branches
- Clippers
- Glue gun and glue sticks
- Binder twine
- Exterior stain

Directions:

1. Collect branches while pruning or walking through the woods. For a rough and rustic look, use larger, bark-covered branches, 7.5 to 10 cm (3" to 4") in diameter. Oak, Scotch pine, spruce, and many fruit trees have good gnarly skins. A sleeker look can be achieved with smaller, 2.5 to 7.5 cm (1" to 3") twigs with a smoother surface. Beech, silver maple, or birch are good.
2. Clip assorted twigs unevenly. They should be 5 to 7.5 cm (2" to 3") longer than your cedar planter is high.
3. One at a time, trace a line of glue down each branch, press it to the planter, and hold a minute.
4. Place each branch snugly against the last, being sure to keep them straight.
5. Stick main branches on until planter is concealed. Fill any gaps with smaller twigs. Let stand for a few minutes.
6. Wrap binder twine around the base and top of the planter.
7. Apply a coat of exterior stain to the twine.

A Quilt

(shown on page 161)

Instructions given are for a queen-size coverlet, which will hang down the sides of a queen-size bed approximately 30 cm (12") all around. The finished size of the quilt will be approximately 216 x 264 cm (85" x 104").

Supplies:

Fabric amounts are based on a 115 cm (45") width fabric. Use a 100% cotton calico for the patchwork. Choose four different fabrics ranging from light to dark. There should be one predominant fabric (usually the darkest) in order for the pattern to show up, and it should be placed in the No. 4 position. A poly-cotton broadcloth may be used for the backing.

- Fabric 1 (light) — 1.2 m (1 1/2 yards)
- Fabric 2 (lightest medium) — 2.2 m (2 3/8 yards) (includes fabric for Border 1)
- Fabric 3 (darkest medium) — 2.6 m (2 3/4 yards) (includes fabric for Border 2)
- Fabric 4 (dark) - 2.8 m (3 yards) (includes fabric for Border 3)
- Backing fabric - 6 m (6 1/2 yards)
- Masking tape
- Bonded polyester Fatt Batt (queen size)
- Chenille or cotton darning needle
- 3 skeins of embroidery floss for tying
- Thread for sewing
- Invisible thread (optional) for stitching in ditch

Directions:

1. Pre-wash all fabric and dry in the dryer before cutting. Press if necessary.

2. Cutting: Carefully cut or tear all strips from selvage to selvage so that the strips are approximately 115 cm (45") long by the width listed below. Be accurate! The very best way to cut the strips is to use a rotary cutter as you can cut many layers at a time and have perfectly accurate strips. You will need the following:

- Eighteen 6 x 115 cm (2 1/4" x 45") strips of each fabric for the quilt blocks
- Eight 10 x 115 cm (4" x 45") strips of lightest medium (No. 2) for Border 1
- Ten 13 x 115 cm (5" x 45") strips of darkest medium (No. 3) for Border 2
- Ten 15 x 115 cm (6" x 45") strips of dark (No. 4) for Border 3

3. Sewing the quilt blocks: Use a 5 mm (1/4") seam allowance and a short stitch length (a number 2 setting if your machine is metric or 12 to 15 stitches per inch) throughout. It is not necessary to back-stitch or pin.

a. Lay the 6 x 115 cm (2 1/4" x 45") strips beside your machine in the order shown in Fig. A. There should be eighteen strips in each pile.

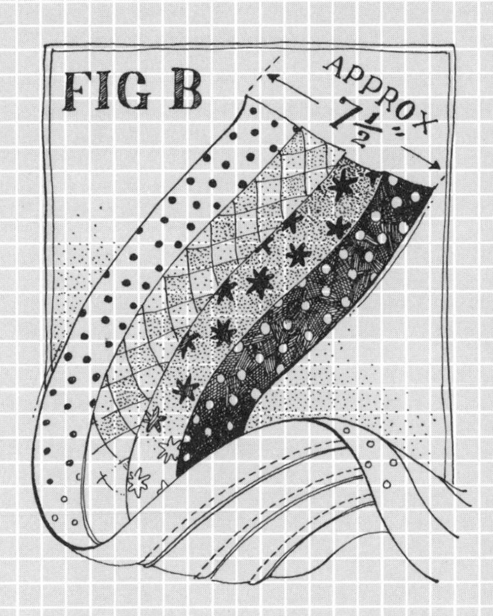

b. Sew the four strips (one of each colour) together along the long edges to form a "strip set" (Fig. B), being careful not to stretch the strips as you sew. Don't worry if the lengths of the strips are not exactly 115 cm (45"). Repeat this step, keeping the fabrics in the same order, until all the 6 cm (2 1/4") strips are used. You will have eighteen strip sets.

4. Press the seams to one side (not open), towards the darkest fabric, being careful not to stretch the strip set as you press. Press lightly on the wrong side in order to establish the direction of the seams; then turn over and press well on the right side. Measure the width of your strip set (approx. 19 cm or 7 1/2").

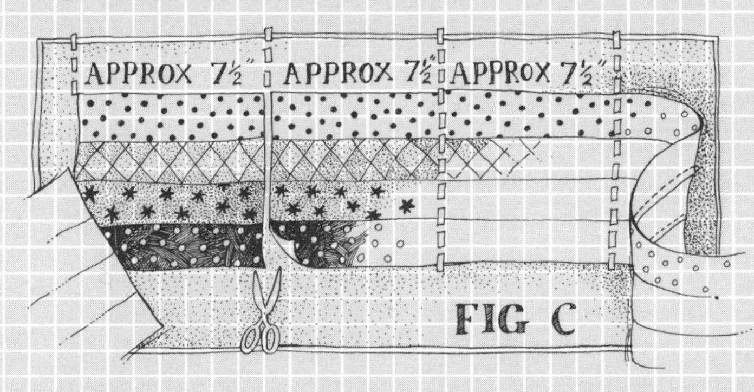

5. Cut the eighteen strip sets into square blocks, using the measurement of the width of your strip set obtained in Step 4 (approx. 19 cm or 7 1/2"). It is important to cut at right angles to the strip set. Even off one end of each strip set and then mark and cut five blocks from each (Fig. C). If using a rotary cutter, you can carefully stack several strip sets and cut through all layers. You need eighty-eight blocks — you will have two extra. Discard these or set them aside.

6. Previewing the quilt top: In a large area, lay out the quilt blocks to preview the quilt top. Your quilt will have eight blocks across and eleven blocks down. The block in the top left corner of the quilt should have the dark strip on the bottom. The block next to it should have the dark strip on the left. Continue to alternate the blocks in this manner with the dark strip on the bottom or the left alternately until all eighty-eight blocks are in place (Fig. D).

7. Sewing the quilt top: Looking at your quilt on the floor, you have eight rows across and eleven blocks down.

a. Flap each of the blocks in Row 2 right sides together to the blocks in Row 1. Starting at the top, pick up the blocks from the top down, keeping them in pairs, and keeping the top two on the top of the pile. Pin a label "Rows 1 and 2" on this pile of blocks. Now gather Row 3 from the top down; then Row 4, and so on, until all eight rows are gathered and labelled Row 3, Row 4, etc. Only the blocks in Rows 1 and 2 are in pairs; the remaining rows are gathered individually.

b. Stitch the vertical Row 1. Pick up the first pair of blocks from the Rows 1 and 2 pile and stitch with a 5 mm (1/4") seam, matching the top and the bottom of the two blocks. Don't cut the thread or lift the pressure foot. Butt the next pair of blocks from that pile up to the first pair and continue to sew, matching the corners of the blocks. Butt the next pair and so on (Fig. E) until you have all eleven pairs from the Rows 1 and 2 pile stitched. Cut the thread only after the last pair of blocks.

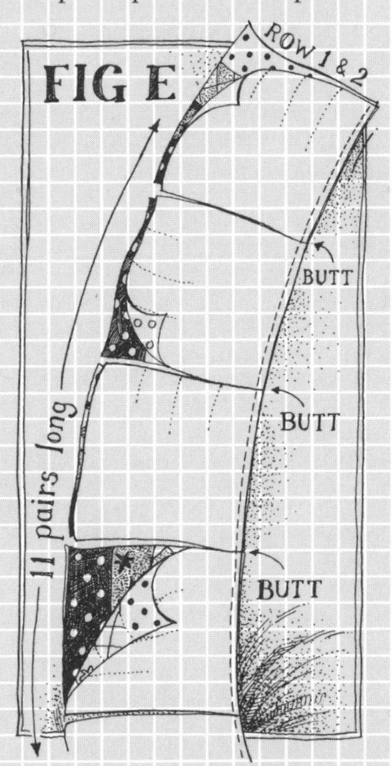

c. Go back up to the top of Rows 1 and 2 and open out the first pair of blocks. Set the pile of blocks labelled Row 3 beside your machine. Take the top block from this pile and flap it right sides together to block 2 and sew using a 5 mm (1/4") seam. Continue to add one block at a time all the way down (Fig. F). When all the blocks from Row 3 are added, go back up to the top and do the same for Row 4 through Row 8. At this point, all the vertical rows will be sewn and the stitches between the blocks will act as pins when you go to sew the horizontal rows.

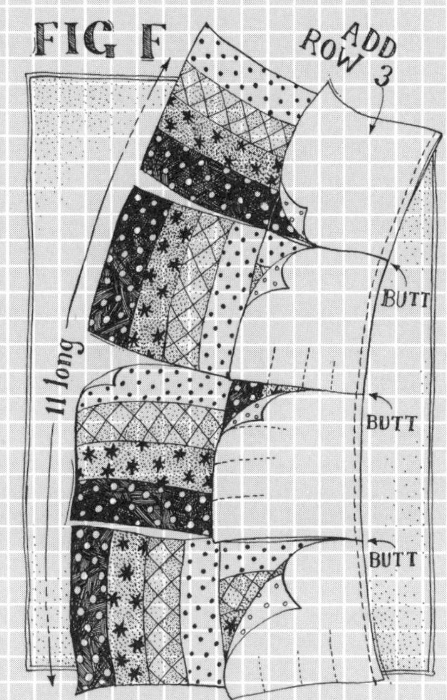

d. Now sew the horizontal rows by flapping the entire top row right sides together onto the next row and stitching all the way across, matching the corners of the blocks where they are joined with a thread. Repeat with each row. Your quilt top is now ready for borders.

8. Border 1 (inside border): Stitch two 115 cm (45") lengths together to make one 230 cm (90") strip for each side of the quilt (i.e., four long strips).

Match the centre seam of one 230 cm (90") border strip to the middle of one long edge of the quilt top, right sides together, and pin. Stitch with 5 mm (1/4") seam. Trim ends of the border strip even with the top and bottom of the quilt top. Repeat with the other long edge of the quilt top. Press these borders out, pressing the seam towards the border. Match the centre seam of one of the remaining 230 cm (90") border strips to the middle of one short end of the quilt top, right sides together, and pin. Stitch with 5 mm (1/4") seam. Repeat with last inside border strip. Trim and press (Fig. G).

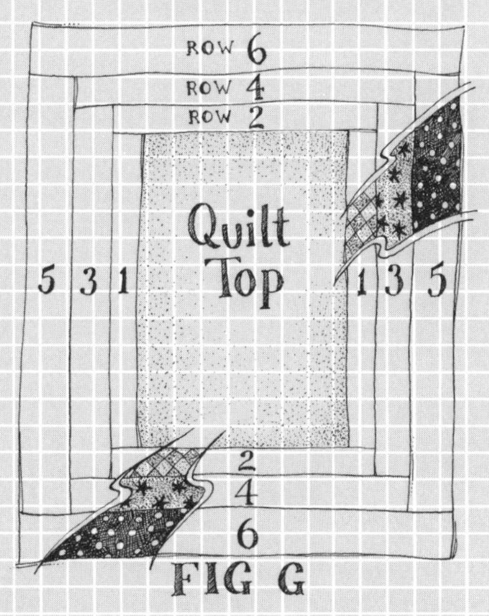

9. Border 2: Stitch two 115 cm (45") lengths together to make one 230 cm (90") strip. Repeat to make a second 230 cm (90") strip. Stitch three 115 cm (45") lengths together to make one 342.5 cm (135") strip; repeat. Using the longer border strips first, match the centre of one border strip with the centre of one long edge of the quilt. Stitch, trim, and press. Repeat with the second long border strip. Then attach the shorter border strips to the top and bottom of the quilt, matching the centres as before. Stitch, trim, and press.

10. Border 3: Same as Border 2.

11. Backing: Cut or tear the 6 m (6 1/2 yard) piece of backing fabric in half so that you have two pieces 115 cm (45") wide by 3 m (3 1/4 yards) long. Join these two pieces together along the long selvage edge to obtain one piece 230 cm (90") wide by 3 m (3 1/4 yards) long.

12. Assembly:

a. Lay the backing on the floor, wrong side up (a wood or tile floor is best). Fasten the backing to the floor with masking tape, smoothing out all wrinkles and puckers (Fig. H).

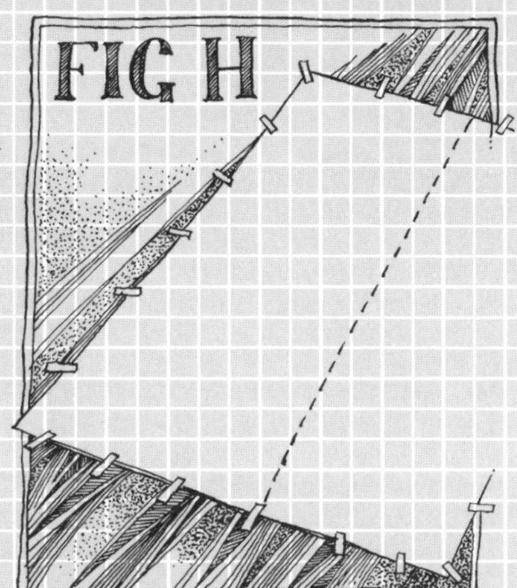

b. Place the quilt batting on top of the backing, smoothing out the wrinkles.

c. Centre the quilt top on the batting, right side up. Pin the quilt top through all three layers every 5 to 7.5 cm (2" to 3") all the way around the outer edge. Smooth out all wrinkles and make sure the quilt is square with the backing (Fig. I).

13. Tying:

a. Use a chenille or cotton darning needle for tying. Cut a long length of embroidery floss (use all six strands) and thread the needle.

b. Starting in the lower right corner of the quilt, take a 5 mm (1/4") stitch in the corner of each block, straddling the seam line and sewing through all thicknesses. Do not cut the floss between stitches and leave a 5 cm (2") end after the last stitch in the row.

c. Clip the floss between stitches and tie the ends with tight square knots (Fig. J). Trim the ends to about 2.5 cm (1") long. Rub between your fingers to fluff them up.

d. Before removing the pins, baste with a long running stitch around the outer edge of the quilt. Remove pins and tape and lift quilt off the floor.

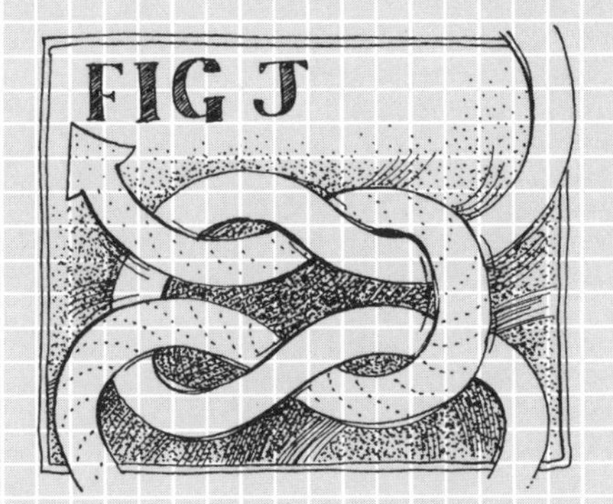

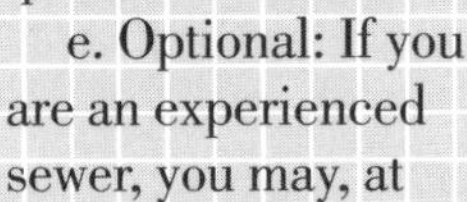

e. Optional: If you are an experienced sewer, you may, at this point, wish to "stitch in the ditch" through all layers right in the seam lines of each border. This is not a good idea for beginners; it is difficult to feed all three layers through the sewing machine without getting puckers.

14. Finishing the edge:

a. Carefully trim the batting even with the edge of the quilt top all around.

b. Trim the backing 4 cm (1 1/2") wider than the quilt top all around (draw a pencil line and cut with scissors, or use a rotary cutter and see-through ruler) (Fig. K).

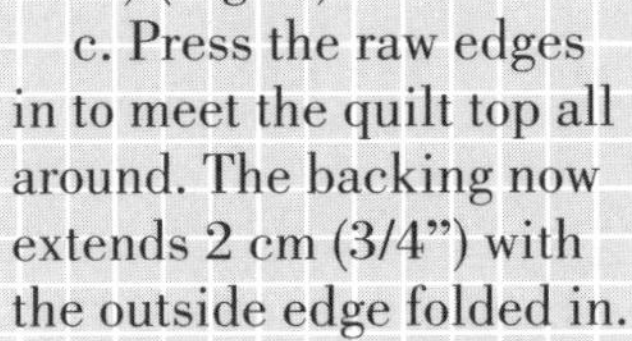

c. Press the raw edges in to meet the quilt top all around. The backing now extends 2 cm (3/4") with the outside edge folded in.

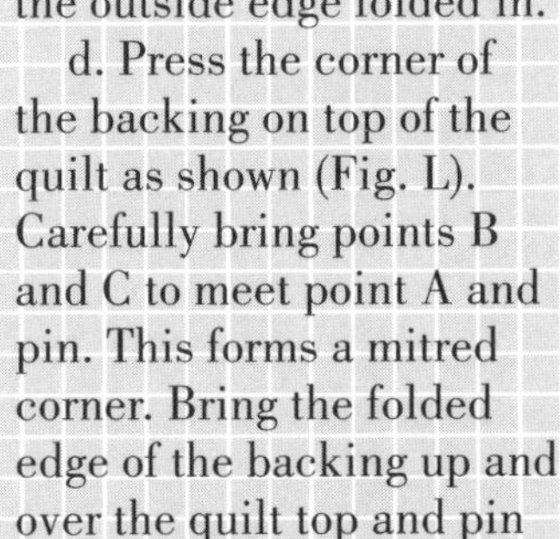

d. Press the corner of the backing on top of the quilt as shown (Fig. L). Carefully bring points B and C to meet point A and pin. This forms a mitred corner. Bring the folded edge of the backing up and over the quilt top and pin in place. Topstitch the edge of the backing to the quilt top, firmly holding the quilt both in front of and behind the pressure foot as you stitch. Keep the portion you are stitching smooth and taut as you sew (Fig. M).

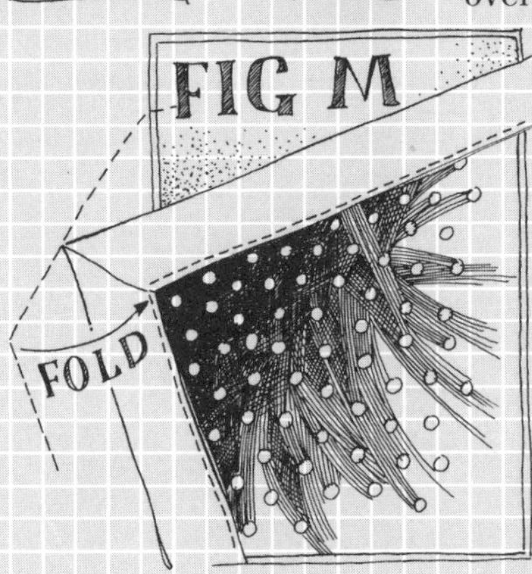

A Twig Table

(shown on page 173)

Supplies:

Frame:

- 4 twigs 66 x 4 cm (26" x 1 1/2") diameter (legs)
- 8 twigs 46 x 2.5 cm (18" x 1") diameter (horizontal members)
- 3 twigs 56 x 2.5 cm (22" x 1") diameter (top members)
- 8 twigs 76 x 1.3 cm (30" x 1/2") diameter (diagonal braces)

Top:

- 25 twigs 56 x 1.3 cm (22" x 1/2") diameter (table-top struts)
- Claw hammer
- Small sledge hammer (optional)
- Small pruning saw or handsaw
- 4 cm (1 1/2") nails
- 5 cm (2") nails
- Drill

Directions:

1. Lay a pair of legs on a flat work surface, keeping in mind that the fat ends will be at the top. Lay a horizontal member across the legs, 10 cm (4") from the bottom, and flush with the outside edge of the legs. Drill a hole of slightly smaller diameter than the 5 cm (2") nails through both the horizontal member and the leg. Nail flush. Lay a second piece across the top of the legs, flushing ends with edges. Drill and nail as before. Repeat this for the other pair of legs. This produces two sides.

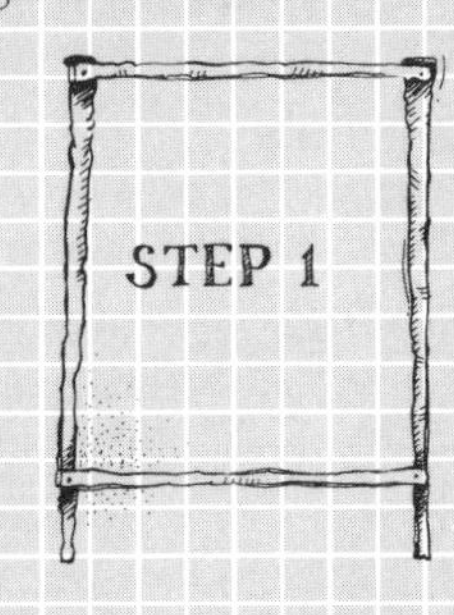

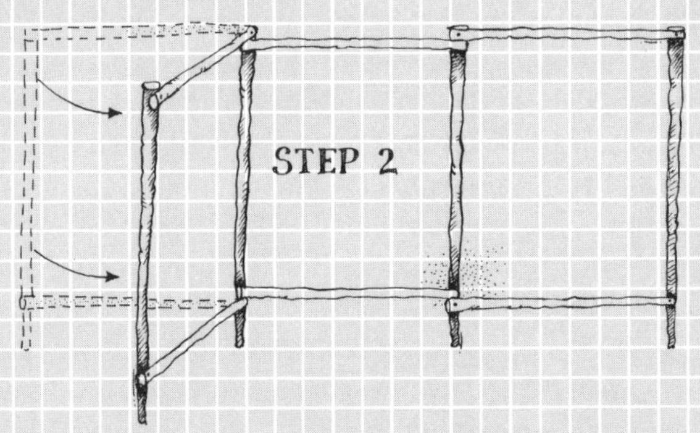

2. Lay the two sides flat and parallel on the work surface, but about 46 cm (18") apart. Take the outer leg of the left side and raise it as though turning the page of a large book. Lay a horizontal member across the legs of opposing sides in contact with the previously nailed

horizontal member but touching on its upper surface. Keep the angle between raised side and developing side close to 90 degrees. Drill and nail as before. Lay a second horizontal member so as to join the left side to the right side but this time just under the horizontal members of the previously constructed sides. Drill and nail. Now turn the right side up like the page of a large book and nail the remaining end of each horizontal member to the leg of the second side.

3. Turn the developing frame so that the missing side is down. Add two horizontal members to complete the union of the sides. A box-like structure will result.

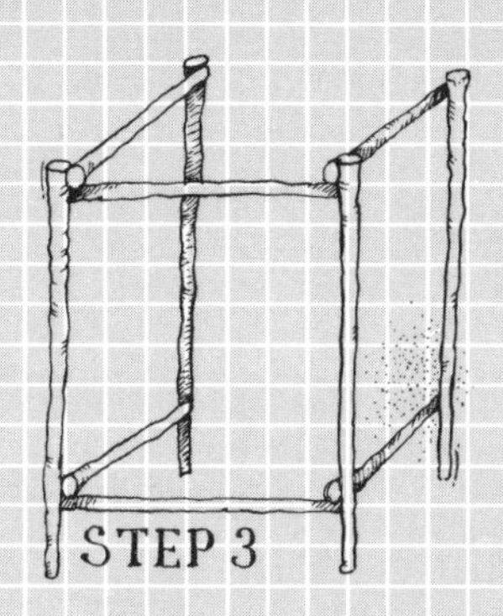

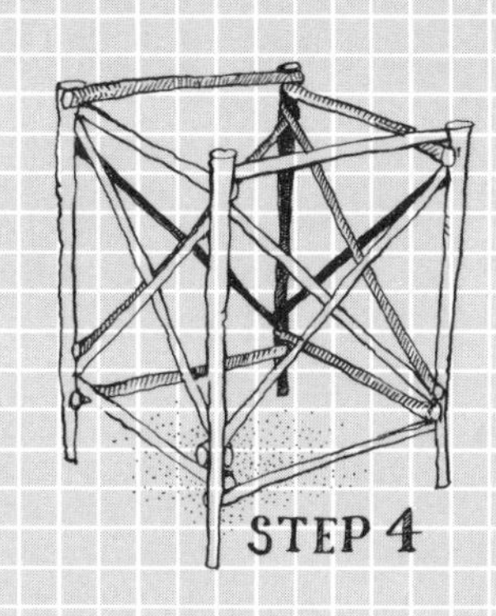

4. Using two of the diagonal braces, attach each with 4 cm (1 1/2") nails from the top inner side of one leg diagonally to the lower inner side of the neighbouring leg. Drill and nail the top ends. Drill and nail the lower ends only after you ascertain that the side you are working on is square. Turn the table so that the braced and now rigid side is upper-most and repeat the bracing procedure on the opposite side. Again, turning the unbraced sides down, complete the bracing of the third and fourth sides. This step is the most critical in ensuring a pleasing and well-balanced look.

5. Place the frame so that it is standing upright. Position one of the top members across the top ends of the legs so that 5 cm (2") of this member protrudes beyond each leg. Drill for the 5 cm (2") nails. Nail flush into the end grain of the leg. Repeat this procedure on the other two leg tops. The third top member is situated between the first two and drilled and nailed flush to the horizontal members installed during Step 4.

6. The final step is to apply the table-top. Using table-top struts, place one strut flush against the ends of the three top members so that 5 cm (2") of the table-top struts protrude beyond each edge of the top members. Drill for 4 cm (1 1/2") nails. Nail. Repeat this procedure at the opposite ends of the three top members. Apply a third strut in the middle of the first two. Continue to apply additional struts in the middle of intervening spaces until nine struts

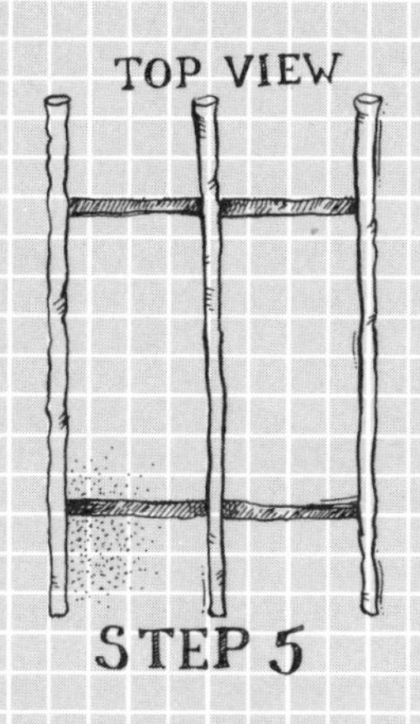

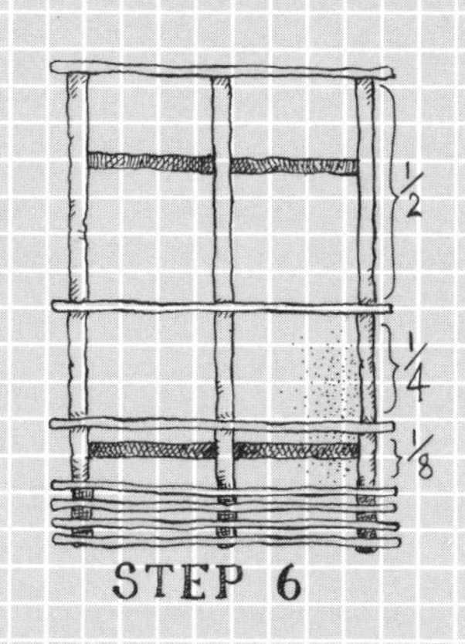

have been applied. Then, apply two additional struts between each of the original nine. The completed table-top will thus have twenty-five struts separated by approximately 1 to 2 cm (1/2" to 3/4").

Instructions courtesy of Nannyberry Woods Twig Furniture

Painting a Chair

(shown on page 185)

Supplies:

- Chair, painted or unpainted
- Oil-based primer (for unpainted chair)
- Sandpaper (for painted chair)
- Artists' acrylic paint — white, red, yellow, blue
- Paintbrushes, including fine artists' brush
- Urethane

Directions:

1. If the wood is raw, cover it with an oil-based primer. Otherwise, sand the surface to rough it up.

2. Mix the acrylic paint colours to get the colours of your choice. Make enough of each that you won't run out, as it's impossible to get the right colour again.

3. Paint each piece of the chair a different colour as follows. Apply one or two overall coats of the colour you have selected as a base colour. Then add a little white to the colour and dry-brush it over the base coat. (To dry-brush, take a very small amount of paint into a dry brush, working it in. Then brush lightly and randomly over the surface.)

4. Now add the decorative dots, dashes, flowers, and swirls with a fine artists' brush. Do this freehand. The colours of the designs will contribute to the over-all zaniness for a wonderful effect. You will have a one-of-a-kind chair.

5. Brush on two or three coats of urethane to protect the finish.

Directions courtesy of folk artist J.C. Brown, Vanderwerff & Brown

THE DIRECTORY OF SOURCES

THE FOLLOWING PAGES CONTAIN NAMES OF STORES AND SUPPLIERS SELLING DECORATING ITEMS AND SERVICES, COLLECTED BY the editors of *Canadian House & Home* magazine over the past several years. This is by no means a complete list of the sources available in Canada, but rather it is our own list of those companies we have sourced for our magazine. Entries have been coded as follows:

(R) Retail Store or Service – available to the public.
(T) Trade Showroom – available through your designer or architect.
(M) Manufacturer or Distributor – telephone for retail outlet closest to you.

When a company has several locations we have listed, where possible, the head office address first. Please call the head office, or check your local telephone directory for the location nearest you. You will find the resource list is national, but with many more sources listed for the Toronto area. This reflects the number of companies with head offices in this area as well as our own familiarity with the city from which we publish.

We are anxious to learn of other good sources from across Canada and hope that you will send us information on your favourites.

Canadian House & Home
Suite 304
60 St. Clair Avenue East
Toronto, Ontario
M4T 1N5

Antiques

Acorn Antiques, The
319 Main Street
Mahone Bay, Nova Scotia
B0J 2E0
Tel: (902) 624-8642 or
(902) 624-9293 (R)

Alan Clairman Antiques
244 Carlton Street
Toronto, Ontario M5A 2L1
Tel: (416) 968-6975 (R)

Ann Wood Antique Prints Inc.
64 Queen Mary's Drive
Toronto, Ontario M8X 1S5
Tel: (416) 925-7459 (R)

Antique Shoppe, The
750 Bank Street
Ottawa, Ontario K1S 3V6
Tel: (613) 232-0840 (R)

Antiquités Hier Pour Demain
C.P. 189
914, route 117
Piedmont, Quebec J0R 1K0
Tel: (514) 227-4231 (R)

Antiquités Phyllis Friedman Inc.
5012, rue Sherbrooke ouest
Montreal, Quebec H3Z 1H4
Tel: (514) 483-6185 (R)

Antiquités Toi et Moi Inc.
965, rue Notre Dame
Lavaltrie, Co. Berthier, Quebec
J0K 1H0
Tel: (514) 586-1495 (R)

Bashford's
736-17th Avenue S.W.
Calgary, Alberta T2S 0B7
Tel: (403) 228-7780 (R)

Beaver Hall Antiques Limited
P.O. Box 490
21 King Street East
Gananoque, Ontario K7G 2V1
Tel: (613) 382-2228 (R)

Budd Sugarman Interior Design & Antiques
19 Hazelton Avenue
Toronto, Ontario M5R 2E1
Tel: (416) 925-4471 (R)

Carol Solway Antiques Limited
88 Yorkville Avenue
Toronto, Ontario M5R 1B9
Tel: (416) 922-0702 (R)

Circa Antiques and Interiors
166 Davenport Road
Toronto, Ontario M5R 1J2
Tel: (416) 961-3744 (R)

Clutter's Curiosity Art Deco Antiques
653 Queen Street East
Toronto, Ontario M4M 1G4
Tel: (416) 461-3776 (R)

Country Furniture and Antiques
2698 Agricola Street
Halifax, Nova Scotia B3K 4C9
Tel: (902) 455-6177 (R)

D & E Lake Ltd.
239 King Street East
Toronto, Ontario M5A 1J9
Tel: (416) 863-9930 (R)

Davenport House Antiques & Interiors
158 Davenport Road
Toronto, Ontario M5R 1J2
Tel: (416) 922-3778 (R)

David Gillies Antiques
66 Avenue Road
Toronto, Ontario M5R 3N8
Tel: (416) 969-8464 (R)

David Robinson (Antiques) Ltd.
1016 Langley Street
Victoria, British Columbia
V8W 1V8
Tel: (604) 384-6425

1236 Yonge Street
Toronto, Ontario M4T 1W3
Tel: (416) 921-4858 (R)

David S. Brown Antiques
1307, rue Ste-Catherine ouest
Montreal, Quebec H3G 1P7
Tel: (514) 844-9866 (R)

Devonshire House
178 1/2 Davenport Road
Toronto, Ontario M5R 1J2
Tel: (416) 927-0279 (R)

Dirstein Robertson Limited
77 Yorkville Avenue
Toronto, Ontario M5R 1C1
Tel: (416) 961-6211 (R)

Donohue & Bousquet
27 Hawthorne Avenue
Ottawa, Ontario K1S 0A9
Tel: (613) 232-5665 (R)

Eleanor Dover Oriental Antiques and Artifacts
25 Ingram Drive
Toronto, Ontario M6M 2L7
Tel: (416) 246-1774 (R)

Faith Grant
1156 Fort Street
Victoria, British Columbia
V8V 3K8
Tel: (604) 383-0121 (R)

Fifty-One Antiques Ltd.
21 Avenue Road
Toronto, Ontario M5R 2V1
Tel: (416) 968-2416 (R)

Florentine Antiques
Unit 8
320 Don Park Road
Markham, Ontario L3R 1J4
Tel: (416) 475-0927 (R)

French Country Antiques Inc.
Suite 210
160 Pears Avenue
Toronto, Ontario M5R 1T2
Tel: (416) 925-8248 (R)

Gerald W. Hamilton Antiques
44 Pine Street North
Port Hope, Ontario L1A 3G6
Tel: (416) 885-8046 (R)

Greenburnie Antiques Ltd.
R.R. 1
Lombardy, Ontario K0G 1L0
Tel: (613) 283-8323 (R)

Guildhall Antiques Ltd.
111 Jarvis Street
Toronto, Ontario M5C 2H4
Tel: (416) 487-7697 (R)

Haidles Antiques
R.R. 1
Oro, Ontario N0N 2E0
Tel: (705) 487-3754 (R)

Harbourfront Antique Market Inc.
390 Queen's Quay West
Toronto, Ontario M5V 3A6
Tel: (416) 340-8377 (R)

Henrietta Antony Inc.
4192, rue Ste-Catherine ouest
Montreal, Quebec H3Z 1P4
Tel: (514) 935-9116 (R)

Heritage Restorations
2833-14th Street S.W.
Calgary, Alberta T2T 3V3
Tel: (403) 245-2124 (R)

Hinton Antiques
65 Queen Street
Orillia, Ontario L3V 1B8
Tel: (705) 325-9666 (R)

Inquisitive
1646 Bayview Avenue
Toronto, Ontario M4G 3C2
Tel: (416) 481-8819 (R)

J. Sorensen Antique Restoration
P.O. Box 671
R.R. 1
Mallorytown, Ontario K0E 1R0
Tel: (613) 659-3874 (M) (R)

J.W. Humphries Antiques Ltd.
9 Russell Street East
Lindsay, Ontario K9V 1Z7
Tel: (705) 324-5050 (R)

James Green Antique Oriental Carpets
190 Davenport Road
Toronto, Ontario M5R 1J2
Tel: (416) 925-5356 (R)

Jane Mitchell Antiques
Unit 101
2 Beechwood Avenue
Vanier, Ontario K1L 8L9
Tel: (613) 749-5267 (R)

John L. Russell Reg'd.
1504, rue Sherbrooke ouest
Montreal, Quebec H3G 1L3
Tel: (514) 935-2129 (R)

Jonny's Antiques
10 Shakespeare Street South
Shakespeare, Ontario N0B 2P0
Tel: (519) 625-8307 (R)

Kershaw — Old Maps & Prints
P.O. Box 7113
442 Wilson Street East
Ancaster, Ontario L9G 3L3
Tel: (416) 648-1991 (R)

L'Atelier Antiques and Decorative Objects
1228 Yonge Street
Toronto, Ontario M4T 1W3
Tel: (416) 966-0200 (R)

Les Antiquités Mucha Inc.
97, rue St-Paul
Quebec City, Quebec G1K 3V8
Tel: (418) 694-0896 (R)

Little Red School House Antiques
R.R. 2
Kilworth, Ontario P0E 1G0
Tel: (705) 689-2419 (R)

Lorenz Antiques
701 Mount Pleasant Road
Toronto, Ontario M4S 2N4
Tel: (416) 487-2066 (R)

Louis Wine Ltd.
848-A Yonge Street
Toronto, Ontario M4W 2H1
Tel: (416) 929-9333 (R)

Michael Reeves Antiques Ltd.
171 Queen Street East
Toronto, Ontario M5C 1S2
Tel: (416) 368-0257 (R)

Michel Taschereau Antiques
176 Cumberland Avenue
Toronto, Ontario M5H 2G1
Tel: (416) 923-3020

1227, rue Sherbrooke ouest
Montreal, Quebec H3G 1G1
Tel: (514) 286-4630 (R)

Neil Clement Antiquaire Inc.
2115, rue de la Montagne
Montreal, Quebec H3G 1Z8
Tel: (514) 849-7934 (R)

P.L. Templeton Antique Carpets Ltd.
131 Avenue Road
Toronto, Ontario M5R 2H7
Tel: (416) 923-2147 (R)

Paisley Shop, The
889 Yonge Street
Toronto, Ontario M4W 2H2
Tel: (416) 923-5830 (R)

Pao & Moltke Limited
118 Yorkville Avenue
Toronto, Ontario M5R 1C2
Tel: (416) 925-2197 (R)

Petit Musée Ltée. Antiquaire
1494, rue Sherbrooke ouest
Montreal, Quebec H3G 1L3
Tel: (514) 937-6161 (R)

Port Dalhousie Trading Company
104 Avenue Road
Toronto, Ontario M5R 2H3
Tel: (416) 920-0323 (R)

Portobello Antiques
3050 Granville Street
Vancouver, British Columbia
V6H 3J8
Tel: (604) 734-2275 (R)

Prince of Serendip Antiques Ltd.
1073 Yonge Street
Toronto, Ontario M4W 2L2
Tel: (416) 925-3760 (R)

R.G. Perkins & Son Antiques Ltd.
1198 Yonge Street
Toronto, Ontario M4T 1W1
Tel: (416) 925-0973 (R)

R.H.V. Tee & Son (England) Ltd.
7963 Granville Street
Vancouver, British Columbia
V6P 2P0
Tel: (604) 263-2791 (R)

Red Indian Art Deco Inc.
507 Queen Street West
Toronto, Ontario M5V 2B4
Tel: (416) 364-2706 (R)

Robert Picard Antiquités Québecoises
C.P. 1170
501, route 138
Lavaltrie, Quebec J0K 1H0
Tel: (514) 586-1575 (R)

Robert Rockland Rare Carpets
1451, rue Sherbrooke ouest
Montreal, Quebec H3G 2S8
Tel: (514) 937-6273 (R)

Rollins Raeburn Interior Design Inc.
146 Davenport Road
Toronto, Ontario M5R 1J1
Tel: (416) 923-5676 (R)

Ronald Windebank Antiques Ltd.
21 Avenue Road
Toronto, Ontario M5H 2G1
Tel: (416) 962-2862 (R)

Ruth Stalker Antiques Ltd.
4447, rue Ste-Catherine ouest
Westmount, Quebec H3Z 1R2
Tel: (514) 931-0822 (R)

Sands of Time Ltd., The
1025 Fort Street
Victoria, British Columbia
V8V 3K5
Tel: (604) 384-2817 (R)

Sergio Bernardi Antiques
120 Yonge Street South
Aurora, Ontario L4G 1M4
Tel: (416) 841-6218 (R)

Some Other Time Antiques
27 Pearl Street
Streetsville, Ontario L5M 1X1
Tel: (416) 826-5218 (R)

Stanley Wagman & Son Antiques Ltd.
111 Avenue Road
Toronto, Ontario M5R 3J8
Tel: (416) 964-1047 (R)

Stewart and Miller Antiques
188 Montague Street
Lunenburg, Nova Scotia
B0J 2C0
Tel: (902) 634-8330 (R)

Stuart Jackson Gallery
119 Yorkville Avenue
Toronto, Ontario M5R 1C4
Tel: (416) 967-9166 (R)

Susan's Antiques
585 Mount Pleasant Road
Toronto, Ontario M4S 2N5
Tel: (416) 487-9262 (R)

Town House Antiques Ltd., The
216 King Street
St. Catharines, Ontario L2R 3J9
Tel: (416) 687-8770 (R)

Town of York Antiques
219 Avenue Road
Toronto, Ontario M5R 2J3
Tel: (416) 925-4720 (R)

Tubtown Gifts & Antiques Ltd.
Bush Street
Belfountain, Ontario L0N 1B0
Tel: (519) 927-5965 (R)

Uno Langmann Ltd.
2117 Granville Street
Vancouver, British Columbia
V6H 3E9
Tel: (604) 736-8825 (R)

Upper Canada House Ltd.
467 Eglinton Avenue West
Toronto, Ontario M5N 1A7
Tel: (416) 489-9110 (R)

Van Schyndel-Lachapelle Antiques
Box 101
Highway 2
Grafton, Ontario K0K 2G0
Tel: (416) 349-2467 (R)

Victoria's Antiques
6430 Chebucto Road
Halifax, Nova Scotia B3L 1L2
Tel: (902) 422-7712 (R)

Waller Antiques Ltd.
828 Fort Street
Victoria, British Columbia
V8W 1H8
Tel: (604) 388-6116 (R)

William Dennis Gallery, The
826 Fort Street
Victoria, British Columbia
V8W 1H8
Tel: (604) 382-2412 (R)

Blinds & Shutters

Canada Custom Shutters
(Phone for nearest dealer)
225 Industrial Parkway South
Unit 21-27
Aurora, Ontario L4G 3V5
Tel: (416) 738-5745 (M)

Contour Window Fashions
Suite 401
3910 Bathurst Street,
Toronto, Ontario M3H 5Z3
Tel: (416) 633-7070 (R)

Hunter Douglas Canada Inc.
(Phone for nearest dealer)
Unit B
2155 Drew Road
Mississauga, Ontario L5S 1S7
Tel: (416) 678-1133 (M)

Kirsch Canada Ltd.
233 Signet Drive
Weston, Ontario M9L 1V3
Tel: (416) 745-8860 (M) (R)

LouverDrape/Abbey Blinds
(Phone for nearest dealer)
6310 Vipond Drive
Mississauga, Ontario L5T 1J9
Tel: (416) 673-2869 (M)

Mastercraft Shutters Inc.
Unit 4
3640 Weston Road,
Weston, Ontario M9L 1W2
Tel: (416) 748-1333 (M) (R)

Polymat Shades Inc.
(Phone for nearest dealer)
260 Enford Road
Richmond Hill, Ontario
L4C 3E8
Tel: (416) 884-9227 (M)

Shutter Mold
(Phone for nearest dealer)
373 Tiffin Street
Barrie, Ontario L4M 4S4
Tel: (705) 721-9269 or
1-800-465-2988 (M)

Sturdi-bilt Wood Products Limited
201 Don Park Road
Markham, Ontario L3R 1C2
Tel: (416) 475-1050 (M) (R)

Wriseo Ltd.
(Phone for nearest dealer)
144 Steelcase Road West
Markham, Ontario L3R 2R8
Tel: (416) 475-9492 (M)

Carpets & Rugs

Aban Persian Rugs
Unit 222
2600 John Street
Markham, Ontario L3R 3W3
Tel: (416) 474-0083 (R)

Anglo Oriental Ltd.
68 Prince Andrew Place
Don Mills, Ontario M3C 2H4
Tel: (416) 445-8111

Unit 13
13520 Crestwood Place
Burnaby, British Columbia
V6V 2M3
Tel: (604) 276-8586 (T)

Appel Ltd.
321 Davenport Road
Toronto, Ontario M5R 1K5
Tel: (416) 922-3935 (T)

Bartex Carpets
2655 Steeles Avenue West
Downsview, Ontario M3J 2Z8
Tel: (416) 665-1500 (R)

Carpet Market Ltd., The
2705 Agricola Street
Halifax, Nova Scotia B3K 4C7
Tel: (902) 455-7904 (R)

Claire Murray, Inc.
Suite 226-7
4030, rue St-Ambroise
Montreal, Quebec H4C 2C7
Tel: (514) 937-9113 (R)

Dominion Rug Inc.
3420 Yonge Street
Toronto, Ontario M4N 2M9
Tel: (416) 485-9488 (R) (T)

Elte Carpets
80 Ronald Avenue
Toronto, Ontario M6E 5A2
Tel: (416) 785-7885 (R)

Franco Belgian Company Ltd.
115 Dupont Street
Toronto, Ontario M5R 1V4
Tel: (416) 967-0115 (T)

Gordon T. Sands Ltd.
40 Torbay Road
Markham, Ontario L3R 1G6
Tel: (416) 475-6380 (T)

H & I Carpet Corporation of Canada
(Phone for nearest dealer)
162 Bedford Road
Toronto, Ontario M5R 2K9
Tel: (416) 961-6891 (T)

Indo-Persian Rug Co. Ltd.
(Phone for nearest location)
1127 Finch Avenue West
Downsview, Ontario L3J 2E8
Tel: (416) 736-7144 (R)

Neeshat
170 West Beaver Creek Road
Richmond Hill, Ontario
L4B 1L6
Tel: (416) 886-0404 (R)

(R) Retail Store/ (T) Trade Showroom/ (M) Manufacturer or Distributor

Peerless Carpet Corp.
(Phone for nearest dealer)
78 Walker Drive
Bramalea, Ontario L6T 4H6
Tel: (416) 458-3100

7791 Alberbridge Way
Richmond, British Columbia
V6X 2A4
Tel: (604) 273-5611 (T)

Perfection Rug Company
(Phone for nearest dealer)
4221, rue Ste-Catherine ouest
Montreal, Quebec H3Z 1P6
Tel: (514) 939-2400

Suite 100
113 Dupont Street
Toronto, Ontario M5R 1V4
Tel: (416) 920-5900

Suite 303
839 Cambie Street
Vancouver, British Columbia
V6B 2P4
Tel: (604) 669-3990 (T)

Santa Fe Legacy Inc.
(By appointment only)
4052 Major Mackenzie Drive
Woodbridge, Ontario L4L 1A6
Tel: (416) 832-5563 (R)

Turco-Persian Rug Co. Limited
452 Richmond Street East
Toronto, Ontario M5A 1R2
Tel: (416) 366-0707 (R)

Vancouver Rug Import
101 Water Street
Vancouver, British Columbia
V6B 1A7
Tel: (604) 688-6787 (R)

Draperies, Custom Sewing Rooms, Upholsterers

Art's Custom Upholstery Inc.
Unit 6
90 Melford Drive
Scarborough, Ontario M1B 2A1
Tel: (416) 321-6612 (R)

B.B. Bargoon's
(Phone for nearest location)
201 Whitehall Road
Markham, Ontario L3R 9Y3
Tel: (416) 475-3172 (R)

Chintz & Co.
(Phone for locations in Victoria, Calgary, and Edmonton)
1180 Marine Drive
North Vancouver,
British Columbia V7P 1S8
Tel: (604) 985-8011 (R)

Chintzy's
1518 Dresden Row
Halifax, Nova Scotia B3J 2K2
Tel: (902) 425-7429 (R)

Draperies Unlimited
300 Nantucket Boulevard
Scarborough, Ontario M1P 2P4
Tel: (416) 285-8288 (M) (T)

Drapes and More Inc.
80 Alexdon Road
Downsview, Ontario M3J 2B3
Tel: (416) 631-7556 (R)

John Mark Designs
1953 Gerrard Street East
Toronto, Ontario M4E 2A9
Tel: (416) 699-6238 (R)

Louis Interiors Inc.
120 Orfus Road
North York, Ontario M6A 1L9
Tel: (416) 785-9909 (M)

Mountain Furniture Co. Ltd.
4640 Pacific Road N.E.
Calgary, Alberta T2E 5S5
Tel: (403) 230-0064 (M) (R)

Paramount Custom Built Upholstering Ltd.
1176 Bloor Street West
Toronto, Ontario M6H 1N1
Tel: (416) 533-8261 (R)

Robert Custom Upholstery Ltd.
1710 Midland Avenue
Scarborough, Ontario M1P 3C7
Tel: (416) 755-3121 (R)

Silva Upholstery Inc.
80 Alexdon Road
Downsview, Ontario M3J 2B3
Tel: (416) 638-9595 (M) (R)

Fabrics, Linens, Wallcoverings

Appel
321 Davenport Road
Toronto, Ontario M5R 1K5
Tel: (416) 922-3935 (T)

Arthur Sanderson & Sons
(Phone for nearest dealer)
Unit 302
1595-16th Avenue
Richmond Hill, Ontario
L4B 3N9
Tel: (416) 731-2570 (M) (R)

B.B. Bargoon's
(Phone for nearest location)
201 Whitehall Road
Markham, Ontario L3R 9Y3
Tel: (416) 475-3172 (R)

Baumann Fabrics Ltd.
302 King Street East
Toronto, Ontario M5A 1K6
Tel: (416) 869-1221 (T)

Boutiques Descamps
(Phone for nearest location)
130 Bloor Street West
Toronto, Ontario M5S lN5
Tel: (4l6) 967-6980 (R)

Brunschwig & Fils
320 Davenport Road
Toronto, Ontario M5R 1K6
Tel: (416) 968-0699 (T)

Chintz & Co.
(Phone for locations in Victoria, Calgary, and Edmonton)
1180 Marine Drive
North Vancouver,
British Columbia V7P 1S8
Tel: (604) 985-8011 (R)

Collections Au Lit Inc.
Suite 404
642, rue de Courcelle
Montreal, Quebec H4C 3C5
Tel: (514) 933-5070 (R)

Dome Fabrics Limited
533 College Street
Toronto, Ontario M6G 1A8
Tel: (416) 924-1178 (R)

Dressmakers' Supply
1325 Bay Street
Toronto, Ontario M5R 2C5
Tel: (416) 922-6000 (R)

Fabric Solution, The
240 Carlton Street
Toronto, Ontario M5A 2L1
Tel: (416) 923-8841 (R)

H. Brown Ribbons Ltd.
530 Adelaide Street West
Toronto, Ontario M5V 1T5
Tel: (416) 364-4397 (M)

Habert Associates Limited
170 Bedford Road
Toronto, Ontario M5R 2K9
Tel: (416) 960-5323 (T)

Hazelton House
234 Davenport Road
Toronto, Ontario M5R lJ6
Tel: (4l6) 925-4779 (T)

Jeff Brown Fine Fabrics Limited
320 Davenport Road
Toronto, Ontario M5R 1K6
Tel: (416) 968-0859 (T)

Joanne Fabrics Inc.
Unit 4
1090 Aerowood Drive
Mississauga, Ontario L4W 1Y5
Tel: (416) 624-2744 (T)

Keyser Collection
(Phone for nearest dealer)
Suite 204
400, rue St-Jacques ouest
Montreal, Quebec H2Y lSl
Tel: (514) 987-1565 (M)

Kobe Fabrics Ltd.
267 Davenport Road
Toronto, Ontario M5R 1J9
Tel: (416) 968-1921 (T)

Kravet Fabrics
320 Davenport Road
Toronto, Ontario M5R 2K9
Tel: (416) 921-1262 (T)

Mills Wallcoverings Ltd.
80 Tycos Drive
Toronto, Ontario M6B 1V9
Tel: (416) 782-1164 (T)

Moore-Pearsall Leathers Ltd.
47 Front Street East
Toronto, Ontario M5E 1B3
Tel: (416) 363-5881 (R)

Nash James International
26 Duncan Street
Toronto, Ontario M5V 2B9
Tel: (416) 977-6274 (M)

Offray Ribbon Canada Inc.
4060, rue Ste-Catherine ouest
Montreal, Quebec H3Z 2Z3
Tel: (514) 931-3721 (M)

Ontario Wallcoverings
462 Front Street West
Toronto, Ontario M5V 1B6
Tel: (416) 593-4519 (T)

Phoenix Floor and Wall Products
111 Westmore Drive
Rexdale, Ontario M9V 3Y6
Tel: (416) 745-4200 (M)

Pratesi Linens of Canada
1448, rue Sherbrooke ouest
Montreal, Quebec H3G 1K4
Tel: (514) 285-8909 (R) (T)

Reid & Lyons Decorative Trims
444 St. Germain Avenue
Toronto, Ontario M5M lX1
Tel: (4l6) 789-0413 (R)

Robert Allen Fabrics (Canada) Ltd.
321 Davenport Road
Toronto, Ontario M5R 1K5
Tel: (416) 323-3493 (T)

Sheridan
87 Avenue Road
Toronto, Ontario M5R 3R9
Tel: (416) 920-6627 (R)

Stitsky's Inc., The Original
754 Bathurst Street
Toronto, Ontario M5S 2R6
Tel: (416) 537-2633 (R)

Sunworthy Wallcoverings
195 Walker Drive
Brampton, Ontario L6T 3Z9
Tel: (416) 791-8788 (M) (R)

Telio & Cie Ltd.
1407, rue de la Montagne
Montreal, Quebec H3G 1Z3
Tel: (514) 842-9116

113 Dupont Street
Toronto, Ontario M5R 1V4
Tel: (416) 968-2020 (T)

Tissa Inc.
146 Dupont Street
Toronto, Ontario M5R 1V2
Tel: (416) 964-8883 (T)

Val Abel Industries Ltd.
777 Alness Street
Downsview, Ontario M3J 2H8
Tel: (416) 661-2235 (T)

W.H. Bilbrough & Company Ltd.
326 Davenport Road
Toronto, Ontario M5R 1K6
Tel: (416) 960-1611 (T)

Flooring & Tiles

A. Peplak Hardwood Flooring Ltd.
Unit 3
4635 Burgoyne Street
Mississauga, Ontario L4N 1V9
Tel: (416) 238-8647 (R)

Acme Slate and Tile Co. Ltd.
21 Golden Gate Court
Scarborough, Ontario M1P 3A4
Tel: (416) 293-3664 (R)

Armstrong World Industries Canada Ltd.
(Phone for nearest dealer)
Suite 201
2233 Argentia Road
Mississauga, Ontario L5N 2X7
Tel: (416) 826-4832 (M)

Barker Tiles
(Phone for nearest dealer)
105, rue Barker
Cowansville, Quebec J2K 2P8
Tel: (514) 263-0222 (M)

Bruce Hardwood Flooring
(Dealers across Canada, phone for nearest location)
16803 Dallas Parkway
Dallas, Texas 75248
Tel: 1-800-334-4064 (M) (R)

C.B. Marble Craft Ltd.
17 Airview Road
Rexdale, Ontario M9W 4P1
Tel: (416) 741-1585 (M) (R)

C.S.F. Interior Finishes
P.O. Box 482
Gormley, Ontario L0H 1G0
Tel: (416) 883-1009 (M) (R)

Caledonia Marble Co. Ltd.
167 Bentworth Avenue
Toronto, Ontario M6A 1P6
Tel: (416) 256-0251 (M)

Canaroma
(Phone for nearest dealer)
3200 Steeles Avenue West
Concord, Ontario L4K 3B2
Tel: (416) 661-8679 (M) (R)

Carrara Marble (1990) Inc.
280 Deerhide Crescent
Weston, Ontario M9M 2Y6
Tel: (416) 745-4506 (M) (T)

Ceratec Inc.
(Phone for nearest location)
100 Rossdean Drive
Weston, Ontario M9L 2S1
Tel: (416) 743-5514 (M)

Congoleum Corp.
(Phone for nearest dealer)
Unit 43
1313 Border Street
Winnipeg, Manitoba R3H 0X4
Tel: (204) 694-1652 (M)

Country Tiles
321 Davenport Road
Toronto, Ontario M5R 1K5
Tel: (416) 922-9214

5337, rue Ferrier
Montreal, Quebec H4P 1L9
Tel: (514) 733-7596 (R)

Crystal Tile & Marble Art
20 Apex Road
North York, Ontario M6A 2V2
Tel: (416) 781-5671 (R)

Domco Industries Limited
(Phone for nearest dealer)
1001, rue Yamaska est
Farnham, Quebec J2N 1J7
Tel: 1-800-363-9276 (M)

(R) Retail Store/ (T) Trade Showroom/ (M) Manufacturer or Distributor

Kahrs Wood Floors
(Phone for nearest dealer)
Goodfellow Inc.
P.O. Box 5001
5155 Highway 5
Burlington, Ontario L7R 3Y8
Tel: (416) 335-5800
Europlex International
Unit 3
2551 Vauxhall Place
Richmond, British Columbia
V6V 1Z5
Tel: (604) 276-9718 (M) (R)

Marchesi Marblecraft
3915 Kitchener Street
Burnaby, British Columbia
V5C 3L9
Tel: (604) 291-9221 (R)

Olympia Floor and Wall Tile Company Ltd.
1000 Lawrence Avenue West
Toronto, Ontario M6B 4A8
Tel: (416) 789-4122 (R)

Pacific Hardwood Ltd.
8 Oak Street
Weston, Ontario M9N 1R8
Tel: (416) 241-8631 (R)

Phoenix Floor & Wall Products
111 Westmore Drive
Rexdale, Ontario M9V 3Y6
Tel: (416) 745-4200 (M)

Ramca Tile Ltd.
(Phone for nearest dealer)
170 Tycos Drive
Toronto, Ontario M6B 1W8
Tel: (416) 781-5521
1085, rue Van Horne
Montreal, Quebec H2V 1J6
Tel: (514) 270-9192 (R)

Roberts Cork Company of Canada Ltd., The
(Phone for nearest dealer)
Unit 10
2576 Dunwin Drive
Mississauga, Ontario L5L 1J5
Tel: (416) 820-1072 (M)

Stradwicks Mississauga Ltd.
850 Dundas Street East
Mississauga, Ontario L4Y 2B8
Tel: (416) 279-4181 (R)

T.M.T. Marble Supply Co. Ltd.
900 Keele Street
Toronto, Ontario M6N 3E7
Tel: (416) 653-6111 (R)

Thomcorp Designs Ltd.
8 Finch Avenue West
Willowdale, Ontario M2N 6L1
Tel: (416) 250-6550 (R)

Trus Joist Canada Ltd.
(Phone for nearest dealer)
10277-154 Street
Surrey, British Columbia
V3R 0N0
Tel: (604) 588-7878 (M) (R)

Florists & Floral Designers

Blossoms Flower Shop
1 Rowanwood Avenue
Toronto, Ontario M4W 1Y5
Tel: (416) 960-8903 (R)

Covent Garden Flower Market
1116-B Yonge Street
Toronto, Ontario M4W 2L6
Tel: (416) 960-5800 (R)

Cruickshank's
1015 Mount Pleasant Road
Toronto, Ontario M4P 2M1
Tel: (416) 488-8292 (R)

Decorative Plants Canada Ltd.
Unit 7-8
5900 Amber Drive
Mississauga, Ontario L4W 2N3
Tel: (416) 624-0509 (T)

Demarco-Perpich
1096 Yonge Street
Toronto, Ontario M4W 2L6
Tel: (416) 967-0893 (R)

Doyle Walker Industries Inc.
Unit 5
2410 Dunwin Drive
Mississauga, Ontario L5L 1J9
Tel: (416) 828-2322 (M)

Earthrise
2954 West 4th Avenue
Vancouver, British Columbia
V6K 1R4
Tel: (604) 736-8404 (R)

Fiori Floral Designs
633 St. Clair Avenue West
Toronto, Ontario M6C 1A7
Tel: (416) 658-0715 (R)

Garden Rooms
1905 West 1st Avenue
Vancouver, British Columbia
V6J 1G7
Tel: (604) 736-6688 (R)

Gardens Antique
3518 Main Street
Vancouver, British Columbia
V5V 3N3
Tel: (604) 867-2311 (R)

Parklane Nurseries
P.O. Box 249
Gormley, Ontario L0H 1G0
Tel: (416) 887-5851 (R)

Pinks
12411 Stony Plain Road
Edmonton, Alberta T5N 3N3
Tel: (403) 488-0957 (R)

Plant Warehouse, The
1290 Bay Street
Toronto, Ontario M5R 2C3
Tel: (416) 964-7020 (R)

Poppies
153 Dunvegan Road
Toronto, Ontario M5P 2N8
Tel: (416) 484-6200 (R)

Rose Patch, The
Suite M6
379 Adelaide Street West
Toronto, Ontario M5V 1S5
Tel: (416) 594-9758 (T)

Sheridan Nurseries
(Phone for nearest location)
4077 Highway 7 East
Unionville, Ontario L3R 1L5
Tel: (416) 477-2253 (R)

Sissinghurst Ltd.
50 Carroll Street
Toronto, Ontario M4M 3G3
Tel: (416) 461-7217 (T)

Thomas Hobbs Florist
2127 West 41st Avenue
Vancouver, British Columbia
V6M 1Z6
Tel: (604) 263-2601 (R)

Weall & Cullen Nurseries
(Phone for nearest location)
4300 Steeles Avenue East
Markham, Ontario L3R 8G8
Tel: (416) 477-4477 (R)

Furniture

Area Group Inc.
334 King Street East
Toronto, Ontario M5A 1K8
Tel: (416) 367-5850 (T)

Artisateck
(Phone for nearest dealer)
108, Carré Gallery
Montreal, Quebec H3C 3R3
Tel: (514) 939-1234 (M)

Aziz Design Inc.
493 Davenport Road
Toronto, Ontario M4V 1B7
Tel: (416) 921-3809 (R)

Bagnald's Heritage Furniture
P.O. Box 177
Windsor Junction, Nova Scotia
B0N 7V0
Tel: (902) 860-1685 (R)

Banister's Furniture
(Phone for nearest dealer)
541 Bailey Street East
Ajax, Ontario L1S 3C2
Tel: (416) 686-4737 (M)

Barrymore Furniture Co Ltd.
1137 King Street West
Toronto, Ontario M6K 1E2
Tel: (416) 532-2891 (M)

Bass River Chairs
(Phone for nearest location)
936 Bedford Highway
Bedford, Nova Scotia B4A 3P1
Tel: (902) 835-5666
60 Highfield Park Drive
Dartmouth, Nova Scotia
B3A 4R9
Tel: (902) 465-2277
Highfield Square
1100 Main Street
Moncton, New Brunswick
E1C 1H4
Tel: (506) 856-7176 (R)

Bateman Furniture Company
Unit 5
230 Bayview Drive
Barrie, Ontario L4N 4Y8
Tel: (705) 722-7775 (R)

Bonaventure Furniture Industries
146 Dupont Street
Toronto, Ontario M5R 1V2
Tel: (416) 961-5900 (T)

Brunschwig & Fils
320 Davenport Road
Toronto, Ontario M5R 1K6
Tel: (416) 968-0699 (T)

Cabinetworks Ltd.
45 Borden Avenue
Dartmouth, Nova Scotia
B3B 1C7
Tel: (902) 468-8118 (R)

Cambridge Interiors Inc.
(Phone for dealer nearest you)
415 Dundas Street
Cambridge, Ontario N1R 5R5
Tel: (519) 740-0322 (M)

Canadian Windsor Chairmaking
Unit 13
422 North Rivermede Road
Concord, Ontario L4K 3R5
Tel: (416) 738-8003 (M) (R)

Cantu Interiors
2562 Eglinton Avenue West
Toronto, Ontario M6M 1T4
Tel: (416) 653-3353 (R)

Capability
493 Davenport Road
Toronto, Ontario M4V 1B7
Tel: (416) 962-1859 (R)

Clutter's Art Deco Gallery
653 Queen Street East
Toronto, Ontario M4M 1G4
Tel: (416) 461-3776 (R)

Codd & Company
Suite 216
160 Pears Avenue
Toronto, Ontario M5R 1T2
Tel: (416) 923-0066 (T)

Concept B
Unit W3
388 Carlaw Avenue
Toronto, Ontario M4M 2T4
Tel: (416) 462-1700 (T)

Copacetic Woodwork & Design Ltd.
284 Carlaw Avenue
Toronto, Ontario M4M 2S8
Tel: (416) 462-1177 (R)

Decor Action
6900 Airport Road
Mississauga, Ontario L4V 1E8
Tel: (416) 247-0026 (R)

Diane Watts International Inc.
Suite 203
160 Pears Avenue
Toronto, Ontario M5R 1T2
Tel: (416) 961-2887 (R) (T)

Foley's Furniture & Appliances
Box 128
511 Hume Street
Collingwood, Ontario L9Y 4H9
Tel: (705) 445-0661 (R)

Fraser's Furniture Showroom
8300, chemin Devonshire
Montreal, Quebec H4P 2P7
Tel: (514) 731-7518 (R)

Gibbard Furniture
(Phone for nearest dealer)
88 Dundas Street East
Napanee, Ontario K7R 3L7
Tel: (613) 354-3331 (M)

Heidecker Interiors
2273 Dundas Street West
Mississauga, Ontario L5K 2L8
Tel: (416) 828-6570 (R)

House of Viking, The
5200 Dixie Road
Mississauga, Ontario L4W 1E4
Tel: (416) 625-8811 (R)

Intarc Limited
147 Davenport Road
Toronto, Ontario M5R 1J1
Tel: (416) 924-7111 (R)

Italinteriors
359 King Street East
Toronto, Ontario M5A 1L1
Tel: (416) 366-9540 (T)

Joan Eiley & Associates Ltd.
326 Davenport Road
Toronto, Ontario M5R 1K6
Tel: (416) 968-0778 (T)

Jordan's Interiors Ltd.
1470 West Broadway
Vancouver, British Columbia
V6H 1H4
Tel: (604) 733-1174 (R)

Kaufman Galleries
(Phone for nearest dealer)
201 Balsam Street
Collingwood, Ontario L9Y 3Y7
Tel: (705) 445-6000 (R)

Kennedy Galleries
109 Kennedy Road South
Brampton, Ontario L6W 3G3
Tel: (416) 453-5213 (R)

Keyser Collection
(Phone for nearest dealer)
Suite 204
400, rue St-Jacques ouest
Montreal, Quebec H2Y 1S1
Tel: (514) 987-1565 (M)

Legends
250 Garyray Drive
North York, Ontario M9L 1P1
Tel: (416) 749-9330 (T)

L'Image Design
7100 Warden Road
Unionville, Ontario L3R 8B5
Tel: (416) 475-7703 (R)

Living Rooms Ltd.
The Murray Premises
Beck's Cove
St. John's, Newfoundland
A1C 6H1
Tel: (709) 753-2099 (R)

Lumacryl
(Phone for nearest dealer)
160 West Beaver Creek Road
Richmond Hill, Ontario
L4B 1G4
Tel: (416) 731-4556 (M) (R)

Manor House
600 Bedford Highway
Halifax, Nova Scotia B3M 2L8
Tel: (902) 445-3250 (R)

Mobilier Philippe Dagenais
(Phone for nearest location)
116, rue Main
Granby, Quebec J2G 2V2
Tel: (514) 372-8366 (R)

(R) Retail Store/ (T) Trade Showroom/ (M) Manufacturer or Distributor

Murray's Ironworks
c/o Joan Eiley & Associates Ltd.
326 Davenport Road
Toronto, Ontario M5R 1K6
Tel: (416) 968-0778 (T)

Nienkamper
300 King Street East
Toronto, Ontario M5A 1K4
Tel: (416) 362-3434 (T)

Northeast Homes Co. Ltd.
P.O. Box 654
Bathurst, New Brunswick
E2A 3Z6
Tel: (506) 546-3301 (R)

Ottoman Empire Inc.
Suite 221
276 Carlaw Avenue
Toronto, Ontario M4M 2A9
Tel: (416) 466-0872 (R)

Pacific Passage Interiors Inc.
(Phone for nearest location)
8400 Woodbine Avenue
Markham, Ontario L3R 2K4
Tel: (416) 479-1050 (R)

Palazzetti Inc.
(Phone for nearest dealer)
431 Carlingview Drive
Rexdale, Ontario M9W 5G7
Tel: (416) 674-2599 (M)

Palliser Furniture
(Phone for nearest dealer)
55 Vulcan Avenue
Winnipeg, Manitoba R3G 1B9
Tel: (204) 988-5600 (M)

Palma Brava
3050 Yonge Street
Toronto, Ontario M4N 2K4
Tel: (416) 488-5636 (R)

Panache Design
361 King Street East
Toronto, Ontario M5A 1L1
Tel: (416) 369-0084 (R) (T)

Paramount Furnishings
Suite 101
5520 Minoru Boulevard
Richmond, British Columbia
V6X 2A9
Tel: (604) 273-0155 (R)

Pascals
(Phone for nearest location)
901, rue de Bleury
Montreal, Quebec H2Z 1M5
Tel: (514) 878-5400 (R)

Patio Comfort
881 Richmond Road
Ottawa, Ontario K2A 0G8
Tel: (613) 728-1773 (R)

Patio Gallery
1701 Avenue Road
Toronto, Ontario M5M 3Y3
Tel: (416) 789-7677 (R)

Patiorama Bourque
16641, rue 117
St. Antoine Mirabel, Quebec
J7Z 5T4
Tel: (514) 438-1134 (R)

Pine Design
Suite 115
401 Richmond Street West
Toronto, Ontario M5V 1Y2
Tel: (416) 340-2532 (M) (R)

Prismatique Designs Limited
265 Davenport Road
Toronto, Ontario M5R 1J9
Tel: (416) 961-7333 (T)

Quess Furniture
157 Princess Street
Toronto, Ontario M5A 4M4
Tel: (416) 366-4744 (M) (R) (T)

Regency Interiors Inc.
105 Howden Road
Scarborough, Ontario M1R 3C7
Tel: (416) 752-0044 (R)

Ridpath's Fine Furniture Ltd.
906 Yonge Street
Toronto, Ontario M4W 2J2
Tel: (416) 920-4441 (R)

Roche Bobois
(Phone for nearest location)
2131 Yonge Street
Toronto, Ontario M4S 2A7
Tel: (416) 487-0222
1010 Mainland Street
Vancouver, British Columbia
V6B 2T6
Tel: (604) 669-5443 (M) (R)

Salco Furniture Corp.
(Phone for nearest dealer)
Units 4 & 5
20 Steelcase Road West
Markham, Ontario L3R 1B2
Tel: (416) 475-8353 (M)

Sata Manufacturing
(Phone for nearest dealer)
63 St. Regis Crescent North
Downsview, Ontario M3J 1Y9
Tel: (416) 638-9235 (M) (T)

Savoia Chair Frames Ltd.
65 Densley Avenue
Toronto, Ontario M6M 2P5
Tel: (416) 244-4900 (T)

Shelagh's of Canada Limited
354 Davenport Road
Toronto, Ontario M5R 1K6
Tel: (416) 924-7331 (R) (T)

Sklar-Pepplar Furniture Galleries
(Phone for nearest dealer)
2815 Matheson Boulevard East
Mississauga, Ontario L4W 4P7
Tel: (416) 238-6762 (M) (R)

Steek's Fine Furniture Ltd.
2627 Portage Avenue
Winnipeg, Manitoba R3J 0P7
Tel: (204) 888-8360 (R)

Steptoe & Wife
322 Geary Avenue
Toronto, Ontario M6H 2C7
Tel: (416) 530-4200 (R)

Suttles and Seawinds
(Phone for nearest location)
466 Main Street
Mahone Bay, Nova Scotia
B0J 2E0
Tel: (902) 624-6177 (R)

Tendex Silko Inc.
264 The Esplanade
Toronto, Ontario M5A 4J6
Tel: (416) 361-1555 (R) (T)

Thomasville Furniture Industries Inc.
(Dealers across Canada, phone for nearest location)
P.O. Box 339
401 East Main Street
Thomasville, North Carolina
27361
Tel: (919) 472-4000 (M)

Triede Design
460, rue McGill
Montreal, Quebec H2Y 2H2
Tel: (514) 398-0602 (T)

UpCountry Canada Inc.
247 King Street East
Toronto, Ontario M5A 1J9
Tel: (416) 366-8806 (R)

Vanderwerff & Brown
136 Hallam Street
Toronto, Ontario M6H 1X1
Tel: (416) 535-1107 (R)

Vogel of Canada
(Phone for nearest dealer)
176 Milvan Drive
Weston, Ontario M9L 1Z9
Tel: 749-2954 (M)

William Switzer & Associates Ltd.
(Phone for nearest dealer)
6-611 Alexander Street
Vancouver, British Columbia
V6A 1E1
Tel: (604) 255-5911 (M) (T)

Windsor Decor
278 Newkirk Road
Richmond Hill, Ontario
L4C 3G7
Tel: (416) 884-8159 (T)

Windsor House Collection
1311 Alness Street
Concord, Ontario L4K 1E8
Tel: (416) 665-9300 (M)

Wise Kalan & Associates
160 Pears Avenue
Toronto, Ontario M5R 1T2
Tel: (416) 975-1564 (T)

Wood Gallery, The
250 Garyray Drive
North York, Ontario M9L 1P1
Tel: (416) 749-9330 (T)

Ziggurat Concept Inc.
254 King Street East
Toronto, Ontario M5A 1K3
Tel: (416) 362-5900 (R)

Housewares & Accessories

A Step Up
Park Lane Mall
5657 Spring Garden Road
Halifax, Nova Scotia B3J 3R4
Tel: (902) 422-9155 (R)

Amos Pewterers Ltd.
589 Main Street
Mahone Bay, Nova Scotia
B0J 2E0
Tel: (902) 624-9547 (R)

At My Table
207 Queen's Quay West
Toronto, Ontario M5J 1A7
Tel: (416) 861-9056 (R)

Balfor & Co.
(Phone for nearest dealer)
1830 Walkley Road
Ottawa, Ontario K1H 8K3
Tel: (613) 731-3275 (M)

Bath n' Bedtime
(Phone for nearest location)
1911 Dundas Street East
Mississauga, Ontario L4X 1N1
Tel: (416) 622-7715 (R)

Bianco by Sarahband
130 Avenue Road
Toronto, Ontario M5R 2H6
Tel: (416) 929-9676 (R)

Birdsall-Worthington Pottery Ltd.
590 Main Street
Mahone Bay, Nova Scotia
B0J 2E0
Tel: (902) 624-9447 (R)

Bleu Nuit
15 Hazelton Avenue
Toronto, Ontario M5R 2E1
Tel: (416) 925-4593
3913, rue St-Denis
Montreal, Quebec H2W 2M4
Tel: (514) 843-5702 (R)

Bronson's China and Gifts
2 Steeles Avenue West
Thornhill, Ontario L4J 1A1
Tel: (416) 881-9930 (R)

Canfloyd Trading Limited
55-F East Beaver Creek Road
Richmond Hill, Ontario
L4B 1E8
Tel: (416) 731-2821 (M)

Ceramica Artistica Inc.
3220 Dufferin Street
Toronto, Ontario M6A 2T3
Tel: (416) 785-0057 (R)

Christofle
(Phone for nearest dealer)
1476, rue Sherbrooke
Montreal, Quebec H3G 1L3
Tel: (514) 987-1242
Ogilvy Building
1307, rue Ste-Catherine ouest
Montreal, Quebec H3G 1P7
Tel: (514) 987-1242 (M)

Clutter's Art Deco Gallery
653 Queen Street East
Toronto, Ontario M4M 1G4
Tel: (416) 461-3776 (R)

Coffee Gourmet Centre
4868, rue Sherbrooke ouest
Westmount
Montreal, Quebec H3Z 1H1
Tel: (514) 369-0368 (R)

Crabtree & Evelyn
(Phone for nearest location)
Unit 5
23 Railside Road
Don Mills, Ontario M3A 1B2
Tel: (416) 391-4200
Pacific Centre Mall
701 West Georgia Street
Vancouver, British Columbia
V7Y 1E7
Tel: (604) 662-7211
Banker's Hall
315-8th Avenue Southwest
Calgary, Alberta T2P 4K1
Tel: (403) 263-0613
Place Montreal Trust
1500, avenue McGill College
Montreal, Quebec H3A 3J5
Tel: (514) 499-9729
Brunswick Square
39 King Street
St. John, New Brunswick
E2L 4W3
Tel: (506) 648-9508 (R)

Danesco Inc.
(Phone for nearest dealer)
18111, route Transcanadienne
Kirkland, Quebec H9J 3K1
Tel: (514) 694-9111 (M)

Dansk International Designs
(Phone for nearest dealer)
60 Horner Avenue
Toronto, Ontario M8Z 4X3
Tel: (416) 259-1127 (M)

Denby Canada Limited
(Phone for nearest dealer)
1780 Sismet Road
Mississauga, Ontario
L4W 1W8
Tel: (416) 624-0490 (M)

Du Verre
307 Queen Street West
Toronto, Ontario M5V 2A4
Tel: (416) 593-0182 (R)

Fancy That
Park Lane Mall
5657 Spring Garden Road
Halifax, Nova Scotia B3J 3R4
Tel: (902) 429-5566 (R)

Fireplace Shop Ltd., The
379 Eglinton Avenue West
Toronto, Ontario M5N 1A3
Tel: (416) 483-4085 (R)

Frida Craft Store Ltd.
39 Front Street East
Toronto, Ontario M5E 1B3
Tel: (416) 366-3169 (R)

General Store, The
Hazelton Lanes
55 Avenue Road
Toronto, Ontario M5R 3L2
Tel: (416) 323-1527 (R)

Goodman's China & Gifts
(Phone for nearest location)
221 Wilmington Avenue
Downsview, Ontario M3H 5K1
Tel: (416) 638-2630 (R)

(R) Retail Store/ (T) Trade Showroom/ (M) Manufacturer or Distributor

Henry Birks & Sons
(Phone for nearest location)
1240, Carré Phillip
Montreal, Quebec H3B 3H4
Tel: (514) 397-2511 (M) (R)

Heritage Pewter
Box 120
5657 Spring Garden Road
Halifax, Nova Scotia B3J 3R4
Tel: (902) 422-7667 (R)

Holt Renfrew Co.
(Phone for nearest location)
50 Bloor Street West
Toronto, Ontario M4W 1A1
Tel: (416) 922-2333 (R)

J.G. Durand Crystal
(Phone for nearest dealer)
Suite 550
14, Place du Commerce
Nun's Island, Quebec H3E 1T5
Tel: (514) 766-7900 (M)

James House of Fine China, The
1869 Upper Water Street
Halifax, Nova Scotia B3J 1S9
Tel: (902) 429-2355 (R)

K. Howling & Associates Inc.
(Phone for nearest dealer)
9-135 East Beaver Creek Road
Richmond Hill, Ontario
L4B 1E2
Tel: (416) 764-5399 (M)

K.R. Thompson Pottery
492 Main Street
Mahone Bay, Nova Scotia
B0J 2E0
Tel: (902) 624-9069 (R)

La Loggia
Suite 311
160 Pears Avenue
Toronto, Ontario M5R 1T2
Tel: (416) 921-8681 (R)

Lato Design
100 Scollard Street
Toronto, Ontario M5R 1G2
Tel: (416) 323-0472 (R)

Les Must de Cartier
(Phone for nearest location)
102 Bloor Street West
Toronto, Ontario M5S 1M8
Tel: (416) 964-0003 (R)

Londens
92-C Scollard Street
Toronto, Ontario M5R 1G2
Tel: (416) 961-9858 (R)

Mad Company
140 Avenue Road
Toronto, Ontario M5R 2H6
Tel: (416) 967-5586 (R)

Main Course, The
1910 Avenue Road
Toronto, Ontario M5M 3Z8
Tel: (416) 787-7742 (R)

Mikasa Import & Domestic Trading Co. of Canada Ltd.
(Phone for nearest dealer)
161 McPherson Street
Markham, Ontario L3R 3L3
Tel: (416) 474-0880 (M)

Mills Brothers Ltd.
5486 Spring Garden Road
Halifax, Nova Scotia B3J 1G4
Tel: (902) 429-6111 (R)

Nastri
609 Mount Pleasant Road
Toronto, Ontario M4S 2M5
Tel: (416) 484-1647 (R)

Nitty Gritty Reproductions Co.
163 Queen Street East
Toronto, Ontario M5A 1S1
Tel: (416) 364-1393 (R)

Noritake Canada Limited
(Phone for nearest dealer)
90 Nugget Avenue
Agincourt, Ontario M1S 3A7
Tel: (416) 291-2946 (M)

Northdale Trading Limited
55-D East Beaver Creek Road
Richmond Hill, Ontario
L4B 1E8
Tel: (416) 731-9535 (M)

Pack-Rat
1062 Yonge Street
Toronto, Ontario M4W 2L5
Tel: (416) 924-5613 (R)

Palate, The
Hazelton Lanes
87 Avenue Road
Toronto, Ontario M5R 3R9
Tel: (416) 944-9400

2 First Canadian Place
18 Lower Concourse
Toronto, Ontario M5X 1C7
Tel: (416) 777-0700 (R)

Pelmar Distributing
(Phone for nearest dealer)
265 Eddystone Avenue
Downsview, Ontario M3N 1H6
Tel: (416) 742-1488 (M)

Primavera Interior Accessories Ltd.
Suites 111 & 215
160 Pears Avenue
Toronto, Ontario M5R 1T2
Tel: (416) 921-3334 (T)

Quasi Modo
789 Queen Street West
Toronto, Ontario M6J 1G1
Tel: (416) 366-8370 (R)

Quintessence
1657 Bayview Avenue
Toronto, Ontario M4G 3C1
Tel: (416) 482-1252 (R)

Roots Canada Ltd.
(Phone for nearest location)
1162 Caledonia Road
Toronto, Ontario M5A 2W5
Tel: (416) 781-3574 (R)

Rosenthal China (Canada) Ltd.
(Phone for nearest dealer)
55-G East Beaver Creek Road
Richmond Hill, Ontario
L4B 1E5
Tel: (416) 886-2270 (M)

Royal Doulton Canada Limited
(Phone for nearest dealer)
850 Progress Avenue
Scarborough, Ontario M1H 3C4
Tel: (416) 431-4202 (M)

Sarahband
118 Yorkville Avenue
Toronto, Ontario M5R 1C2
Tel: (416) 927-0971 (R)

Second Story, The
207 Queen's Quay West
Toronto, Ontario M5J 1A7
Tel: (416) 868-6519 (R)

Southwest Mex Atlas Design
1132 Queen Street West
Toronto, Ontario M6J 1J3
Tel: (416) 535-6868 (R)

Summerhill Hardware Limited
24 Birch Avenue
Toronto, Ontario M4V 1C8
Tel: (416) 962-0471 (R)

Umbra Shades Ltd.
2358 Midland Avenue
Scarborough, Ontario M1S 1P8
Tel: (416) 299-0088 (M)

Urban Mode Inc.
389 Queen Street West
Toronto, Ontario M5V 2A5
Tel: (416) 591-8834 (R)

Villeroy & Boch Tableware Ltd.
(Phone for nearest dealer)
55-A East Beaver Creek Road
Richmond Hill, Ontario
L4B 1E8
Tel: (416) 731-6260 (M)

Waterford Wedgwood Canada Inc.
(Phone for nearest dealer)
20 West Beaver Creek Road
Richmond Hill, Ontario
L4B 3L6
Tel: (416) 886-6400 (M)

William Ashley China
50 Bloor Street West
Toronto, Ontario M4W 3L8
Tel: (416) 964-2900 (R)

William Smith & Sons / Portmerion
(Phone for nearest dealer)
20 Voyageur Court South
Rexdale, Ontario M9W 5M7
Tel: (416) 675-3755 (M)

Lighting

Accent Lighting
5570 Kennedy Road
Mississauga, Ontario L4Z 2A9
Tel: (416) 890-7366 (M)

Angle International Showroom
296, rue St-Paul ouest
Montreal, Quebec
Tel: (514) 284-2619 (T)

Artemide
9200, Place Picasso
Montreal, Quebec H1P 3J8
Tel: (514) 325-2690 (M)

Au Courant
354 Davenport Road
Toronto, Ontario M5R 1K6
Tel: (416) 922-5611

4201, rue Ste-Catherine
Montreal, Quebec H3Z 1P6
Tel: (514) 932-3415 (R)

Avenue Lighting
110 Avenue Road
Toronto, Ontario M5R 2H4
Tel: (416) 967-0799 (R)

Frederick Ramond
(Dealers across Canada, phone for nearest location)
16121 South Carmenita Road
Cerritos, California 90701
Tel: (213) 926-1361 (M)

Harris & Roome Supply Limited
P.O. Box 935
260 Brownlow Avenue
Dartmouth, Nova Scotia
B2Y 3Z6
Tel: (902) 468-3887 (R)

Lamp Shades Unlimited Inc.
Unit 45
2721 Markham Road
Scarborough, Ontario M1S 3B2
Tel: (416) 299-3113 (M)

Lighting Unlimited
(Phone for nearest location)
131 Cartwright Avenue
Toronto, Ontario M6A 1V4
Tel: (416) 781-5691 (R)

Lightolier Canada Ltd.
(Phone for nearest dealer)
3015, rue Louis A. Amos
Lachine, Quebec H8T 1C4
Tel: (514) 636-0670 (M)

Magic Lite Ltd.
(Phone for nearest dealer)
Unit 3
1075 Meyerside Drive
Mississauga, Ontario L5T 1M3
Tel: (416) 564-0026 (M)

Nadair
(Phone for nearest dealer)
2600, boulevard Le Corbusier
Laval, Quebec H7S 2G3
Tel: (514) 686-0770 (M)

Raak of Canada
(Phone for nearest dealer)
149 Church Street
Toronto, Ontario M5B 1Y4
Tel: (416) 863-1990 (M) (R)

Sescolite Lighting
1461 Castlefield Avenue
Toronto, Ontario M6M 1Y4
Tel: (416) 651-6570 (R)

Sistemalux
(Phone for nearest dealer)
251 King Street East
Toronto, Ontario M5A 1K2
Tel: (416) 362-9611

365 Eglinton Avenue West
Toronto, Ontario
M5A 1N3
Tel: (416) 322-6422 (R)

Sunrise Lighting Distributors (Mar.) Ltd.
5755 Young Street
Halifax, Nova Scotia B3K 1Z9
Tel: (902) 454-8565 (R)

Tai Pan Lighting Company
(Phone for nearest dealer)
Unit 11
1521 Trinity Drive
Mississauga, Ontario L5T 1P6
Tel: (416) 670-3260 (M)

Turn of the Century Lighting
112 Sherbourne Street
Toronto, Ontario M5A 2R2
Tel: (416) 362-6203 (R)

Union Electric
(Phone for nearest dealer)
1491 Castlefield Avenue
Toronto, Ontario M6M 1Y5
Tel: (416) 652-2800 (M) (R)

Paint & Wallpaper

Ark Industries
R.R. 1
Bridgewater, Nova Scotia
B4V 2V9
Tel: (902) 543-5308 (R)

Arthur Sanderson & Sons
(Phone for nearest dealer)
Unit 302
1595-16th Avenue
Richmond Hill, Ontario
L4B 3N9
Tel: (416) 731-2570 (M) (R)

Benjamin Moore & Co.
(Phone for nearest dealer)
139 Mulock Avenue
Toronto, Ontario M6N 1G9
Tel: (416) 766-1173

7625-19th Street
Burnaby, British Columbia
V3N 2Z2
Tel: (604) 522-3931

9393, boulevard St-Michel
Montreal, Quebec H1Z 3H3
Tel: (514) 321-3330 (M)

ColorWorks Inc.
3667 Strawberry Hill
Halifax, Nova Scotia B3K 5A8
Tel: (902) 455-1335 (R)

Color Your World
(Phone for nearest dealer)
10 Carson Street
Toronto, Ontario M8W 3R5
Tel: (416) 259-3251 (R)

Crown Wallpaper Company
(Phone for nearest dealer)
88 Ronson Drive
Rexdale, Ontario M9W 1B9
Tel: (416) 245-2900 (T)

Decorlux (Division of International Wallcoverings)
(Phone for nearest dealer)
151 East Drive
Brampton, Ontario L6T 1B5
Tel: (416) 791-1547 (M)

Durabond Products
(Phone for nearest dealer)
59 Underwriter Road
Scarborough, Ontario M1R 3B4
Tel: (416) 759-4133 (M)

Exclusive Paints Ltd.
284 College Street
Toronto, Ontario M5T 1R9
Tel: (416) 921-5751 (R)

Glidden Paints
(Phone for nearest dealer)
8200 Keele Street
Concord, Ontario L4K 2A5
Tel: (416) 669-1020 (M)

Heritage Paint and Wallpaper
6438 Quinpool Road
Halifax, Nova Scotia B3L 1A8
Tel: (902) 429-4799 (R)

Homestead House Paint Co. Inc.
(Phone for nearest dealer)
109 Niagara Street
Toronto, Ontario M5V 1C3
Tel: (416) 864-1984 (M)

Metro Wallcoverings
(Phone for nearest dealer)
Unit B
2600 Steeles Avenue West
Concord, Ontario L4K 3C8
Tel: (416) 738-5177 (T)

Minwax
(Phone for nearest dealer)
245 Edward Street
Aurora, Ontario L4G 3M7
Tel: (416) 841-7600 (M)

Olympic Home Care Products
(Dealers across Canada, phone for nearest location)
37 South
1 PPG Place
Pittsburgh, Pennsylvania
15272
Tel: (412) 434-3768 (M)

Paint Colours Unlimited
502 Adelaide Street West
Toronto, Ontario M5V 1T2
Tel: (416) 366-2941 (R)

Para Inc.
(Phone for nearest dealer)
11 Kenview Boulevard
Brampton, Ontario L6T 5G5
Tel: (416) 792-0940 (M)

Plasti-Kote Incorporated
(Phone for nearest dealer)
7655 Tranmere Drive
Mississauga, Ontario L5S 1L4
Tel: (416) 671-8333 (M)

Pratt & Lambert Inc.
(Dealers across Canada, phone for nearest location)
P.O. Box 22
Buffalo, New York 14240
Tel: (716) 873-6000 (M)

Sico Inc.
(Phone for nearest dealer)
2505, avenue de la Metropole
Longeuil, Quebec J4G 1E5
Tel: (514) 527-5111 (M)

St. Clair Paint & Paper
(Phone for nearest location)
2600 Steeles Avenue West
Concord, Ontario L4K 3C8
Tel: (416) 738-0080 (R)

Sunworthy Wallcoverings
(Phone for nearest dealer)
195 Walker Drive
Brampton, Ontario L6T 3Z9
Tel: (416) 791-8788 (M)

Wallpaper Wagon
(Phone for nearest location)
Unit 6
3555 Don Mills Road
Willowdale, Ontario M2H 3N3
Tel: 1-800-461-0778 (R)

Special Decorative Effects

Applied Contracting & Decorating Ltd.
196 Wicksteed Avenue
Toronto, Ontario M4G 2B6
Tel: (416) 467-8920 (R)

Barbara Griffin
58-A Valhalla Boulevard
Scarborough, Ontario M1N 3B3
Tel: (416) 690-6487 (R)

Classic Architectural Coatings
Unit 23
2700 Dufferin Street
Toronto, Ontario M6B 3R1
Tel: (416) 789-7887 (M)

Creative Painting and Decorating
29 Wethered Street
London, Ontario N5Y 1G8
Tel: (519) 453-8539 (R)

David Bermann
25 Maclennan Avenue
Toronto, Ontario M4W 2Y5
Tel: (416) 972-6891 (R)

David Moss Special Effects Ltd.
3-37 Metcalfe Street
Toronto, Ontario M4X 1R7
Tel: (416) 921-2443 (T)

DeForest Studios Corp.
42 Victoria Park Avenue
Toronto, Ontario M4E 3R9
Tel: (416) 691-8971 (T)

Imperial Sales Agency
Unit 7
1170 Sheppard Avenue West
Downsview, Ontario M3K 2A3
Tel: (416) 636-1075 (T)

Octopus Products Ltd.
200 Geary Avenue
Toronto, Ontario M6H 2B9
Tel: (416) 531-5051 (R)

Plum's Emporium
131 Miranda Avenue
Toronto, Ontario M6P 3W8
Tel: (416) 782-9135 (R)

Ritins Studio
110 Parkhurst Boulevard
Toronto, Ontario M4G 2E6
Tel: (416) 467-8920 (T)

Stencil Shoppe, The
(By appointment only)
113 Roslin Avenue
Toronto, Ontario M4N 1Z3
Tel: (416) 483-5816 (R)

Tony Arnett Architectural Painting
Suite 2312
44 St. Joseph Street
Toronto, Ontario M4Y 2W4
Tel: (416) 963-4349 (T)

General

(Stores carrying a broad range of decorative items)

Absolutely Inc.
6 Roxborough Street West
Toronto, Ontario M5R 1T8
Tel: (416) 324-8351 (R)

Area Group Inc.
334 King Street East
Toronto, Ontario M5A 1K8
Tel: (416) 367-5850 (R)

Art Shoppe, The
2131 Yonge Street
Toronto, Ontario M4S 2A7
Tel: (416) 487-3211 (R)

Ashbrooks Department Store
(Phone for other locations)
Square One Shopping Centre
100 City Centre Drive
Mississauga, Ontario L5B 2C9
Tel: (416) 897-1611 (R)

B.B. Bargoon's
(Phone for nearest location)
201 Whitehall Drive
Markham, Ontario L3R 9Y3
Tel: (416) 475-3172 (R)

Babcock Zanner
118 Avenue Road
Toronto, Ontario M5R 1N5
Tel: (416) 920-8162 (R)

Bombay Company, The
(Phone for nearest location)
5905 Kennedy Road
Mississauga, Ontario L4Z 2G3
Tel: (416) 890-8800 or
1-800-668-1136 (R)

Chintz & Co.
(Phone for locations in Victoria, Calgary, and Edmonton)
1180 Marine Drive
North Vancouver,
British Columbia V7P 1S8
Tel: (604) 985-8011 (R)

Cricket on the Hearth
1360 Bedford Highway
Halifax, Nova Scotia B4A 1E2
Tel: (902) 835-5314 (R)

Cullen Country Barns
4300 Steeles Avenue East
Markham, Ontario L3R 8G8
Tel: (416) 477-4475 (R)

DeBoer's Furniture Ltd.
(Phone for nearest location)
275 Drumlin Circle
Concord, Ontario L4K 3E4
Tel: (416) 669-9455 (R)

Deck and Den
244-1st Avenue North
Saskatoon, Saskatchewan
S7K 1X1
Tel: (306) 653-5033 (R)

Decorating Shop, The
5980 Spring Garden Road
Halifax, Nova Scotia B3H 1Y7
Tel: (902) 425-3933 (R)

Eaton's
(Phone for nearest location)
290 Yonge Street
Toronto, Ontario M5B 1C8
Tel: (416) 343-2111 (R)

En Provence Inc.
68 Scollard Street
Toronto, Ontario M5R 1G2
Tel: (416) 975-9400 (R)

Filigree
1210 Yonge Street
Toronto, Ontario M4T 1W1
Tel: (416) 961-5223 (R)

Four Corners Gallery
5322 Yonge Street
North York, Ontario M2N 5R4
Tel: (416) 221-0653 (R) (T)

Hayward Interiors
203 Kenmount Road
St. John's, Newfoundland
A1B 3P9
Tel: (709) 720-3452 (R)

Heritage Interiors
224 Davenport Road
Toronto, Ontario M5R 1J8
Tel: (416) 922-6448 (R)

Hudson's Bay Co., The
(Phone for nearest locaton)
2 Bloor Street East
Toronto, Ontario M4W 3H7
Tel: (416) 972-4000 (R)

Idomo Furniture International
(Phone for nearest location)
4250 Dufferin Street
Downsview, Ontario M3H 5W4
Tel: (416) 630-3622 (R)

Ikea
(Phone for nearest location)
1065 Plains Road East
Burlington, Ontario L7T 2B7
Tel: (416) 637-9447 (R)

Joan Eiley & Associates Ltd.
326 Davenport Road
Toronto, Ontario M5R 1K6
Tel: 968-0778 (T)

Jordan's Interiors Ltd.
1470 West Broadway
Vancouver, British Columbia
V6H 1H4
Tel: (604) 733-1174 (R)

La Cache
Cornell Trading
(Phone for nearest location)
1619, rue William
Montreal, Quebec H3J 1R1
Tel: (514) 935-9295 (R)

Laura Ashley Shops
(Phone 1-800-363-3830 for other locations)
1171 Robson Street
Vancouver, British Columbia
V6E 1B5
Tel: (604) 688-8729

2110, rue Crescent
Montreal, Quebec H3G 2B8
Tel: (514) 284-9225

18 Hazelton Avenue
Toronto, Ontario M5R 2E2
Tel: (416) 922-7761 (R)

Mattinson-White Interior Design Ltd.
1259 Barrington Street
Halifax, Nova Scotia B3J 1Y2
Tel: (902) 422-2275 (R)

Oggo
221 Tenth Avenue S.W.
Calgary, Alberta T2R 0A4
Tel: (403) 237-6446 (R)

Pack-Rat Ltd.
1062 Yonge Street
Toronto, Ontario M4W 2L5
Tel: (416) 924-5613 (R)

Pier 1 Imports
(Phone for nearest location)
3015, rue Brabant-Marineau
Ville St. Laurent, Quebec
H4S 1R8
Tel: 1-800-361-6677 (R)

Pierre Deux
20 Hazelton Avenue
Toronto, Ontario M5R 2E2
Tel: (416) 944-1352 (R)

Ralph Lauren Home Collection
Hazelton Lanes
87 Avenue Road
Toronto, Ontario M5R 2G3
Tel: (416) 968-8686

1316, rue Sherbrooke ouest
Montreal, Quebec H3G 1H9
Tel: (514) 288-3988 (R)

Ridpath's Fine Furniture Ltd.
906 Yonge Street
Toronto, Ontario M4W 2J2
Tel: (416) 920-4441 (R)

Robert Simpson Co.
(Phone for nearest location)
176 Yonge Street
Toronto, Ontario M5C 2L7
Tel: (416) 861-9111 (R)

Sears Canada Inc.
(Phone for nearest location)
222 Jarvis Street
Toronto, Ontario M5B 2B8
Tel: (416) 362-1711 (R)

Shaw-Pezzo and Associates Inc.
80 Wingold Street
Toronto, Ontario M6B 1P5
Tel: (416) 784-4400 (T)

Taos Design
2009 Avenue Road
Toronto, Ontario M5M 4A5
Tel: (416) 322-3959 (R)

GLOSSARY

Accent A bright colour that contrasts with the basic colour scheme of a room.
Advancing colour A colour that makes rooms seem smaller by appearing to come towards the observer.
Antiquing A painting technique used to give a surface an aged appearance.
Apron The section of a sofa, chair, or table that connects the legs. It is also called a skirt.
Armoire A wardrobe, usually wooden, usually with double front doors.
Art Deco An architectural and design style popular in the 1920s and 1930s, featuring streamlined, geometric shapes.
Art Nouveau An architectural and design style first popular at the end of the nineteenth century and featuring elegant, stylized forms.
Aubusson A French carpet or tapestry, after the village of the same name. Usually a flat weave of soft pastel colours and floral patterns.
Ball foot The rounded turning at the base of the legs of a chest of drawers or chair. Commonly used on Mary and William furniture.
Baluster A less common name for banister. A spindle used to support a railing.
Banding A contrasting decorative strip of veneer inlay framing drawer fronts or table-tops. The banding's grain usually runs counter to the surface veneer.
Banquette A built-in bench or seat, usually upholstered.
Baroque A sixteenth-century style of design. Noted for extravagant curves, rich detailing, and bold, exaggerated scale.
Baseboard A board around the base of walls. Also called a skirting board.
Batik A Javanese technique for dyeing fabric with various colours. Wax is used to make parts of the material resistant to colouring.
Bauhaus A German school of design, founded by architect and designer Walter Gropius in 1919. Bauhaus made use of new technology and mass production. Often referred to as the beginning of Modernism.
Bay window A window projecting outward from walls of building.
Beading Small, semi-circular moulding used to outline the edges of a drawer.
Berber carpet A fleeced carpet with a nubbly pile.
Bergère A Louis Quinze and Seize chair with open upholstered sides and back.
Blanket box A trunk made of wood used for storing blankets and linens. Often kept at the foot of a bed.
Bonnet top The rounded top of a cabinet, made to resemble a woman's bonnet.
Bowfront The bulging front or sides of a chest. Common on French and Italian furniture of the late eighteenth century.
Bracket A right-angle support for a shelf.
Breakfront A cabinet for the display of china or books. Usually large.
Broadloom Carpet produced in widths over 1.8 m (6').
Brocade A heavy fabric with embossed pattern, used for drapes and upholstery.
Broken pediment A decorative triangle, with an interrupted apex, located at the top of a large bookcase, cabinet, or doorway.
Bureau A desk with built-in drawers. Sometimes known as a secretary.
Burl A decorative veneer. Usually golden brown.
Cabriole The curving leg of a chair, sofa, or table. The curve is usually completed by a tapered ankle and carved foot. A distinguishing feature of early Chippendale.
Café curtains Curtains suspended from a rod halfway up a window.
Camel back A sofa with an upward curving back. Commonly used in Chippendale-style sofas.
Canopy Fabric draped above a bed from the wall or a frame.
Canvas A heavy, closely woven fabric, usually made from cotton or synthetics.
Capital The top of a column. Different designs of capitals denote different architectural styles.
Carpet tiles Squares of carpet with finished, sealed edges.
Casement window A hinged window, usually opening its whole length.
Ceiling rose Decorative plasterwork, usually in the centre of a ceiling, from which light fixtures are suspended.
Chair rail The moulding above wall panelling at the level of a chair back. Originally intended to protect plaster. Also called a dado.
Chaise longue An upholstered reclining chair with a long seat or attached ottoman.
Chesterfield A sofa on short legs. Especially popular during the Victorian and Edwardian periods.
Chest-on-chest Also called a highboy or tallboy. Two stacked wooden chests, with the top usually smaller than the bottom.
Cheval glass A full-length, swinging mirror, hung between wooden posts on a stand.
Chiffonier A tall narrow chest with numerous shallow drawers of identical size.
Chintz A printed cotton fabric, usually with floral designs.
Chipboard Building material comprising wooden particles bonded together. Also known as particle board.
Classicism The style in which architectural details and decorative elements are based on the designs of ancient Greece and Rome.
Claw-and-ball foot The end of a chair or table leg

carved to resemble an animal's paw clutching a ball.
Combing Painting technique that creates a pattern by tracing a comb across wet surface of paint.
Commode A small, low chest, usually with drawers or doors.
Console A long, narrow table usually placed against a wall or behind a sofa. Also called a sofa table.
Cord A low-looped woven carpet with ribbed appearance.
Cornice Also called crown moulding. The decorative band where the wall meets the ceiling. Also the decorative top of a bookcase or cabinet.
Coromandel A dark ebony with the texture of rosewood. Often used in antique oriental screens.
Cove A concave band of moulding where the wall meets the ceiling.
Credenza A buffet usually used for displaying silverware.
Crewel work A colourful Colonial American embroidery, using yarns on natural linen.
Dado See Chair rail.
Damask A fine, lightweight material, usually silk, with a subtle pattern on one or both sides.
Dentils Equally spaced rectangular blocks in cornice moulding.
Dhurrie An Indian woven carpet of cotton or silk with geometric designs.
Distressing A painting technique and plastering method that give surfaces an appearance of age and antiquity.
Divan A sumptuously upholstered couch, without back or sides.
Dormer Protruding vertical walls built into a sloping roof.
Dowel A slender wooden rod, often used in pockets of Roman blinds to allow the blind to be raised or lowered in horizontal folds.
Dragging A painting technique that reveals the colour beneath a glaze by dragging a brush across the wet surface of the glaze.
Dresser A chest of drawers, usually with an attached mirror.
Eclectic The mixing of various different styles.
Eggshell An oil-based paint with a slight sheen.
Egyptian cotton A fine, silky cotton.
Enamel paint A dense, oil-based paint used for woodwork and metal.
Escritoire A writing desk with numerous drawers. Also called a secretary.
Fauteuil An upholstered armchair.
Faux bois A painting technique used to create the appearance of wood grain.
Faux marbre A painting technique used to create the appearance of marble.
Festoon blinds Window blinds in which fabric is attached to a heading and is raised in loops of ruched swags.
Finial The decorative top of a banister post or the upright section of a piece of furniture. Usually shaped like an urn or pineapple.
Flocked wallpaper Wallpaper with a raised pattern.
Fluorescent Tube lighting, often harsh and institutional.
Fluting Narrow vertical grooves carved in columns or legs of furniture.
Frieze A horizontal decorative plaster band around a room.
Georgian Style of English furniture produced during the reigns of George I, George II, and George III (1714-1820).
Gilt The decorative use of gold-leaf or gold paint.
Gingham A cotton cloth whose familiar check is created by a striped warp and weft.
Glaze A transparent or semi-transparent colour used to enhance and deepen a base coat.
Grout A sealing filler used between the edges of tile.
Halogen lighting Produces a bright, white light. Usually used for task lighting.
Harvest table A long, narrow table, usually of plain pine.
Hassock An upholstered footstool.
Highboy A tall chest of drawers, often built in two parts. Also known as a tallboy.
Hue A single colour. A tint is a hue with white added. A shade is a hue with grey or black added.
Hunt table A semicircular table, often made with drop-end leaves.
Interlining The extra fabric between the surface of a curtain and its lining, providing extra weight and insulation qualities.
Jardinière A tall vase.
Kilim A woven rug without pile. Usually has geometric patterns and quiet colouring.
Lacquer The many-layered application of varnish used to create a deep, polished sheen.
Ladder-back A plain wooden chair with a back built to resemble the rungs of a ladder. Also called slat-back.
Latex paint A water-based paint.
Lawson A sofa of largely square proportions.
Louis Quatorze A style of furniture and design popular during the reign of Louis XIV (1643-1715). Also known as French baroque.
Louis Quinze A style of furniture and design popular during the reign of Louis XV (1715-1774). Employed elaborate rococo ornamentation.
Louis Seize A style of furniture and design popular during the reign of Louis XVI (1775-1793). A revival of interest in the straight line and simplicity of Classicism.
Louis Treize A style of furniture and design popular during the reign of Louis XIII (1610-1643).
Louvre Horizontal, usually slanted slats on doors or shutters.
Lowboy A low chest or table.
Marbling See Faux marbre.
Marquetry A patterned inlay of contrasting wood into a surface.
Matt A flat, non-reflective paint finish.
Monochromatic Describes a colour scheme based on variations of the same colour.

Moulding A decorative trim of wood or plaster.
Mullion The bars that divide a pane of glass into smaller squares or rectangles.
Muslin A plain weave cotton. Its heavier weights are often useful in soft furnishings.
Neoclassic A revival of Classicism.
Organza A stiff, textured sheer fabric.
Ormolu A metal decoration on a piece of furniture. Often gold or gold-painted.
Patina The colour, texture, and sheen of a surface, often associated with aging.
Pattern repeat The drop or distance between repeating elements of a pattern.
Pediment A triangular decorative feature at the top of a sideboard, cabinet, or bookcase.
Pelmet Wood or fabric covering the top of a window.
Pickled finish A white stain simulating the look of pine that has had its paint stripped.
Picture rail A moulded wooden rail on a wall below ceiling level.
Pilaster A decorative false column.
Plinth The slab or block that forms the lowest part of the base of a column.
Poplin A lightweight cotton with a lustrous finish.
Primer The first coat of paint that protects and seals a surface, and prevents the absorption of subsequent coats.
Quarter-round Small moulding with the cross-section of a quarter circle.
Ragging A painting technique that creates a pattern on a base colour by wiping the surface with rags dipped in glaze or thinned paint.
Receding colours Colours that seem to make a room seem larger by appearing to recede from the observer.
Refectory table A long narrow table.
Rococo A style popular during the reign of Louis XV, marked by exaggerated curves and extravagant ornamentation.
Roman blind A fabric blind that is raised vertically in pleats.
Rosette A carved wooden ornamentation, usually of leaves pointing outward from a central point.
Sailcloth A heavy-duty, canvas-like cotton.
Sea-island cotton A fine lustrous cotton, originally from the coast of Georgia.
Secretary A desk with drawers and often with an attached bookcase above the writing surface.
Selvage The finished border on a piece of fabric.
Shellac A natural resin, soluble in alcohol, commonly used in varnishes.
Sideboard A buffet, often used for china.
Sisal matting Floor matting made from plant fibres.
Skirt See Apron.
Skirting board See Baseboard.
Slat-back See Ladder-back.
Sleigh bed A bed frame with curved or scrolled head and foot.
Slipper chair A small, feminine bedroom chair.
Sponging A painting technique that applies additional colour and pattern to the base coat with a sponge dipped in paint.
Stencilling Tracing patterns made by using cut-out designs.
Stippling A painting technique that creates a dappled effect by flicking paint at a surface.
Stretcher The piece of wood that braces the legs of a table or chair.
Swagged drapery The elaborate folds of drapery around a window.
Tabouret A low, upholstered footstool.
Tallboy See Highboy.
Template A cutting guide, used like a paper pattern.
Tester The frame of a four-poster bed intended to support the fabric of the canopy.
Ticking A strong fabric in twill weave with a warp stripe. Traditionally black and white or blue and white.
Toile de Jouy A light printed fabric decorated with pastoral or historical themes. Generally printed in one colour.
Torchière A floor lamp that directs light towards the ceiling.
Trompe-l'oeil A painting technique used to create the illusion of distance or of objects such as bookcases, windows, etc. Literally, to trick the eye.
Trundle bed A low mattress and frame that could be rolled beneath a larger bed.
Undercoat A coat of paint between primer and topcoat.
Valence The horizontal covering section at the top of drapery.
Vanity A dressing table.
Veneer A thin, polished surface of wood applied over a rougher wooden surface.
Victorian A style period defined by the reign of Queen Victoria (1837-1901).
Vitrine A glass-fronted cabinet.
Wainscoting Panelling, usually wood, that covers the lower section of a wall.
Warp Lengthwise threads in a woven fabric.
Weft Crosswise threads in a woven fabric.
Wilton A kind of carpet with a close velvet pile.
Windsor chair A simple wooden chair, with splayed legs and a hoop back inset with many spindles.
Wing chair A large upholstered chair with a high back that has wings curving inwards on each side.

RECOMMENDED READING

General Interior Design and Decorating

Antiques at Home, Barbara Milo Ohrbach. New York: Clarkson N. Potter, 1989.
Color in Decoration, Annie Sloan and Kate Gwynn. Boston: Little, Brown & Co., 1990.
The Complete Book of Home Design, Rev. Ed., Mary Gilliatt. Boston: Little, Brown & Co., 1989.
The Conran Beginner's Guide to Decorating, Jocasta Innes and Jill Blake. London: Conran Octopus, 1988.
Craftsmanship Revival in Interior Design, J. Ronald Reed. Toronto: Stoddart, 1989.
Design and Detail: The Practical Guide to Styling a House, Tricia Guild and Elizabeth Wilhide. London: Conran Octopus, 1988.
Designs on Your Home, Dagny Duckett. London: Unwin Hyman, 1988.
Dictionary of Furniture, Charles Boyce. New York: Roundtable, 1985.
Finishing Touches, Elizabeth Hilliard. London: Conran Octopus, 1990.
Floorworks, Akiko Busch. New York: Bantam, 1988.
A History of English Furniture, Percy MacQuoid. London: Bracken, 1988.
Interiors, Minn Hogg. New York: Clarkson N. Potter, 1988.
The Laura Ashley Complete Guide to Home Decorating, Charyn Jones, ed. New York: Crown, 1989.
Living Details, Thomas Cowan. Toronto: Stoddart, 1986.
Low Cost High Style, Elizabeth Wilhide and Andrea Spencer. London: Conran Octopus, 1987.
Mary Gilliatt's New Guide to Decorating, Mary Gilliatt. Boston: Little, Brown & Co., 1988.
Osborne and Little The Decorated Room, Lorraine Johnson and Gabrielle Townsend. London: Webb & Bower, 1988.
Planning and Designing Lighting, Edward Effron. Boston: Little, Brown & Co., 1986.
Porch Presence, Sally Fennell Robbins. New York: Michael Friedman, 1990.
The Textile Art in Interior Design, Melanie Payne. New York: Simon & Schuster, 1990.
White by Design, Bo Niles. New York: Stewart, Tabori & Chang, 1984.
William Morris and the Arts and Crafts Movement: A Source Book, Linda Parry. London: Studio Editions, 1989.

Specific Styles

American

American Country Classic, Mary Emmerling. New York: Crown, 1990.
American Family Style, Mary Randolph Carter. New York: Penguin, 1988.
Nantucket Gardens and Homes, Scott Heard. Boston: Little, Brown & Co., 1990.
The New England Colonial, Anne Elizabeth Powell. New York: Bantam, 1988.
The Town House, American Design, Chippy Irvine and Joe Viesti. New York: Bantam, 1988.

Country

The Barn Book, Kate Corbett-Winder. London: Random Century, 1990.
Country, Barbara Radcliffe Rogers. Toronto: Harper & Collins, 1989.
The Country Home Book, Miranda Innes. New York: Simon & Schuster, 1989.
Formal Country, Pat Ross. New York: Penguin, 1989.
Simple Country Style, Mary Trewby. Toronto: Stoddart, 1990.

English

English Country Style, Mary Gilliatt. Boston: Little, Brown & Co., 1986.
The Englishman's Room, Alvilde Lees-Milne. New York: Penguin, 1986.
English Style, Suzanne Slesin and Stafford Cliff. New York: Clarkson N. Potter, 1984.

French

French Style, Susan Slesin and Stafford Cliff. New York: Clarkson N. Potter, 1982.
Pierre Deux's French Country, Pierre Moulin, Pierre Le Vec, and Linda Dannenberg. New York: Clarkson N. Potter, 1984.
Pierre Deux's Normandy, Pierre Moulin, Pierre Le Vec, and Linda Dannenberg. New York: Crown, 1988.

Southwest

American Country West, Mary Emmerling. New York: Clarkson N. Potter, 1985.
Casa Mexicana, Tim Street-Porter. New York: Stewart, Tabori & Chang, 1989.
The Desert Southwest, Nora Burba, Paula Panich, and Terrence Moore. New York: Bantam, 1987.
Sante Fe Style, Christine Mather and Sharon Woods. New York: Rizzoli, 1986.

Miscellaneous

Italian Country, Catherine Sabino. New York: Clarkson N. Potter, 1988.
Period Details, Martin Miller and Judith Miller. New York: Crown, 1987.
Period Style, Mary Gilliatt. London: Conran Octopus, 1990.
Scandinavia Living Design, Elizabeth Gaynor. New York: Stewart, Tabori & Chang, 1987.
Shaker Design, June Sprigg. New York: Penguin, 1989.
Spain, Angus Mitchell and Tom Bell. Boston: Little, Brown & Co., 1990.
Victorian Details, Joanne Wissinger. Vancouver: Raincoast, 1990.

Children's Rooms

Children's Rooms, Jane Lott. Toronto: Stoddart, 1989.
In My Room: Designing for and with Children, Antonio Torrice and Ro Logrippo. New York: Random House, 1989.
Nursery Design, Barbara Aria. New York: Bantam, 1990.

Do-It-Yourself and Crafts

Classic Crafts: A Practical Compendium of Traditional Skills, Martina Margetts, ed. Toronto: Stoddart, 1989.
The Country Diary Book of Stencilling, Jane Cheshire and Rowena Stott. London: Webb & Bower, 1988.
Decorating with Fabric, Donna Lang and Lucretia Robertson. New York: Clarkson N. Potter, 1986.
Decorative Paint Techniques, Annie Sloan and Kate Gwynn. New York: Portland House, 1990.
Decorative Style, Kevin McCloud. London: Dorling Kindersley, 1990.
Displaying Pictures and Photographs, Caroline Clifton-Mogg and Piers Feetham. New York: Crown, 1988.
DIY by Design, Terence Conran. London: Conran Octopus, 1989.
Fabric Magic, Melanie Paine. New York: Random House, 1987.
Fabric Painting, Kazz Ball. Toronto: Harper & Collins, 1989.
Glorious Needlepoint, Kaffe Fassett. London: Century Hutchinson, 1987.
Master Strokes: A Practical Guide to Decorative Paint Techniques, Jennifer Bennell. Australia: Century Hutchinson, 1988.
Paintworks: The Art of Decorative Paint, Althea Wilson. London: Century Hutchinson, 1988.
Papier-Mâché Today, Sheila McGraw. Toronto: Firefly, 1990.
The Stencil Book, Amelia Saint George. Toronto: Stoddart, 1988.
The Stenciled House, Lyn Le Grice. London: Dorling Kindersley, 1988.
Vogue Sewing for the Home, Peggy Bendel. New York: Harper & Row, 1987.

Flower Arranging and Indoor Gardens

The Backyard Book, Rachel Carley. New York: Penguin, 1988.
The Container Garden, Nigel Colborn. London: Conran Octopus, 1990.
Cultivated Pleasures: The Art of Romantic Gardening, Elizabeth Saft. New York: Penguin, 1989.
Designing with Flowers, Tricia Guild. New York: Crown, 1986.
Dried Fresh Flowers from Your Garden, Elizabeth Bullivant. New York: Penguin, 1989.
The Five Minute Flower Arranger, Jan Newdick. New York: Crown, 1989.
The Flower Arranger's Garden, Rosemary Verey. Toronto: Stoddart, 1989.
Flower Arranging: A Step-by-Step Guide, Susan Conder, Sue Phillips, and Pamela Westland. London: Hamlyn, 1990.
Herbs: Gardens, Decorations and Recipes, Emelie Tolley and Chris Mead. New York: Clarkson N. Potter, 1985.
Highrise Horticulture: A Guide to Gardening in Small Places, David Tarrant. Vancouver: Whitecap, 1989.
Paradise Contained, William Stites. New York: Doubleday, 1990.
The Scented Room, Barbara Milo Ohrbach. New York: Clarkson N. Potter, 1986.

SHOPPING INFORMATION

For more information about the suppliers listed here, please refer to The Directory of Sources

Book Jacket: tassels – Reid & Lyons Decorative Trims; fringe – Brunschwig & Fils; plastic laminates – Octopus Products; braid – Brunschwig et Fils. Pages 2-3: fabric – Pierre Deux; tile – Country Tiles; tassel – Reid & Lyons Decorative Trims. Pages 96-97: tiles – Country Tiles; print fabric – Brunschwig & Fils; plain fabric – Nash James International.

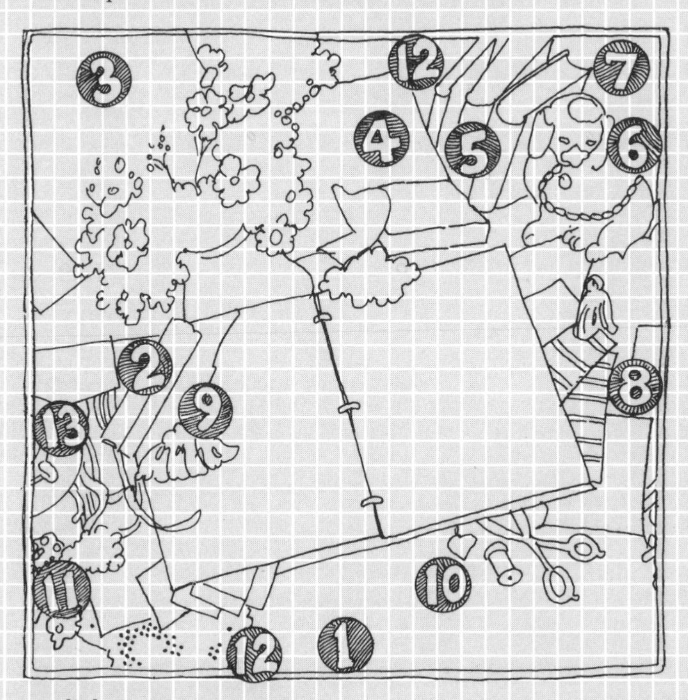

English Country How-To

Page 114-115 (see diagram above): 1. table – The Paisley Shop; 2. tiles – Country Tiles; 3. wallpaper border – Laura Ashley Shops; 4. lacquer collection – The Paisley Shop; 5. books – Plum's Emporium; 6. Staffordshire reproduction – Plum's Emporium; 7. leather – Moore-Pearsall Leathers; 8. fabrics – Arthur Sanderson Canada; 9. tassels – Reid & Lyons Decorative Trims; 10. silver heart – Filigree; 11. faux ivory brooches – Filigree; 12. lace – Filigree; 13. cup and saucer – Ralph Lauren Home Collection.

Page 118: tassels - Reid & Lyons Decorative Trims; Page 119: tile – Country Tiles; Page 120: cup and saucer – Ralph Lauren Home Collection; Page 121: chintz – Arthur Sanderson Canada; Page 123: wallpaper border – Laura Ashley Shops; Page 124: tile – Country Tiles.

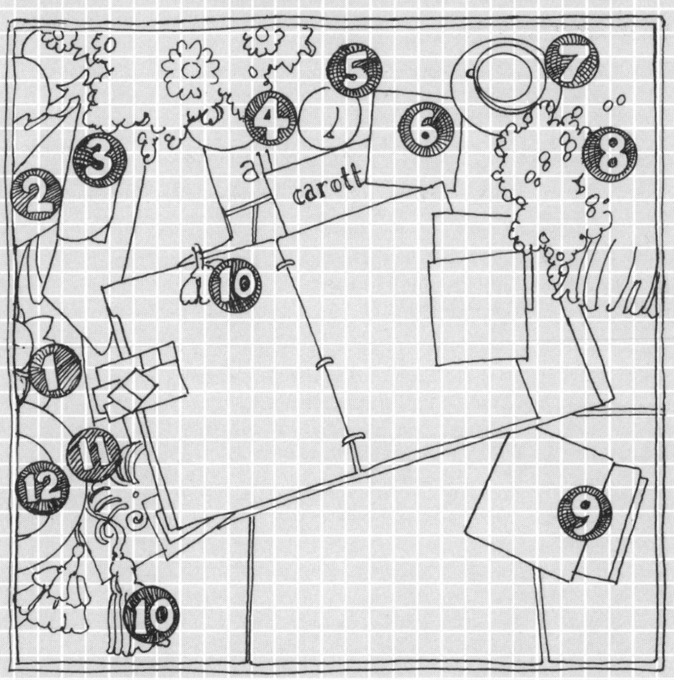

French Country How-To

Page 128-129 (see diagram above): 1. carved fruit wall sconce – En Provence; 2. fabrics – En Provence, Pierre Deux; 3. wallpaper border – Pierre Deux; 4. pitcher – En Provence; 5. marble peach – En Provence; 6. tiles – Country Tiles; 7. demi-tasse – Pierre Deux; 8. dried flowers – Demarco-Perpich; 9. fabrics – Pierre Deux; 10. tassels – Reid & Lyons Decorative Trims; 11. plate – En Provence; 12. marble figure – En Provence.

Page 130: fabric – Pierre Deux; Page 131: tiles – Country Tiles; Page 133: tiles – Country Tiles; tassel – Reid & Lyons Decorative Trims; Page 134: fabrics – Pierre Deux; Page 135: cup and saucer – Pierre Deux.

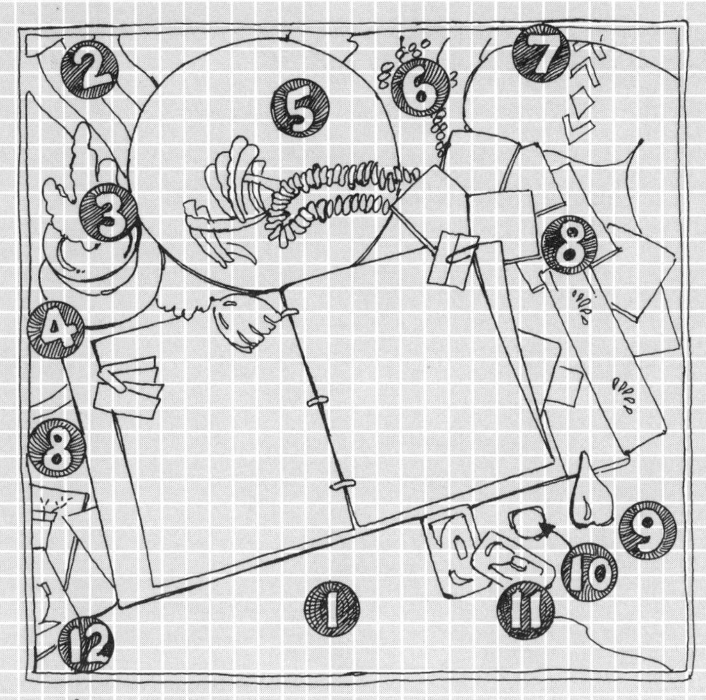

Southwest How-To

Page 140-141 (see diagram above): 1. drum table – Taos Design; 2. serapes – Taos Design; 3. cactus – The Plant Warehouse; 4. Kachina doll – Four Corners; 5. willow tray – Four Corners; 6. necklaces – Taos Design; 7. rug – Ralph Lauren Home Collection; 8. plain and border tiles – Country Tiles; 9. leather – Moore-Pearsall Leathers; 10. miniature canteen – Four Corners; 11. buckle (on right) – Four Corners; 12. Hopi tiles – Four Corners.

Page 143: tiles – Country Tiles; Page 144: tiles – Country Tiles; Page 146: bowl – Ralph Lauren Home Collection; Page 148: necklace – Taos Design; buckle – Harbourfront Antique Market.

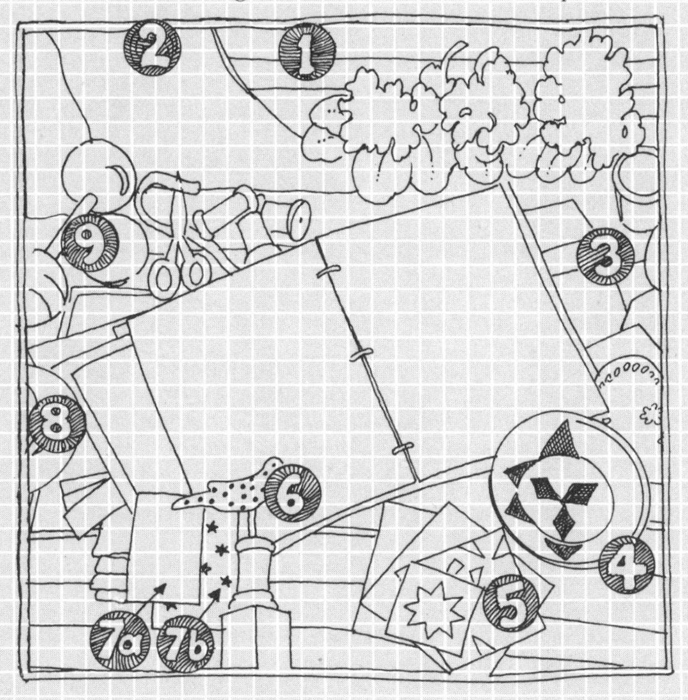

Folk How-To

Page 152-153 (see diagram bottom left): 1. hooked rug – The Port Dalhousie Trading Company; 2. ticking fabric – B.B. Bargoon's; 3. wallpapers – Ralph Lauren Home Collection; 4. bowl – Ralph Lauren Home Collection; 5. tiles – Country Tiles; 6. bird – The Port Dalhousie Trading Company; 7a. red checked fabric – Ralph Lauren Home Collection; 7b. star pattern fabric – Habert Associates; 8. cup and saucer – Ralph Lauren Home Collection; 9. juggler's sticks – The Port Dalhousie Trading Company.

Page 155: tiles – Country Tiles; Page 156: wallpapers – Ralph Lauren Home Collection; Page 157: fabric – Ralph Lauren Home Collection; Page 158: bowl – Ralph Lauren Home Collection; Page 160: folk art bird – The Port Dalhousie Trading Company.

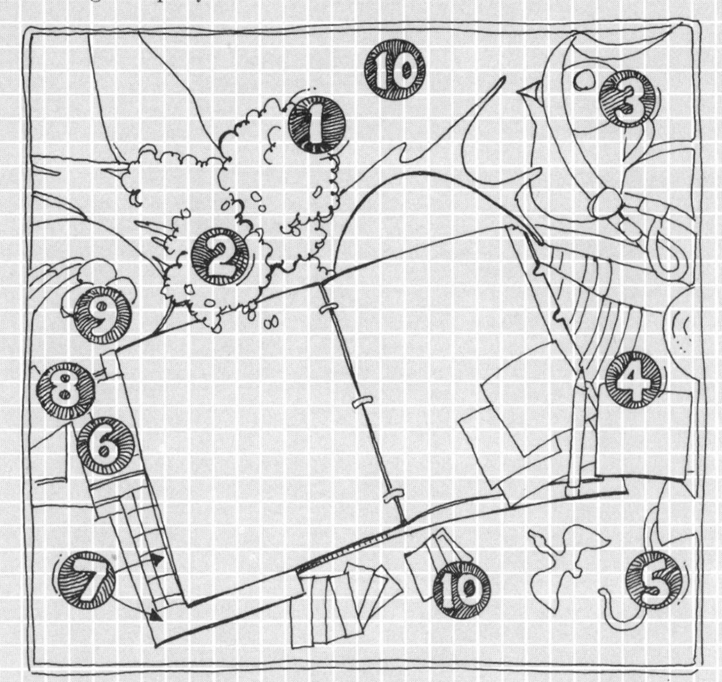

True North How-To

Page 164-165 (see diagram above): 1. white flowers – Demarco-Perpich; 2. coloured flowers – At My Table; 3. enamel coffee pot – At My Table; 4. fabrics (Indian blanket patterns, denim, checks) – Ralph Lauren Home Collection; 5. iron wall hook – Filigree; 6. wallpapers (blue-and-red handkerchief pattern and blue-and-white stripe) – Ralph Lauren Home Collection; 7. blue-and-white checked fabric – Pierre Deux; black-and-white fabric – Old Sturbridge Village Collection by Waverly; 8. stone tiles – Country Tiles; 9. speckled china dish – At My Table; 10. leather – Moore-Pearsall Leathers.

Page 167: wallpaper – Ralph Lauren Home Collection; Page 168: solid fabric – Ralph Lauren Home Collection; check fabric – Old Sturbridge Village Collection by Waverly; Page 170: twig chair – Pack-Rat; fabrics – Ralph Lauren Home Collection; Page 172: quillbox – Roots Canada.

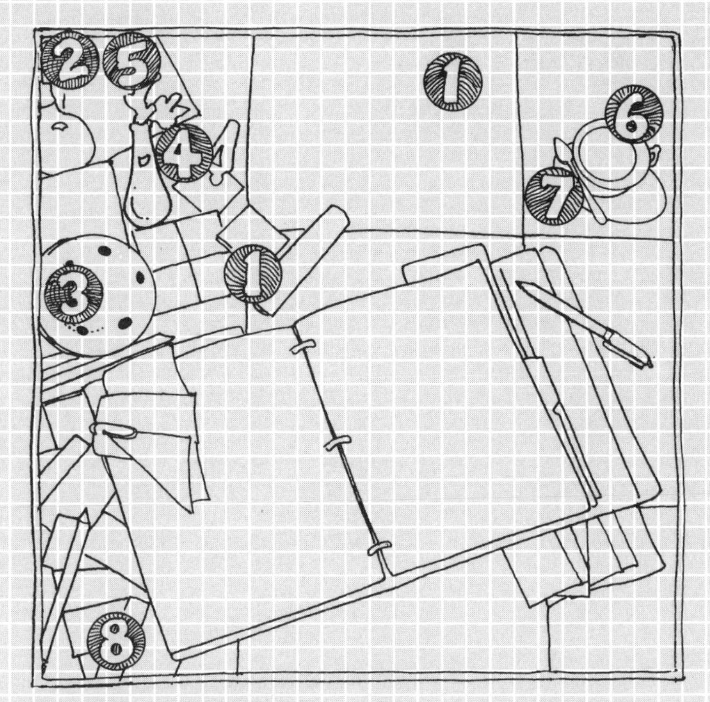

Contemporary How-To

Page 177-178 (see diagram above): 1. tiles – Ramca Tile; 2. fabrics – Telio & Cie; 3. bowl – At My Table; 4. glass perfume bottles – Triede Design; 5. decorative paper – Mediterranean by Fred Cole for Crown Wallpaper Company; 6. cup and saucer – Triede Design; 7. spoon – Triede Design; 8. plastic laminates – Octopus Products.

Page 179: plastic laminates – Octopus Products; glass tiles – Ramca Tile; Page 180: tiles – Ramca Tile; Page 181: tiles – Ramca Tile; Page 182: tiles – Ramca Tile; fabric – Telio & Cie; bowl – At My Table; Page 185: fabric – Telio & Cie; Page 186: sugar bowl – Triede Design; perfume bottles – Triede Design; Page 187: plastic laminates – Octopus Products.

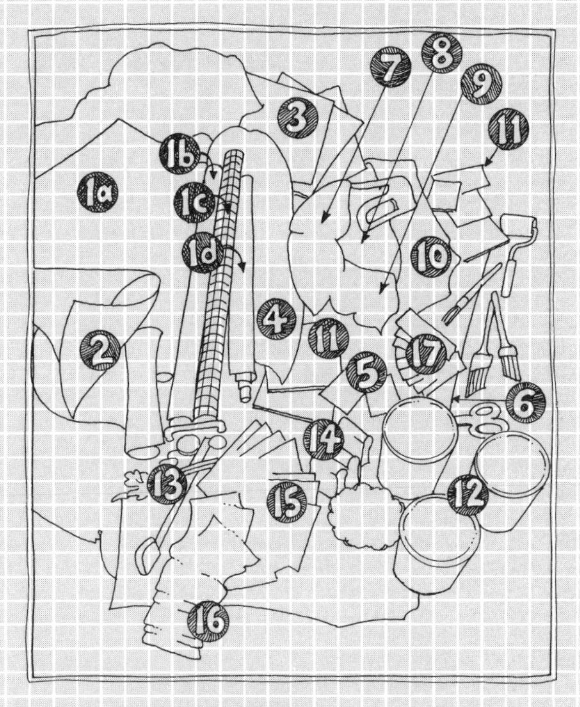

Sources and Resources

Page 192 (see diagram above): 1a. yellow wallpaper – Pierre Deux; 1b. red plaid wallpaper – Ralph Lauren Home Collection; 1c. blue plaid wallpaper – Ralph Lauren Home Collection; 1d. white print wallpaper – Pierre Deux; 2. wallpaper border – Laura Ashley Shops; 3. linoleum tiles – Exclusive Paints; 4. rug samples – Elte Carpets; 5. carpet samples – Elte Carpets; 6. sisal matting – Elte Carpets; 7. red fabric – Pierre Deux; 8. blue fabric – Pierre Deux; 9. brown print fabric – Schumacher, Crown Wallpaper Company; 10. plain blue fabric – The Original Stitsky's; 11. tiles – Country Tiles; 12. paintbrushes, paint, rollers – Exclusive Paints; 13. drawer pulls – Summerhill Hardware; 14. milk paint – Homestead House Paint; 15. decorative papers – Folly Parterre by Osborne & Little, Habert & Associates; 16. polished cottons – H. Brown Ribbons Ltd.; 17. paint swatches – Color Your World.

PHOTO CREDITS

We want to acknowledge and thank the following copyright holders of the photographs. The names in brackets are people who the copyright holder or the authors also wish to acknowledge.

Jacket background: Photographer - The Jackson Klömstad Partnership
Jacket-front inset: Photographer - Ted Yardwood (Designer - Charlotte Ambridge/Dirstein Robertson Limited)
Jacket-back insets (clockwise from top right): Photographer - Michael Mahovlich; Photographer - Michael Mahovlich (Location - UpCountry); Photographer - David Allen; Photographer - Michael Mahovlich; Photographer - Michael Mahovlich; Photographer - The Jackson Klömstad Partnership
Page 2-3: Photographer - The Jackson Klömstad Partnership
Page 3 (inset): Photographer - Ted Yarwood
Page 9: Photographer - Nigel Dickson
Page 12 (upper left): Photographer - Masao Abe
Page 12 (middle right): En Provence
Page 12 (lower left): Photographer - Michael Mahovlich
Page 13 (upper left): Photographer - Masao Abe
Page 13 (middle right): Photographer - John Sherlock
Page 13 (lower left): Photographer - Michael Mahovlich
Page 14: Photographer - Masao Abe
Page 15: Photographer - John Sherlock
Page 16-17: Photographer - Ted Yarwood
Page 18: Photographer - Michael Mahovlich
Page 19 (left): Photographer - Masao Abe
Page 19 (right): Photographer - Masao Abe
Page 20: Designer - Robert Dirstein/Dirstein Robertson Limited (Photographer - Peter Vitale)
Page 21 (right): Photographer - The Jackson Klömstad Partnership
Page 22: Photographer - Christopher Dew
Page 23: Photographer - Michael Mahovlich
Page 24 (top left): Photographer - Robert Burley/Design Archive
Page 24 (bottom left): Photographer - Joy Von Tiedemann
Page 24-25: Photographer - Michael Mahovlich
Page 26: Photographer - Pat Lacroix
Page 27 (top): Photographer - Michael Mahovlich
Page 27 (bottom): Photographer - Joy Von Tiedemann
Page 28: Photographer - Michael Mahovlich
Page 29: Pierre Deux (Photographer - Robert Grant)
Page 30-31: Photographer - Michael Mahovlich
Page 32: Photographer - Shin Sugino
Page 33: Photographer - Michael Mahovlich
Page 34: Pierre Deux (Photographer - Robert Grant)
Page 35: Pierre Deux (Photographer - Joe Standart)
Page 36: Photographer - Michael Mahovlich
Page 36-37: Photographer - Masao Abe
Page 38: Pierre Deux (Photographer - Fabrizio Ferri)
Page 39: Photographer - Margaret Belisle/Jim Eager
Page 40: Photographer - Joy Von Tiedemann
Page 41 (left): Photographer - Roger Brooks and Associates
Page 41 (right): Photographer - David Allen
Page 42: Photographer - Roger Brooks and Associates
Page 43: Photographer - Michael Mahovlich
Page 44-45: Photographer - John Sherlock (Architect - Werner Forster)
Page 46: Photographer - The Jackson Klömstad Partnership
Page 47: Photographer - Marc Romanelli/The Image Bank Canada
Page 48-49: Photographer - John Sherlock
Page 50: Photographer - Robert Burley/Design Archive
Page 51 (top): Photographer - Christopher Dew
Page 51 (bottom): Photographer - Ted Yarwood
Page 52 (top): Designer - Joan Eiley & Assoc. Ltd.
Page 52 (bottom): Photographer - Michael Mahovlich
Page 53: Photographer - Masao Abe
Page 54: Photographer - The Jackson Klömstad Partnership
Page 55 (top): Photographer - Ian Samson
Page 55 (bottom): Designer - Randy Knox Interior Design
Page 56: Photographer - Masao Abe (Sharon & Ken Murray)
Page 57: Photographer - Michael Mahovlich
Page 58-59: Photographer - Michael Mahovlich (Kathy & Ray Goodman)
Page 60: Photographer - Ian Samson
Page 61 (top): Photographer - The Jackson Klömstad Partnership
Page 61 (bottom): Photographer - Chris Reardon
Page 62: Photographer - Michael Mahovlich
Page 63 (top): Photographer - Michael Mahovlich
Page 63 (bottom): Photographer - Masao Abe
Page 64-65: Photographer - Clive Webster
Page 67 (left): Photographer - Masao Abe
Page 67 (right): Photographer - Masao Abe
Page 68: Photographer - Michael Mahovlich
Page 69: Photographer - Ted Yarwood
Page 70-71: Ralph Lauren Home Collection
Page 72: Photographer - Christopher Dew
Page 73 (top left): Photographer - John Sherlock (Mr. & Mrs. Killam)
Page 73 (top right): Photographer - John Sherlock (Mr. & Mrs. Killam)
Page 73 (bottom left): Photographer - John Sherlock (Mr. & Mrs. Killam)
Page 73 (bottom right): Photographer - John Sherlock (Mr. & Mrs. Killam)
Page 74: Photographer - Christopher Dew
Page 75: Photographer - John Sherlock (Furniture designer - Ronae Theabeau/Willow Lane Designs)
Page 76-77: Photographer - Margaret Belisle/Jim Eager
Page 77 (top): Photographer - Michael Mahovlich
Page 77 (bottom): Photographer - Joy Von Tiedemann
Page 78: Photographer - The Jackson Klömstad Partnership
Page 79 (top): Ralph Lauren Home Collection
Page 79 (bottom): Ralph Lauren Home Collection
Page 80: Photographer - John Sherlock
Page 81: Photographer - Michael Mahovlich
Page 82: Photographer - John Sherlock (Location - Artemis Antiques Showroom)
Page 83: Photographer - David Allen (Architect - Kenney Nickerson)
Page 85 (top): Photographer - Michael Mahovlich
Page 85 (bottom): Photographer - Ted Yarwood
Page 86: Photographer - Christopher Dew
Page 87 (top): Photographer - Ted Yarwood
Page 87 (bottom): Photographer - Christopher Dew
Page 88-89: Photographer - Christopher Dew
Page 90: Photographer - Christopher Dew
Page 91: Photographer - Ted Yarwood
Page 92: Photographer - Michael Mahovlich

Page 93: Photographer - Michael Mahovlich
Page 96-97: Photographer - The Jackson Klömstad Partnership
Page 98: Photographer - Michael Mahovlich
Page 99: Photographer - Masao Abe
Page 100-101: Photographer - Ted Yarwood
Page 103: Photographer - Ted Yarwood
Page 104: Photographer - John Sherlock (Designers - Thomas Hobbs & Brett Beattie)
Page 105: Photographer - Michael Mahovlich (Jim Allen)
Page 106: Photographer - Michael Mahovlich
Page 107: Photographer - Masao Abe
Page 108-109: Photographer - The Jackson Klömstad Partnership
Page 110-111: Photographer - The Jackson Klömstad Partnership
Page 112-113: Photographer - The Jackson Klömstad Partnership
Page 114-115 (background): Photographer - The Jackson Klömstad Partnership
Page 114-115 (photo in workbook): Photographer - Ted Yarwood
Page 116-117: Photographer - Michael Mahovlich
Page 116-187 (close-cropped photographs): Photographer - The Jackson Klömstad Partnership
Page 117 (top right): Photographer - Michael Mahovlich
Page 118: Photographer - The Jackson Klömstad Partnership
Page 119: Photographer - The Jackson Klömstad Partnership
Page 120: Photographer - David Allen
Page 121 (top): Photographer - Ted Yarwood
Page 121 (bottom): Photographer - Michael Mahovlich
Page 122: Brunschwig & Fils
Page 123 (background): Photographer - Shin Sugino
Page 123 (inset): Photographer - Shin Sugino
Page 124: Photographer - Masao Abe (Designer - Rollins Raeburn)
Page 125: Photographer - Michael Mahovlich
Page 126-127: Photographer - Michael Mahovlich (Designer - Edward Welker Interiors Ltd.)
Page 128-129 (background): Photographer - The Jackson Klömstad Partnership
Page 128-129 (photo in workbook): Photographer - Clive Webster (Designer - Gary Zanner)
Page 129: Photographer - Michael Mahovlich
Page 130-131: Photographer - David Allen
Page 131 (right): Photographer - John Sherlock (Designers - Thomas Hobbs & Brent Beattie)
Page 132 (top): Designer - Norma King Design Inc.
Page 132 (bottom): Photographer - Michael Mahovlich
Page 133: Photographer - The Jackson Klömstad Partnership
Page 134-135: En Provence
Page 135: Photographer - Michael Mahovlich
Page 136: Photographer - Michael Mahovlich
Page 137: Photographer - Masao Abe
Page 138-139: Photographer - Michael Mahovlich (Designer - Leo LaFerme)
Page 140-141 (background): Photographer - The Jackson Klömstad Partnership
Page 140-141 (photo in workbook): Photographer - Michael Mahovlich (Designer - Stephen Bailey)
Page 141: Photographer - The Jackson Klömstad Partnership
Page 142-143: Photographer - Masao Abe (Designer - Christopher Robinson & Judy Davies)
Page 143: Designer - Randy Knox Interior Design
Page 144-145: Photographer - Robert Burley/Design Archive
Page 145: Photographer - Michael Mahovlich
Page 146-147: Photographer - Robert Burley/Design Archive
Page 147: Photographer - The Jackson Klömstad Partnership
Page 148 (top): Photographer - Michael Mahovlich
Page 148-149: Photographer - Shin Sugino
Page 149 (right): Photographer - The Jackson Klömstad Partnership (Floorcloth designer & artist - Kathy Chandler/The Stencil Shoppe)
Page 150-151: Photographer - Michael Mahovlich
Page 152-153 (background): Photographer - The Jackson Klömstad Partnership
Page 152-153 (photo in workbook): Photographer - C. Nöel (Designer - Dorothy Ames)
Page 153: Photographer - Shin Sugino
Page 154: Photographer - Michael Mahovlich (Location - UpCountry)
Page 155: Photographer - The Jackson Klömstad Partnership
Page 156: Photographer - Michael Mahovlich (Trudie Nelson & Craig Dyer)
Page 157 (top): Photographer - The Jackson Klömstad Partnership (Stencil artist - Kathy Chandler/The Stencil Shoppe)
Page 157 (bottom): Photographer - Michael Mahovlich
Page 158 (top): Photographer - Masao Abe
Page 158 (bottom): Photographer - John Sherlock
Page 159 (bottom left): Photographer - Michael Mahovlich
Page 159 (top right): Photographer - The Jackson Klömstad Partnership (Chuck MacIntosh/Homestead House Paint Inc.)
Page 160: Photographer - Chris Reardon
Page 161 (top): Photographer - Margaret Belisle/Jim Eager
Page 161 (bottom): Photographer - David Allen
Page 162-163: Photographer - John Sherlock (Designer - Josette Whist)
Page 164-165 (background): Photographer - The Jackson Klömstad Partnership
Page 164-165 (photo in workbook): Photographer - Michael Mahovlich (Designer - Stephen Bailey)
Page 165: Photographer - Michael Mahovlich
Page 166-167: Photographer - Joy Von Tiedemann
Page 167: Photographer - Michael Mahovlich
Page 168: Photographer - Joy Von Tiedemann
Page 169 (top): Photographer - Michael Mahovlich
Page 169 (inset): Photographer - Michael Mahovlich (Designer - Stephen Bailey)
Page 170: Photographer - The Jackson Klömstad Partnership
Page 170-171: Photographer - Michael Mahovlich (Kathy & Ray Goodman)
Page 172-173: Photographer - Chrisopher Dew
Page 173: Photographer - The Jackson Klömstad Partnership
Page 174-175: Photographer - Margaret Belisle/Jim Eager (Designer - Marshall Cummings)
Page 176-177 (background): Photographer - The Jackson Klömstad Partnership
Page 176-177 (photo in workbook): Photographer - Taffi Rosen (Designer - Taffi Rosen)
Page 177: Photographer - Michael Mahovlich
Page 178: Designer - Norma King Design Inc. (Photographer - Scott Frances)
Page 178-179: Photographer - Ted Yarwood
Page 180: Photographer - Roger Brooks and Associates
Page 181: Photographer - Joy Von Tiedemann
Page 183: Photographer - Taffi Rosen
Page 184: Photographer - David Allen
Page 185: Photographer - Michael Mahovlich (Artist - J.C. Brown/Vanderwerff & Brown)
Page 186: Photographer - Christopher Dew
Page 187: Photographer - Michael Mahovlich (Designer - Tim Lawrence)
Page 188-189: Photographer - Ted Yarwood (Designer - Sinclair Russell)
Page 192: Photographer - The Jackson Klömstad Partnership

INDEX

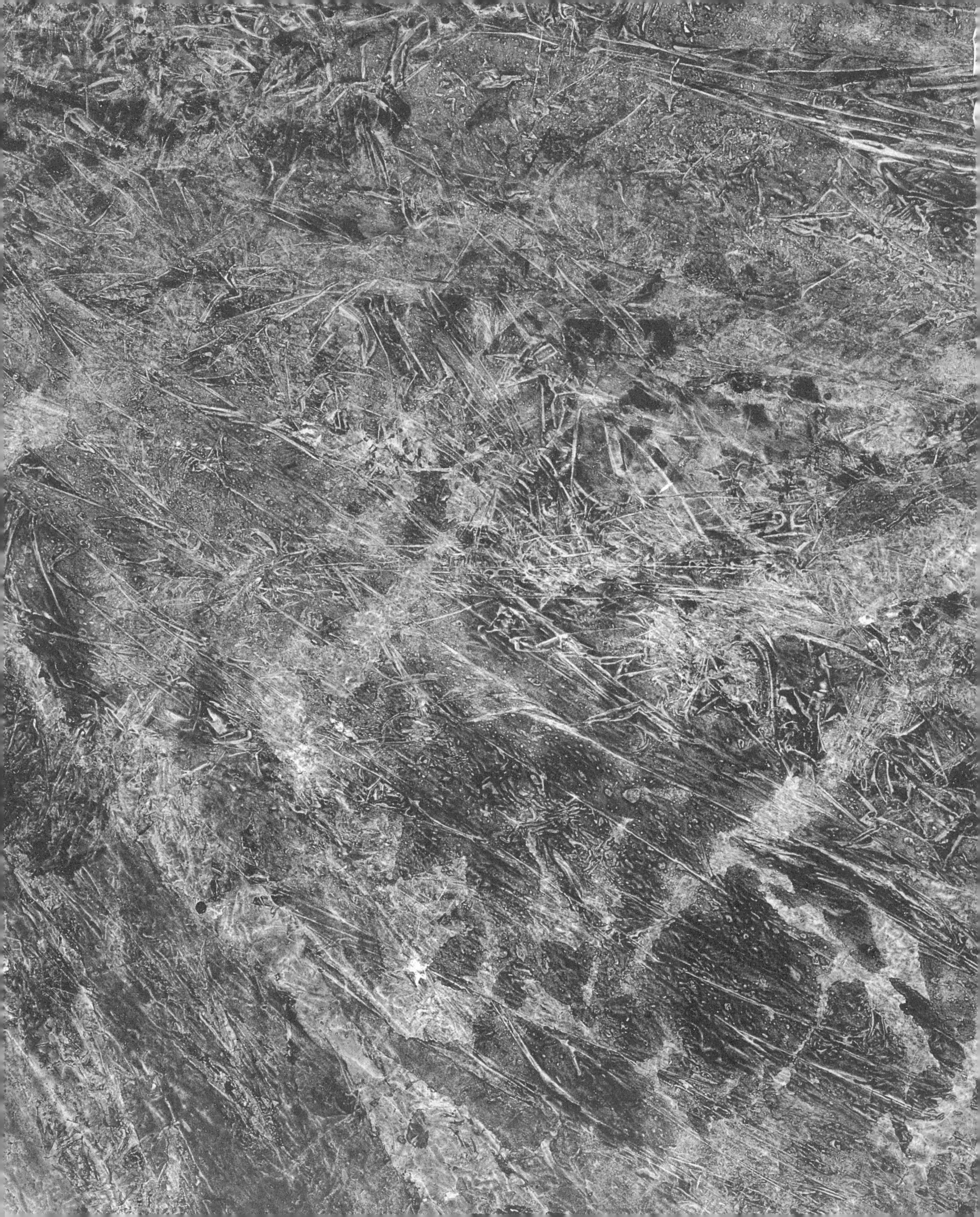